Quantitative Methods in derivatives pricing

Founded in 1807, John Wiley & Sons is the oldest independent publishing company in the United States. With offices in North America, Europe, Australia, and Asia, Wiley is globally committed to developing and marketing print and electronic products and services for our customers' professional and personal knowledge and understanding.

The Wiley Finance series contains books written specifically for finance and investment professionals as well as sophisticated individual investors and their financial advisors. Book topics range from portfolio management to e-commerce, risk management, financial engineering, valuation and financial instrument analysis, as well as much more.

For a list of available titles, visit our Web site at www.WileyFinance.com.

Quantitative Methods in
derivatives pricing

*An Introduction
to Computational Finance*

Domingo Tavella

John Wiley & Sons, Inc.

Published by John Wiley & Sons, Inc., New York.
Published simultaneously in Canada.

This publication is designed to provide accurate and authoritative information in regard to the subject matter covered. It is sold with the understanding that the publisher is not engaged in rendering professional services. If professional advice or other expert assistance is required, the services of a competent professional person should be sought.

ISBN 0-471-39447-5

Printed in the United States of America.

10 9 8 7 6 5 4 3 2

To
Rudolph and Natalie

T he emergence of computational finance as a discipline in its own right is relatively recent. The first international conference on computational finance took place in 1995 at Stanford University, where, as far as the author is aware, the name for this new discipline was coined. The *Journal of Computational Finance* was created shortly thereafter, and its success and popularity soon demonstrated that there was a body of work of sufficient mass and extent to rightfully configure the emergence of a new discipline, complete with its views, paradigms, and methods.

The use of computational methods for solving engineering problems allows us to analyze systems of such scale and complexity that their analysis would not be conceivable through empirical study through purely analytical means. Computational chemistry, computational fluid dynamics, the numerical simulation of astronomical structures, structural analysis, and so on, are examples where the use of sophisticated numerical techniques allows us to gain a type of understanding of the nature of the problem that could not be gained otherwise.

Just as physicists and engineers solve problems by solving so-called "conservation equations," financial engineers price financial instruments by solving their corresponding pricing equations. The *conservation equations of physics* establish relationships between the rates of convection, diffusion, creation, and disappearance of mass, momentum, and energy. Typically, these relationships are in the form of partial differential equations (PDEs). The pricing equations of financial instruments state the way the price of the instrument depends on time and the value of other instruments or processes. Typically, these pricing equations are also PDEs.

While the *conservation equations of physics* are derived by considering the detailed balance of mass, momentum, and energy flows, the pricing equations of financial instruments are derived by considering arbitrage (rather, the absence of arbitrage) and expectations. Are there significant differences in the computational challenges presented by physical problems and financial problems? Although this question is hard to answer with generality, there are observations we can make about how financial engineers perceive these challenges vis-à-vis their colleagues in other disciplines. In engineering fields such as structural analysis or fluid dynamics, engineers can deal with a relatively well-established set of PDEs with which he or she can solve a very large number of problems by simply changing the boundary conditions. This relative consensus and stability of the mathematical framework makes it possible to develop large and flexible software systems to implement particular solution approaches applicable to particular areas of engineering. These systems can be used to solve a large variety of problems by simply changing boundary values and the way boundaries are treated. These systems will typically implement a particular numerical approach, such as finite elements or finite differences, applicable to large classes of problems. Structural engineers, for example, can deal with a large array of problems using a single computational methodology, such as finite elements. Aerodynamicists can work on projects ranging from small aircraft to reentry vehicles and still use the same methodology, such as finite differences.

This situation is significantly different in financial engineering. The pricing of financial contracts is not just a matter of repeatedly applying the same numerical methodology with different boundary conditions. In many cases, the pricing equation is very specific to the particular financial instrument being considered. In other cases, the pricing equation is not known. Yet in other cases the pricing equation is extremely ill-suited for certain types of numerical techniques. This means that the financial engineer must be fluent in a number of computational techniques appropriate for dealing with different instruments.

This book is designed as a graduate textbook in financial engineering. It was motivated by the need to present the main techniques used in quantitative pricing in a single source adequate for Master level students. Students are expected to have some background in algebra, elementary statistics, calculus, and elementary techniques of financial pricing, such as binomial trees and simple Monte Carlo simulation. The book includes a brief introduction to the fundamentals of stochastic calculus.

The book is divided into seven chapters covering an introduction to stochastic calculus, a summary of asset pricing theory, simulation applied to pricing, and pricing using finite difference solutions. The topic of trees as a tool for pricing is touched on at the end of the finite differences chapter. Although trees are a popular pricing technique, finite differences, of which trees are a particularly simple case, are a far more powerful and flexible approach. Significant effort is dedicated to the fundamentals of early exercise simulation. This methodology is rapidly taking the lead as a preferred way to price highly dimensional early exercise instruments.

Chapter 1 is a brief introduction to single-period pricing with the objective of motivating the idea that the price of a financial instrument is given by an expectation.

Chapter 2 is a summary introduction to the basic elements of stochastic calculus. The material is presented in a nonrigorous way and should be easy to follow by anyone with a basic background in elementary calculus.

Chapter 3 is a brief description of pricing in continuous time, where the main objectives are to more precisely determine the price as an expectation under a suitable measure and to derive the relevant pricing equation.

Chapter 4 focuses on the generation of scenarios for simulation. In practical implementations of simulation, the generation of scenarios of appropriate quality is essential. Issues of accuracy are discussed in detail.

Chapter 5 is dedicated to simulation applied to computing expectations for European pricing. This chapter gives a summary with selected case studies of the main approaches that have demonstrated practical value in financial pricing.

Chapter 6 deals with simulation applied to early exercise pricing. At the time of this writing, this is a rapidly evolving subject. For this reason, this chapter must be viewed as an update of the most established aspects of simulation for early exercise pricing. The chapter presents a brief historical account of the various techniques, but the emphasis is on linear squares Monte Carlo, the technique that has marked a breakthrough in this area.

Chapter 7 summarizes the use of finite differences in option pricing. The material is presented in a concise manner, with an emphasis on the fundamentals.

DOMINGO TAVELLA

San Francisco, California
March 2002

acknowledgments

During the preparation of this book, I benefited from discussions with colleagues. I am especially indebted to Dr. Ervin Zhao for his valuable suggestions on the manuscript. My thanks are also due to Dr. Joshua Rosenberg and Mr. Didier Vermeiren for their helpful comments.

D.T.

contents

CHAPTER 1

Arbitrage and Pricing

The purpose of this short chapter is to motivate the notion that the price of a financial instrument is expressed in the form of an expectation of suitably discounted future values or cash flows. To accomplish this, we will work in a single period framework, where we will show that the price of a security is an expectation where the probabilities used to compute the expectation are determined by a normalizing asset, known as the *numeraire asset*. We will not elaborate on discrete time pricing beyond this initial chapter. The reader interested in additional details of discrete time pricing can consult the excellent work by Dotham (1990). The reason we will not dwell on discrete time modeling is that the power of the numerical pricing methods we will consider originates in their application to continuous time models.

THE PRICING PROBLEM

We will obtain intuitive derivation of pricing formulation by the following line of reasoning.

■ Absence of arbitrage implies the existence of state prices. State prices are the values of elementary securities known as *Arrow-Debreu securities*.
■ State prices, when properly rescaled by the values of other instruments or portfolios of instruments, can be interpreted as probabilities.
■ The derivative's price is an expectation with respect to a probability measure determined by the rescaling of state prices (a probability measure assigns probabilities to outcomes.)
■ When the underlying processes that determine the derivative's price are Ito processes, the expectation can be expressed as the solution to a parabolic partial differential equation. This is the pricing equation.

Arbitrage

We will consider a market that at payoff time T may achieve one of S states. Assume there are N traded securities, whose values at $t = 0$ are denoted by $V_n(0)$, $n = 1,..., N$, and whose payoffs at time $t = T$ are indicated by $F_{s,n}(T)$, $s = 1,..., S$, $n = 1,..., N$. The matrix $\tilde{F}(T)$, whose elements are $F_{s,n}(T)$, is called the *payoff matrix*. Each column of the payoff matrix represents the payoffs of a given security for the different market states. Each row represents the payoffs of the different securities for a given market state.

We now define the concept of Arrow-Debreu securities. We will use this concept in establishing the arbitrage conditions in the discrete time model. An Arrow-Debreu security is a security that pays \$1 at time T if a particular state materializes and pays \$0, otherwise.

If at time $t = 0$, we purchase the jth Arrow-Debreu security in the amount $F_{j,n}(T)$, we will get a payoff at time T equal to $F_{j,n}(T)$ if the jth state materializes, and zero, otherwise. This means that if we purchase the jth Arrow-Debreu security in the amount $F_{j,n}(T)$, we will match the payoff of the nth asset in state j.

If we purchase a portfolio of Arrow-Debreu securities, such that $F_{1,n}(T)$ is the amount of Arrow-Debreu security 1, $F_{2,n}(T)$ is the amount of Arrow-Debreu security 2, and ... $F_{S,n}(T)$ is the amount of Arrow-Debreu security S, we will match the payoffs of the nth asset in all states at time T. The value of this portfolio is equal to $\sum_{s=1}^{s=S} F_{s,n}(T)\pi_s$, where π_s is the value of the sth Arrow-Debreu security. The present value of the nth asset must be equal to the value of this portfolio, because their payoffs are the same. (See Equation 1.1.)

$$V_n(0) = \sum_{s=1}^{s=S} F_{s,n}(T)\pi_s, \quad n = 1,..., N \tag{1.1}$$

If this relationship were not satisfied, it would be possible to make a riskless profit. If the portfolio of Arrow-Debreu securities were more valuable than the asset, we would short-sell the portfolio of Arrow-Debreu securities and buy the asset. If the asset were more valuable than the portfolio of Arrow-Debreu securities, we would do the opposite. In either case, the difference would be a riskless profit.

State Prices

The values of the Arrow-Debreu securities are called *state prices*. If somehow we can determine these prices, we can use them to price other securities whose payoffs are known. If we limit our definition of arbitrage to the situation we described in the last section and we assume that there are as many independent assets as there are possible market states, we can find the state prices from observed asset prices by solving the algebraic system

$$\sum_{s=1}^{s=S} F_{s,n}(T)\pi_s = V_n(0), \quad n = 1,\ldots, N \tag{1.2}$$

where $N = S$.

If there is a market for Arrow-Debreu securities, solving this system will give us their prices. If we know their prices, we can price any other security whose payoffs are known. We could then argue that the existence of state prices implies the absence of arbitrage, and vice versa. Since the state prices are the values of securities with positive payoffs, the state prices are positive.

A more precise definition of absence of arbitrage is to say that any investment with nonnegative payoff in every possible market outcome at a future time must have a nonnegative initial cost. Loosely speaking, this statement simply says that we cannot get something for nothing. Mathematically, this means that if we hold amounts x_n, $n = 1,\ldots, N$ of assets whose initial values are $V_n(0)$, $n = 1,\ldots, N$, we must have the conditional:

$$\text{If } \sum_{n=1}^{n=N} F_{s,n}(T) \; x_n \geq 0, \, s = 1,\ldots, S, \; \text{ then } \sum_{n=1}^{n=N} V_n(0)x_n \geq 0$$

With this formulation of arbitrage, it is possible to show that also in the case where the number of market states is greater than the number of securities, $S \geq N$, absence of arbitrage implies the existence of positive state prices $\pi_s \geq 0$, $s = 1,\ldots, S$, such that

$$V_n(0) = \sum_{s=1}^{s=S} \pi_s F_{s,n}(T) \tag{1.3}$$

(The proof of this statement uses arguments from operations research: for details, please refer to Varian (1987) or Duffie (1996).) It is clear that each π_s can be interpreted as the values of a security that has a payoff of \$1 at time T if the state s materializes and \$0, otherwise. We can see this by setting the payoff matrix F equal to the identity matrix.

In summary, the present value, $V(0)$, of a security with payoff $V_s(T)$ at time T, if state s materializes, is given by

$$V(0) = \sum_{s=1}^{s=S} \pi_s V_s(T) \tag{1.4}$$

If there are as many market states as there are independent securities, the state prices π_i are unique and the market is called *complete*. If there are more market states than independent securities, the market is called *incomplete*. In this case, the state prices are not unique.

Equation 1.4 is the starting point for pricing a derivative as an expectation of future values.

Present Value as an Expectation of Future Values

Consider two instruments whose present values are denoted by $A(0)$ and $B(0)$ and whose payoff vectors are $A(T)$ and $B(T)$. We write down the ratio of their present values, using the last equation, as:

$$\frac{A(0)}{B(0)} = \frac{\pi_1 B_1(T)}{\pi_1 B_1(T) + \cdots + \pi_S B_S(T)} \frac{A_1(T)}{B_1(T)}$$
$$+ \cdots \frac{\pi_S B_S(T)}{\pi_1 B_1(T) + \cdots + \pi_S B_S(T)} \frac{A_S(T)}{B_S(T)} \tag{1.5}$$

This expression can be written as

$$\frac{A(0)}{B(0)} = \sum_{i=1}^{i=S} p_i \frac{A_i(T)}{B_i(T)} \tag{1.6}$$

where

$$p_i = \frac{\pi_i B_i(T)}{\pi_1 B_1(T) + \cdots + \pi_S B_S(T)} \tag{1.7}$$

Notice that the p_is are all nonnegative, and they add up to 1. Hence, since there are as many p_is as there are possible market outcomes, the p_is can be interpreted as probability masses. The market outcomes have probabilities of occurrence of their own, which we call *objective* or *market probabilities*. The probabilities we have just derived are different from the objective probability of the market outcomes. In fact, the market objective probabilities do not appear explicitly in the derivation. We refer to the probabilities in Equation 1.7 as *induced* by the asset in the denominator of Equation 1.5. The asset in the denominator is called the *numeraire asset.*

If the asset in the denominator of Equation 1.5 does not vanish for the market outcomes of interest, the induced probabilities will be different from zero for the outcomes where the objective probabilities are different from zero. A probability measure assigns probabilities to outcomes. Probability measures that assign probabilities with this property are called *equivalent probability measures.* We can infer that absence of arbitrage means that the price of a traded asset, normalized with the price of another traded asset or portfolio of traded assets, equals the expectation of the normalized value at time T with respect to a probability measure induced by the normalizing asset.

This means that the present value of an asset can be written as

$$A(0) = B(0)E^B \frac{A(T)}{B(T)} \tag{1.8}$$

where E^B denotes expectation with respect to probabilities induced by B.

If asset B is an investment of \$1 that pays a known compound return r at time T, we get the more familiar formula

$$\begin{aligned} A(0) &= E^Q \exp(-rT)A(T) \\ &= \exp(-rT)E^Q A(T) \end{aligned} \tag{1.9}$$

where Q indicates that the expectation is taken with respect to probabilities induced by the continuously compounded \$1 investment. This familiar formula says that the present value of an asset with uncertain payoffs is the discounted expectation of the payoffs (assuming that the interest rate is known), where the probabilities of market outcomes are said to be *risk neutral.*

How are the objective probabilities of market outcomes related to the probabilities induced by the numeraire asset? This relationship is captured by the so-called "Radon-Nikodym derivative," defined as

$$Z_i = \frac{p_i}{p_i^M} \tag{1.10}$$

where p_i^M is the objective, or market probability mass, for the ith market outcome. The Radon-Nikodym derivative has the property

$$E^M Z = 1 \tag{1.11}$$

where E^M indicates expectation with respect to the market or objective measure. For any random variable X,

$$E^B X = E^M(ZX) \tag{1.12}$$

We can now summarize our observations:

- If the number of possible market outcomes is equal to the number of independent assets with payoffs associated with these market outcomes, the market is called *complete*. A unique set of state prices determines a unique probability measure induced by a normalizing asset, and there is no arbitrage.
- If the number of possible market outcomes is greater than the number of independent assets with payoffs associated with these outcomes, the market is called *incomplete*. State prices rule out arbitrage but are not unique and there is a nonunique probability measure induced by a normalizing asset.
- If there are more independent assets than market states, there are no state prices, there are no probabilities induced by a normalizing asset, and there is arbitrage.

So far, we have motivated the formulation of the pricing problem as an expectation of future payoffs. This expectation is taken with respect to probabilities associated with a given normalizing asset. The goal of quantitative pricing is to compute this expectation. As we will see, this expectation can be computed according to different methodologies. Each methodology for computing the expectation gives rise to a different specialization of quantitative financial pricing. The main approaches are as follows.

- Direct analytical evaluation of the expectation: This approach may give closed-form solutions. We will see some simple examples in Chapter 3.
- Numerical computation of the expectation by simulation: A variety of Monte Carlo techniques can be used with varying degrees of success. We will discuss these techniques in Chapters 5 and 6.
- Transformation of the expectation into a partial differential equation (PDE) or an integro-partial differential equation (IPDE): This allows us to resort to the vast field of numerical analysis applied to parabolic PDEs. We will discuss this in Chapter 7.

Before tackling the pricing problem with any particular methodology, we must enrich the framework for formulating the expectation we discussed. The reason for this is that a number of questions arise that are not contemplated in this extremely simplistic model. For example: What happens if payoffs are distributed in time? What happens if payoffs occur at unknown times? What happens if the holder of a security can make decisions regarding payoffs as time evolves? To address these issues, we will formulate the pricing problem in continuous time. It also happens that working in continuous time allows us to introduce powerful methodologies that would not be possible otherwise, such as numerical solutions of stochastic differential equations and partial differential equations.

The fundamental tool for working with financial pricing in continuous time is stochastic calculus. This textbook assumes no prior knowledge of stochastic calculus on the part of the reader. The next chapter is a brief summary of the main concepts of stochastic calculus that we will need to work effectively with the rest of the chapters.

Before moving on, however, we must keep in mind that the pricing framework that we just postulated, where the price of a security is an expectation, hinges on the absence of arbitrage. Unlike physicists, who do not have to worry about the validity of the conservation principles on which they base their calculations, financial engineers must be concerned about the validity of their fundamental principle, the absence of arbitrage. Although the physical world does not violate its conservation equations, the market may, in fact, "violate" the absence of arbitrage. If this happens, the framework and methodologies this book concerns itself with will not work.

Before deciding on a computational methodology, the validity of the nonarbitrage pricing framework must be determined. It is useful to ask these questions:

■ Are the instruments of interest and its hedging securities sufficiently liquid?
■ Are there any restrictions on trading that would be relevant to the instrument in question, such as the inability to perform short sales?
■ Are there significant transaction costs associated with the instrument or its hedging securities?

Clearly, effort in developing a sophisticated pricing approach is not warranted if the fundamental assumption on which the approach is based is invalid.

CHAPTER 2

Fundamentals of Stochastic Calculus

T his chapter provides a summary of the concepts of stochastic calculus needed in financial engineering calculations. This chapter is an attempt to condense the fundamentals of a complex subject in a manner that is accessible to readers with a modest mathematical background. Readers who already have a background in stochastic calculus can go directly to the next chapter. The exposition in this chapter is nonrigorous and intuitive. For a more comprehensive treatment of stochastic calculus, the reader may consult the excellent works of Karatzas and Shreve (1988) and Protter (1995). The book by Oksendal (1995) is applications-oriented and highly recommended.

BASIC DEFINITIONS

Unlike regular calculus, which deals with deterministic functions, integrals, and differential equations, stochastic calculus deals with stochastic processes, functions of stochastic processes, integrals involving processes, and differential equations involving processes.

A stochastic process is defined in a *probability space*. Before discussing stochastic processes in detail, we elaborate on the elements of the probability space.

PROBABILITY SPACE

A stochastic process is defined in a probability space, which we denote by (Ω, F, P). In the probability space we have the following elements.

- Ω is the space of all possible outcomes of an observation or experiment, also known as the *sample space*.
- F is known as the *filtration*. The filtration is a set of so-called "σ-fields," or "σ-algebras." The filtration determines, or encodes, the

information that is revealed by observing the time evolution of the stochastic process.

■ P is the *probability measure*. It assigns probabilities to subsets of Ω.

We will now describe these items in greater detail.

Sample Space

The outcomes contained in the sample space Ω depend on what we are interested in observing. For example, if we are considering the number of times a stock price has moved upward within a period of time, Ω would be a set of integers, where each integer represents a possible number of upward moves by the stock, namely $\Omega = \{0, 1, ..., n\}$.

A more relevant example, which will serve as a basis for discussion in the next few sections, is when we are interested in the trajectories of up and down moves of a stock price in a given period of time. Ω would then be the set of up and down sequences that can be observed in that period of time. For example, if the period of time contains three observations, Ω will consist of $2^3 = 8$ sequences, each one indicating the succession of up and down moves, namely, $\Omega = \{uuu, uud, udu, udd, duu, dud, ddu, ddd\}$. The observations we are interested in are realizations of stochastic processes. (The price of a stock, as we will see later, can be characterized by a stochastic process.) Therefore, the sample space of interest to us is the set of possible trajectories of a stochastic process in a given time interval.

Filtration and the Revelation of Information

Information about the true outcome is represented by subsets of Ω. Considering our three-observation example, before any observation is made, we can say the following about the true outcome of the stock trajectory: The true trajectory will not be part of the empty set, $\varnothing$, and will be part of the sample space, Ω.

Therefore, before any observation is made, information about the true outcome of the price trajectory is represented by the following set of subsets of Ω:

$$F_0 = \{\varnothing, \Omega\} \tag{2.1}$$

At the first observation of our three observation example, we can say the following about the eventual trajectory that will turn out to be true: a) The true trajectory will not be contained in the empty set, $\varnothing$, and will be contained in the sample space, Ω; and b) The true trajectory will be part of either the set $U = \{uuu, uud, udu, udd\}$ or the set $D = \{duu, dud, ddu, duu\}$.

At the first observation, the information about the true outcome is represented by the following set of subsets of Ω:

$$F_1 = \{\varnothing, \Omega, U, D\} \tag{2.2}$$

At the second observation, we can say the following: a) The true trajectory will not be contained in the empty set, $\varnothing$, and will be contained in the sample set Ω; b) The true trajectory will be part of one of the sets $UU = \{uuu, uud\}$, $UD = \{udu, udd\}, DU = \{duu, dud\}, DD = \{ddu, ddd\}$; and c) The true trajectory will be part of the union of these sets.

At the second observation, information about the true outcome is represented by the following set of subsets of Ω:

$$F_2 = \{\varnothing, \Omega, UU, UD, DD, UU \cup UD, ...\} \tag{2.3}$$

These sets of subsets of Ω, which reveal increasingly more information about the true outcome, are called *σ-fields* or *σ-algebras*. The indexed collection of these σ-algebras is called a *filtration*, $F = \{F_0, ..., F_n\}$. Each element of the filtration encodes information revealed by observation of the up and down moves of the stock price. In this case, we can refer to the filtration as generated by the up and down moves of the stock price. The filtration $\{F_0, F_1, F_2\}$ is generated by the first two observations of the up and down moves. It is clear that the σ-algebras generated by the up and down moves before time t are subsets the σ-algebra generated at by the up and down moves at time t:

$$F_0 \subset F_1 \subset F_2 \cdots \tag{2.4}$$

Probability Measure

A probability measure is a set function. A set function assigns values to sets. A probability measure assigns a real number in the interval $[0, 1]$ to the *disjoint* sets of sets of Ω in such a way that these numbers add up to one (it assigns zero to $\varnothing$ and one to Ω). A probability measure gives us the probability that the true outcome (in the case of the stock price, the true trajectory) is contained in a particular set. Changing the measure means changing the function that assigns values to the sets in Ω. One probability measure of particular interest is the *market measure*. This measure assigns probabilities that are consistent with actual market movements. Other measures are also possible. Chapter 1 introduced the concept of probability measures associated with different normalizing assets. These alternative probability measures are useful because they allow us to formulate the pricing problem in terms of quantities we know, or because they facilitate the mathematical formulation. We will discuss this in detail in Chapter 3. The reader interested in more detailed information on probability measures is referred to the excellent book by Billingsley (1994).

RANDOM VARIABLES

A *random variable* is a function that maps the elements of Ω to the set of real numbers. For the same sample space, we can have different random variables. In our example, the stock price at an observation time is a random variable. The number of times the stock price exceeds a given amount is another random variable.

By observing a random variable we can determine information about the true outcome of an experiment. In our example, by observing the stock price we can determine information about the true outcome of the stock trajectory. This information is represented by σ-algebras generated by the random variable.

If the stock price is described by a recombining binomial tree, we will get less information by observing the stock price than we get by observing the stock trajectories directly. Let's elaborate on the σ-algebras generated by the stock price when the binomial tree is recombining.

Let's denote by $\sigma(S_i)$ the σ-algebra generated by the stock price at the ith observation, where S_i is the random variable that characterizes the stock price at the ith observation. Before any observation is made and at the first observation, the σ-algebras generated by the stock price are the same as F_0 and F_1:

$$\sigma(S_0) = \{\varnothing, \Omega\} \tag{2.5}$$

$$\sigma(S_1) = \{\varnothing, \Omega, U, D\} \tag{2.6}$$

At the second observation time, however, the fact that the stock price follows a recombining tree does not allow us to distinguish between trajectories in DU and UD. From here on, the σ-algebras generated by the stock price contain less information than we can get from observing the samples directly:

$$\sigma(S_2) = \{\varnothing, \Omega, UU, UD \cup DU, DD, UU \cup (UD \cup DU), \ldots\} \tag{2.7}$$

We are now in a position to define a stochastic process.

STOCHASTIC PROCESS

A *stochastic process* is a set of random variables parameterized by time, such as S_t, $0 \le t \le T$, defined in a probability space $\{\Omega, F, P\}$.

Measurable Stochastic Process

A stochastic process S_t is F_t-measurable if every set in the σ-algebra generated by S_t, $\sigma(S(t))$, is in F_t. This means that if we know the information in F_t, we know S_t. By this we mean that if we know the outcomes up to and including the observation at time t, we can evaluate S_t.

Adapted Process

A stochastic process S_t is adapted to F_t if S_t is F_t-measurable.

Conditional Expectation

The expectation of X, conditional on the information contained in the σ-algebra F_t, is denoted as follows:

$$Y = E[X|F_t] = E_t[X] \tag{2.8}$$

where we adopt a simple notation for the conditional expectation operator. Y is an F_t-measurable random variable. If X is adapted to F_t,

$$X = E_t[X] \tag{2.9}$$

Iterated Expectations   If we assume two σ-algebras, G and H, such that the information in G is contained in H, then the *iterated expectation* of a random variable simplifies as follows:

$$E[E[X|H]|G] = E[X|G] \tag{2.10}$$

We will typically be referring to conditional expectations when the σ-algebras are elements of a filtration F. In this case, since $F_t \subset F_s$, $t \le s$, we have

$$E_t[X] = E_t[E_s[X]], \ t \le s \tag{2.11}$$

Martingales

Assume that S_t is a stochastic process adapted to F_t, $0 \le t \le T$. The process S_t is a *martingale* if the expectation of its value at a future time, s, conditional on information at an earlier time, t, is equal to the value of the process at the earlier time t:

$$E_t[S_s] = S_t, \ 0 \le t \le s \le T \tag{2.12}$$

WIENER PROCESS

The *Wiener process,* also known as *Brownian motion,* is the basic process of continuous-time financial modeling.

To visualize a Wiener process, consider a sequence of up and down moves of the price process, S_t. The up or down moves are determined at times $t_k = t_{k-1} + \Delta t$, $k = 0, ..., n$. At each t_k, the up or down amount is determined by sampling from a normal distribution with mean 0 and variance Δt:

$$W(t_{k+1}, \omega) = W(t_k, \omega) + \sqrt{\Delta t} Z \qquad (2.13)$$

Here, Z is a standard normal distribution and ω is a sample point in the sample space Ω. The sample point represents a sequence of up and down moves along the trajectory of the Wiener process. We would get a standard Wiener process by letting $\Delta t \to 0$. The properties of the Wiener process are the following:

■ For each sample $\omega \in \Omega$, $W(t, \omega)$ is a continuous function of t.
■ The initial condition of a Wiener process is $W(t = 0, \omega) = 0$ a.s. Almost surely (a.s.) means that the probability of $W(0, \omega) = 0$ is 1.
■ The increments of the Wiener process are normal and independent. This means

$$E_0[W_s - W_t] = 0, \; t \le s,$$
$$\text{var}[W_s - W_t] = s - t, \; t \le s, \qquad (2.14)$$
$$\text{cov}[(W_s - W_t),(W_v - W_u)] = 0, \; t \le s \le u \le v$$

For simplicity, we omit reference to the sample point ω, and use subscripts for the time dependence.

A Wiener process is adapted to a σ-algebra F_t. The filtration $\{F_t\}_{t \ge 0}$ can be the one generated by the Wiener process itself, or it can be one generated by the Wiener process as well as other processes, as long as the other processes don't reveal information about future movements of the Wiener process.

The following are additional properties of the Wiener process:

■ The Wiener process is Markovian. This means that for $0 \le t \le s$, conditional on F_t, everything random about W_s (such as the mean, variance, and so forth) depends only on W_t.
■ The statement above implies that the Wiener process is a martingale: $E_t[W_s] = W_t, \; t \le s$.
■ The Wiener process is an infinitely "wiggly" function that does not have a defined slope or tangent. The mathematical concept that captures the infinite wiggliness of a process is called *second variation* or *quadratic variation*. Differentiable functions have zero second variation. The Wiener process has finite second variation.

To motivate the notion of *second variation* (SV) as a characterization for the Wiener process, we will first discuss the *first variation* (FV) and the second variation of a differentiable function.

First Variation of a Differentiable Function

The first variation of a differentiable function is finite, whereas the first variation of the Wiener process is infinite.

Define points in time

$$0 = t_0 \le t_1 \le \cdots \le t_n = T \qquad (2.15)$$

and define

$$\Delta = \max (t_{i+1} - t_i), \, 0 \le i < n \qquad (2.16)$$

The first variation, also called simply the *variation* of a function $f(t)$, is defined as

$$FV(f) = \lim_{\Delta \to 0} \sum_{i=0}^{i=n} |f(t_{i+1}) - f(t_i)| \qquad (2.17)$$

If the function $f(t)$ is differentiable, the mean value theorem and a little algebra give

$$FV(f) = \int_{t=0}^{t=T} \left| \frac{df(t)}{dt} \right| dt \qquad (2.18)$$

This means that, in general, the first variation of a differentiable function will be different from zero.

First Variation of the Wiener Process

The first variation of the Wiener process is infinite. The reason for this will become clear after we discuss the second variation of the Wiener process.

Second Variation of a Differentiable Function

The second, or quadratic, variation is defined as

$$SV(f) = \lim_{\Delta \to 0} \sum_{i=0}^{i=n} |f(t_{i+1}) - f(t_i)|^2 \qquad (2.19)$$

Applying the mean value theorem and some algebra, we find

$$SV(f) = \lim_{\Delta \to 0} \Delta \int_{t=0}^{t=T} \left| \frac{df(t)}{dt} \right|^2 dt \qquad (2.20)$$

Since in a differentiable function the integrand is bounded, the second variation of a differentiable function is zero:

$$SV(f) = 0 \qquad (2.21)$$

Second Variation of the Wiener Process

Some algebra shows that the second variation of the Wiener process is equal to its variance:

$$SV(W(t = T)) = T \qquad (2.22)$$

This also says that the first variation of the Wiener process is infinite:

$$
\begin{aligned}
FV(W(T)) &= \lim_{\Delta \to 0} \sum_{i=0}^{i=n} |W(t_{i+1}) - W(t_i)| \\
&\geq \frac{1}{\max(\Delta W)} \lim_{\Delta \to 0} \sum_{i=0}^{i=n} |W(t_{i+1}) - W(t_i)|^2 \qquad (2.23) \\
&\geq \frac{SV(W(T))}{\max(\Delta W)}
\end{aligned}
$$

Since the second variation is finite and the Wiener process is continuous, this shows that the first variation is infinite.

Products of Infinitesimal Increments of Wiener Processes

In using stochastic calculus as a practical tool, the product of two infinitesimal increments of Wiener processes is *not* a stochastic quantity.

First Practical Result: *dWdW = dt*

From the derivation of the second variation of the Wiener process we found that

$$\text{var}[(W(t + \Delta t) - W(t))^2 - \Delta t] = 2\Delta t^2 \qquad (2.24)$$

The quantity $(W(t + \Delta t) - W(t))^2 - \Delta t$ is a stochastic process whose variance vanishes like Δt^2 as $\Delta t \to 0$. We also know that $E[(W(t + \Delta t) - W(t))^2] = \Delta t$, or equivalently, $E[(W(t + \Delta t) - W(t))^2 - \Delta t] = 0$. This means that $(W(t + \Delta t) - W(t))^2 - \Delta t$ tends to zero as $\Delta t \to 0$. We can write,

$$(W(t + \Delta t) - W(t))^2 \to \Delta t \text{ as } \Delta t \to 0 \qquad (2.25)$$

Using differential notation, this means

$$dWdW = dt \qquad (2.26)$$

This is result is striking in that, to lowest order, the product of these two *random* quantities is a deterministic quantity.

Second Practical Result: $dW_1 dW_2 = 0$ If W_1 and W_2 Are Independent

Corollary: $dW_1 dW_2 = \rho dt$ If W_1 and W_2 Are Correlated

This is a straightforward consequence of the last result. Assume that Z_1 and Z_2 are independent Wiener processes. We can construct correlated Wiener processes W_1 and W_2 as follows:

$$dW_1(t) = dZ_1(t) \qquad (2.27)$$

$$dW_2(t) = \rho dZ_1(t) + \sqrt{1-\rho^2} dZ_2(t) \qquad (2.28)$$

It is straightforward to verify that the correlation between dW_1 and dW_2 have variance dt and correlation coefficient ρ:

$$\text{var}[dW_1(t)] = \text{var}[dZ_1(t)] = dt \qquad (2.29)$$

$$\begin{aligned} \text{var}[dW_2(t)] &= \text{var}[dZ_1(t)] + \text{var}[dZ_2(t)] \\ &= \rho^2 dt + (1-\rho^2)dt \\ &= dt \end{aligned} \qquad (2.30)$$

$$\begin{aligned} \text{cov}[dW_1(t)dW_2(t)] &= \rho dZ_1 dZ_2 + \sqrt{1-\rho^2} dZ_1 dZ_2 \\ &= \rho dt \end{aligned} \qquad (2.31)$$

Here we made use of $dZ_1 dZ_2 = 0$. The correlation coefficient between dW_1 and dW_2 is

$$\begin{aligned} \rho &= \frac{\text{cov}[dZ_1, dZ_2]}{\sqrt{\text{var}[dZ_1]}\sqrt{\text{var}[dZ_2]}} \\ &= \frac{\rho dt}{\sqrt{dt}\sqrt{dt}} \\ &= \rho \end{aligned} \qquad (2.32)$$

The product of the increments of two correlated Wiener processes is

$$\begin{aligned} dW_1(t)dW_2(t) &= \rho dZ_1^2(t) + \sqrt{1-\rho^2} dZ_2(t)dZ_1(t) \\ &= \rho dt \end{aligned} \qquad (2.33)$$

STOCHASTIC INTEGRALS

Consider a function $g(Y(t), t)$, where $Y(t)$ is a stochastic process and t is time. We want to work with integrals of the form:

$$I(t) = \int_0^t g(Y(s), s)dW(s) \tag{2.34}$$

Before describing how we interpret this integral, consider the case of the *Riemann integral* of a deterministic function, $f(t)$:

$$J(t) = \int_0^t f(s)ds \tag{2.35}$$

We define points in time $0 = t_0 \le t_1 \le \cdots \le t_n = t$ and $\Delta = \max(t_{i+1} - t_i)$, $0 \le i < n$. In this case, we define the sequence of partial sums as

$$J_n(t) = \sum_{i=1}^{i=n-1} f(\tau_i)(t_{i+1} - t_i) \tag{2.36}$$

where $t_i \le \tau_i \le t_{i+1}$, $i = 1, \ldots, n-1$. The Riemann integral is the limit of these partial sum sequences:

$$J(t) = \lim_{\Delta \to 0} J_n(t) \tag{2.37}$$

The important thing to remark about the Riemann integral is that the result *does not depend* on the choice of τ_i.

The stochastic integral is also defined as a limit of sequences of partial sums. In this case, however, the result does depend on the choice of τ_i. The Ito integral corresponds to the specific choice $\tau_i = t_i$. The limit used in defining the *Ito integral* is the *mean square limit*, or *limit in the mean*.

Mean Square Limit

A sequence $g_n(t)$ is said to converge to a function $g(t)$ in the mean square if

$$\lim_{n \to \infty} E \int_0^t [g_n(t) - g(t)]^2 dt = 0 \tag{2.38}$$

The notation used to express this convergence is

$$g(t) = \operatorname*{ms-lim}_{n \to \infty} g_n(t) \tag{2.39}$$

Ito Integral

The Ito integral corresponds to the case where the integrand is evaluated at the *beginning* of the subintervals used to define the partial sums. This is the integral of interest in financial pricing. We assume that $g(Y(t), t)$ is adapted to the filtration generated by $W(t)$ and that $E[\int_0^t g^2 ds] < \infty$:

$$I_n(t) = \sum_{i=1}^{i=n-1} g(Y(t_i), t_i)(W(t_{i+1}) - W(t_i)) \tag{2.40}$$

The definition of the Ito integral is then

$$I(t) = \underset{n \to \infty}{\text{ms-lim}} \, I_n(t) \tag{2.41}$$

If we chose a different point within the subintervals to evaluate the integrand in the partial sums, we would get a different result for $I(t)$. For example, if we choose to evaluate the integrand at the midpoint in the Wiener process interval, we get the *Stratanovich integral*.

Why are we interested in the Ito integral in finance, as opposed to other definitions of the stochastic integral, such as the Stratanovich integral? As we will see later, the fact that the integrand is evaluated at the beginning of the Wiener process interval is precisely what makes the definition of the Ito integral an adequate choice in finance. Intuitively, we can say that this corresponds to the fact that financial positions are changed *in response* to unexpected changes.

Properties of the Ito Integral

These properties of the Ito integral are useful in getting solutions to stochastic differential equations and other applications.

The Ito Integral Is a Martingale   This means that for $\xi \geq t$,

$$E_t\left[\int_0^s g(Y(\xi), \xi)dW(\xi)\right] = \int_0^t g(Y(\xi), \xi)dW(\xi) \tag{2.42}$$

We can see why this is the case by representing the integral as

$$\int_0^s g(Y(\xi), \xi)dW(\xi) = \int_0^t g(Y(\xi), \xi)dW(\xi) + \int_t^s g(Y(\xi), \xi)dW(\xi) \tag{2.43}$$

When represented as the limit of partial sums, the second integral on the right is the sum of terms of the form $g(Y(\xi_i), t_i)(W(\xi_{i+1}) - W(\xi_i))$. Since

Y is determined by the information generated at time t_i, the terms that make up these partial sums all have zero mean. This tells us that $E_t[\int_t^s g(Y(\xi),\,\xi)dW(\xi)] = 0$. Therefore,

$$E_t\left[\int_0^s g(Y(\xi),\,\xi)dW(\xi)\right] = E_t\left[\underbrace{\int_0^t g(Y(\xi),\,\xi)dW(\xi)}_{\text{known at time } t}\right] \tag{2.44}$$

$$= \int_0^t g(Y(\xi),\,\xi)dW(\xi)$$

Variance of the Ito Integral   The variance of the Ito integral is

$$\text{var}\left[\int_0^t g(Y(s),\,s)dW(s)\right] = E\left[\int_0^t (g(Y(s),\,s))^2 ds\right] \tag{2.45}$$

To prove this result, first notice that since the Ito integral is a martingale,

$$E\left[\int_0^t g(Y(s),\,s)dW(s)\right] = 0 \tag{2.46}$$

From the definition of variance,

$$\text{var}\left[\int_0^t g(Y(s),\,s)dW(s)\right]$$

$$= E\left[\int_0^t g(Y(s),\,s)dW(s)\int_0^t g(Y(s),\,s)dW(s)\right] - \underbrace{\left(E\left[\int_0^t g(Y(s),\,s)dW(s)\right]\right)^2}_{=0}$$

$$= E \lim_{n\to\infty}\left[\sum_{i,j=1}^{i,j=n-1} g(Y(s_i),\,s_i)(W(s_{i+1}) - W(s_i))g(Y(s_j),\,s_j)(W(s_{j+1}) - W(s_j))\right]$$

$$\tag{2.47}$$

Since the cross terms have zero expectation,

$$\text{var}\left[\int_0^t g(Y(s),\,s)dW(s)\right] = E \lim_{n\to\infty}\left[\sum_{i=1}^{i=n-1} g(Y(s_i),\,s_i)^2(s_{i+1} - s_i)\right]$$

$$= E\left[\int_0^t (g(Y(s),\,s))^2 ds\right] \tag{2.48}$$

Covariance of Ito Integrals Following similar arguments as in the last paragraph, one can show that the covariance of two Ito integrals is given by

$$
\text{cov}\left[\int_0^t g_1(X(s), s)dW(s), \int_0^t g_2(X(s), s)dW(s)\right]
$$
$$
= \text{E}\left[\int_0^t g_1(X(s), s)dW(s)\int_0^t g_2(X(s), s)dW(s)\right]
$$
(2.49)

where $g_1()$ and $g_2()$ are functions adapted to the filtration generated by $W(t)$. A little algebra leads to

$$
\text{cov}\left[\int_0^t g_1(X(s), s)dW(s), \int_0^t g_2(X(s), s)dW(s)\right]
$$
$$
= \int_0^t \text{E}[g_1(X(s), s)g_2(X(s), s)]ds
$$
(2.50)

ITO PROCESSES

Ito processes are also called *Ito diffusions* (Oksendal 1995). We will also refer to these processes as *drift-diffusion processes*. In one dimension, the differential form of an Ito process is

$$
dX(t) = a(X(t), t)dt + b(X(t), t)dW(t)
$$
(2.51)

where $a(.)$ and $b(.)$ are adapted to the filtration generated by $W(t)$.

The integral form of this process is

$$
X(t) = X(0) + \int_0^t a(X(s), s)ds + \int_0^t b(X(s), s)dW(s)
$$
(2.52)

where the second integral on the right is interpreted as an Ito integral. $a(.)$ is called the *drift*, and $b(.)$ is called the *volatility* (b^2 is the variance of the process change per unit time).[1] We usually work with the differential form of Ito processes, but we must keep in mind that this is only meaningful if the

---

[1]In practice, volatility refers to the standard deviation of the relative process change, $\frac{dx}{x}$. Here, we will apply this terminology to either the relative or absolute process change, depending on context.

integral form of the process is consistent with the Ito interpretation of the Ito stochastic integral.

A very common form of Ito process used in finance is

$$\frac{dX(t)}{X(t)} = \mu(X(t), t)dt + \sigma(X(t), t)dW(t) \tag{2.53}$$

In this case, $\mu(.)$ is also called the *drift* and $\sigma(.)$ is referred to as the *volatility*.

In several dimensions, we could have a *multidimensional process* $\{X_1, ..., X_N\}$, where each component is driven by a multidimensional Wiener process $\{W_1, ..., W_M\}$ and where M and N are not necessarily equal. We will elaborate on this in the next section.

MULTIDIMENSIONAL PROCESSES

There are several ways to represent a multidimensional stochastic process. This section is meant to clarify the notation that we may encounter.

Multidimensional Wiener Processes

We briefly discussed multidimensional Wiener processes earlier this chapter. A multidimensional Wiener process $\vec{W}$ is a (column) vector $\{W_1, W_2, ..., W_K\}^T$ of correlated Wiener processes W_i. As we saw earlier, the product of any two components of $d\vec{W}$ is the covariance between those components:

$$\begin{aligned} dW_i dW_j &= \text{cov}\,[dW_i, dW_j] \\ &= \rho_{ij}dt \end{aligned} \tag{2.54}$$

We can build correlated Wiener processes by taking combinations of uncorrelated Wiener processes. If $\vec{Z}$ is a (column) vector of uncorrelated Wiener processes, $\{Z_1, Z_2, ..., Z_K\}^T$, we can get the multidimensional Wiener process $\vec{W}$ through a suitable matrix-vector multiplication as follows:

$$dW_i = \sum_{j=1}^{j=K} a_{ij}dZ_j, \, i = 1,..., K \tag{2.55}$$

As we will see in Chapter 4, the matrix with components a_{ij} is the lower *Choleski factor* of the correlation matrix of the dW_i.

The covariance between any two components of $d\vec{W}$ can now be expressed as

$$dW_n dW_m = \text{cov}\,[dZ_n, dZ_m]$$

$$= \left(\sum_{j=1}^{j=K} a_{nj} dZ_j\right)\left(\sum_{j=1}^{j=K} a_{mj} dZ_j\right) \tag{2.56}$$

$$= a_{n1}a_{m1} + \cdots + a_{nK}a_{mK}$$

In vector notation,

$$dW_n = \vec{a}_n^T d\vec{Z} \tag{2.57}$$

$$dW_m = \vec{a}_m^T d\vec{Z} \tag{2.58}$$

where $\vec{a}_n$ and $\vec{a}_m$ are (column) vectors. The covariance is

$$dW_n dW_m = \underbrace{\vec{a}_n^T \vec{a}_m}_{\text{inner vector product}}\, dt \tag{2.59}$$

Multidimensional Ito Processes

As an example, consider a two-dimensional drift-diffusion process, with components $X(t)$ and $Y(t)$:

$$dX = \mu_X dt + \sigma_X dW_X \tag{2.60}$$

$$dY = \mu_Y dt + \sigma_Y dW_Y \tag{2.61}$$

In this case, dW_X, dW_Y, σ_X, and σ_T are scalars, and the product $dX\,dY$ is

$$dX dY = \sigma_X \sigma_Y \text{cov}\,(dW_X dW_Y)$$
$$= \sigma_X \sigma_Y \rho_{XY} dt \tag{2.62}$$

We can also use vector notation for the Wiener part of these processes:

$$dX = \mu_X dt + \vec{\sigma}_X^T d\vec{W} \tag{2.63}$$

$$dY = \mu_Y dt + \vec{\sigma}_Y^T d\vec{W} \tag{2.64}$$

Notice that here we have incorporated the coefficients of the linear combination in Equation 2.58 into the definition of $\vec{\sigma}$. The covariance of dX and dY is

$$dX dY = \text{cov}\,(dX, dY)$$
$$= \vec{\sigma}_X^T \vec{\sigma}_Y dt \tag{2.65}$$

We can have an even more compact notation for multidimensional Ito processes by defining an array $\vec{X}(t) = \{X_1(t), ..., X_K(t)\}$. In this case, we use matrix notation for the Wiener components:

$$d\vec{X}(t) = \vec{\mu}dt + \tilde{\sigma}d\vec{W} \qquad (2.66)$$

where $\tilde{\sigma}$ is a matrix.

When dealing with multidimensional processes, we will typically favor the vector representation of the Wiener part, shown in Equation 2.64. For simplicity, we will normally not use the arrow and the transpose signs, however. In such a case, we would write two-dimensional processes as

$$dX = \mu_X dt + \sigma_X dW \qquad (2.67)$$

$$dY = \mu_Y dt + \sigma_Y dW \qquad (2.68)$$

with covariance

$$\begin{aligned} dXdY &= \text{cov}(dX, dY) \\ &= \sigma_X \sigma_Y dt \end{aligned} \qquad (2.69)$$

where it is understood that σ_X and σ_Y are vectors, and dW is a vector of uncorrelated Wiener processes.

ITO'S LEMMA

Ito's lemma, also known as Ito's *formula,* gives us the drift-diffusion process of a function of a drift-diffusion process.

An informal derivation of Ito's formula is straightforward. Assume a function $G(X, t)$, where $X(t)$ is an Ito process:

$$dX(t) = a_X(X, t)dt + b_X(X, t)dW(t) \qquad (2.70)$$

We are interested in $dG(t)$, which represents the total change of G as a result of changes in X, W, and t. We apply *Taylor's expansion* to G and keep the second order term in dX. To do this we need to assume that $G(X, t)$ is twice differentiable with respect to X:

$$dG(t) = \frac{\partial G}{\partial t}dt + \frac{\partial G}{\partial X}dX + \frac{1}{2}\frac{\partial^2 G}{\partial X^2}(dX)^2 \qquad (2.71)$$

Notice that there is nothing out of the ordinary in expanding $G(X, t)$ in terms of changes in X and t, even if the changes in X are stochastic.

In ordinary calculus we would only keep first-order terms. In our case, however, $(dX)^2$ is of order dt:

$$(dX)^2 = [a_X(X, t)dt + b_X(X, t)dW(t)]^2$$

$$= \underbrace{(a_X dt)^2}_{O(dt^2)} + \underbrace{2a_X b_X dt dW}_{O(dt^{1.5})} + \underbrace{b_X^2(X, t)(dW)^2}_{=dt} \tag{2.72}$$

$$= b_X^2(X, t)dt$$

Replacing in Equation 2.71,

$$dG(t) = \frac{\partial G}{\partial t}dt + \frac{\partial G}{\partial X}(a_X dt + b_X dW) + \frac{1}{2}\frac{\partial^2 G}{\partial X^2}b_X^2 dt \tag{2.73}$$

Ito's formula then becomes

$$dG(t) = \left(\frac{\partial G}{\partial t} + \frac{\partial G}{\partial X}a_X + \frac{1}{2}\frac{\partial^2 G}{\partial X^2}b_X^2\right)dt + \frac{\partial G}{\partial X}b_X dW \tag{2.74}$$

This is the practical form of Ito's formula. To get the process $G(t)$, we integrate this equation, giving the proper interpretation to the stochastic integral.

$$G(s) = G(0) + \int_0^s\left(\frac{\partial G}{\partial t}dt + \frac{\partial G}{\partial X}a_X + \frac{1}{2}\frac{\partial^2 G}{\partial X^2}b_X^2\right)dt + \int_0^s\frac{\partial G}{\partial X}b_X dW(t) \tag{2.75}$$

Multidimensional Ito's Lemma

The derivation of Ito's formula in several dimensions is straightforward. We illustrate the case of two dimensions. Extensions to more dimensions are trivial. Assume a function $G(X(t), Y(t), t)$ of the Ito processes

$$dX(t) = \mu_X dt + \sigma_X dWdY(t) = \mu_Y dt + \sigma_Y dW \tag{2.76}$$

where σ_X, σ_Y are vectors, and dW is a vector of uncorrelated Wiener processes. Expanding $dG(X(t), Y(t), t)$ in terms of dt, $dX(t)$, and $dY(t)$, and keeping second-order terms, we get

$$\begin{aligned}
dG(t) = &\frac{\partial G}{\partial t}dt \\
&+ \frac{\partial G}{\partial X}dX + \frac{\partial G}{\partial Y}dY \\
&+ \frac{1}{2}\frac{\partial^2 G}{\partial X^2}(dX)^2 \\
&+ \frac{\partial^2 G}{\partial X\partial Y}(dXdY) \\
&+ \frac{1}{2}\frac{\partial^2 G}{\partial Y^2}(dY)^2
\end{aligned} \tag{2.77}$$

Replacing for $(dX)^2$, $(dY)^2$, and $dXdY$, we get

$$
\begin{aligned}
dG(t) = &\frac{\partial G}{\partial t}dt \\
&+ \frac{\partial G}{\partial X}dX + \frac{\partial G}{\partial Y}dY \\
&+ \frac{1}{2}\frac{\partial^2 G}{\partial X^2}\sigma_X\sigma_X dt \\
&+ \frac{\partial^2 G}{\partial X\partial Y}\sigma_X\sigma_Y dt \\
&+ \frac{1}{2}\frac{\partial^2 G}{\partial Y^2}\sigma_Y\sigma_Y dt
\end{aligned}
\tag{2.78}
$$

Collecting terms, we get

$$
\begin{aligned}
dG(t) = &\left(\frac{\partial G}{\partial t} + \frac{\partial G}{\partial X}\mu_X + \frac{\partial G}{\partial Y}\mu_Y \right. \\
&\left. + \frac{1}{2}\frac{\partial^2 G}{\partial X^2}\sigma_X\sigma_X + \frac{\partial^2 G}{\partial X\partial Y}\sigma_X\sigma_Y + \frac{1}{2}\frac{\partial^2 G}{\partial Y^2}\sigma_Y\sigma_Y\right)dt \\
&+ \left(\frac{\partial G}{\partial X}\sigma_X + \frac{\partial G}{\partial Y}\sigma_Y\right)dW
\end{aligned}
\tag{2.79}
$$

Here we understand that σ_X, σ_Y, and dW are vectors. This will be our preferred notation. However, for the sake of completeness, consider the case where the Wiener part of the Ito processes is expressed in scalar form:

$$
dX(t) = \mu_X dt + \sigma_X dW_X \quad dY(t) = \mu_Y dt + \sigma_Y dW_X
\tag{2.80}
$$

Here, σ_X and σ_Y are scalars (although the notation is the same as above), and dW_X, dW_Y are one-dimensional correlated Wiener processes. In this case, Ito's formula is

$$
\begin{aligned}
dG(t) = &\left(\frac{\partial G}{\partial t} + \frac{\partial G}{\partial X}\mu_X + \frac{\partial G}{\partial Y}\mu_Y \right. \\
&\left. + \frac{1}{2}\frac{\partial^2 G}{\partial X^2}\sigma_X^2 + \frac{\partial^2 G}{\partial X\partial Y}\sigma_X\sigma_Y\rho_{XY} + \frac{1}{2}\frac{\partial^2 G}{\partial Y^2}\sigma_Y^2\right)dt \\
&+ \frac{\partial G}{\partial X}\sigma_X dW_X + \frac{\partial G}{\partial Y}\sigma_Y dW_Y
\end{aligned}
\tag{2.81}
$$

This form is also very common in the finance literature.

STOCHASTIC DIFFERENTIAL EQUATIONS

A *stochastic differential equation* (SDE) is written as follows:

$$dX(t) = a(X, t)dt + b(X, t)dW(t) \tag{2.82}$$

If $X(t_0)$ is an initial value, the solution of the SDE is

$$X(t) = X(t_0) + \int_0^t a(X, s)ds + \int_0^t b(X, s)dW(s) \tag{2.83}$$

where we agree that the last term in Equation 2.83 is an Ito integral.

Solution of SDEs We would like to get an expression for $X(t)$ such that integrals involving $X(t)$ or functions of $X(t)$ do not appear on the right-hand side. This explicit solution of the SDE is the most useful in practice.

This is straightforward in only a few simple cases and is in general quite difficult. We will explore some simple examples.

In the trivial case of an SDE with constant a and b subject to the initial condition $X(0) = X_0$,

$$dX(t) = adt + bdW(t) \tag{2.84}$$

the solution at time t is

$$X(t) = X_0 + at + bW(t) \tag{2.85}$$

where we use the fact that $W(0) = 0$. To be able to say that this solution is the one given by Equation 2.83, we must also say that the trajectory of $W(t)$ in the interval $0, t$ is the same in both cases. This means that both solutions are the same if the event ω in $W(t, \omega)$ is the same in both cases.

The case where the a and b are functions of time but do not depend on $X(t)$ is slightly more elaborate. In this case the SDE is

$$dX(t) = a(t)dt + b(t)dW(t) \tag{2.86}$$

and the solution is

$$X(t) = X(0) + \int_0^t a(s)ds + \int_0^t b(s)dW(s) \tag{2.87}$$

Here we know that the last integral on the right is a normal process with mean zero and variance

$$\text{var}\left[\int_0^t b(s)dW(s)\right] = \int_0^t b^2(s)ds \tag{2.88}$$

With this result, we can write Equation 2.87 as follows:

$$X(t) = X(0) + \int_0^t a(s)ds + \sqrt{\frac{1}{t}\int_0^t b^2(s)ds}\, W(t) \tag{2.89}$$

where we made use of the fact that $\text{var}[W(t)] = t$. Again, we must assume that the trajectory of $W(t)$ is the same in Equations 2.89 and 2.87.

A slightly more complicated example that is frequently used in finance is the following:

$$dX(t) = X(t)a(t)dt + X(t)b(t)dW(t) \tag{2.90}$$

Applying Ito's lemma to $Y(t) = \log X(t)$ we get

$$dY(t) = \frac{dX}{X} - \frac{1}{2}\left(\frac{dX}{X}\right)^2 \tag{2.91}$$

Replacing $\frac{dX}{X}$, we get

$$\begin{aligned}
dY(t) &= a(t)dt + b(t)dW(t) - \frac{1}{2}(a(t)dt + b(t)dW(t))^2 \\
&= a(t) - \frac{1}{2}b(t)^2 dt + b(t)dW(t)
\end{aligned} \tag{2.92}$$

This can now be integrated:

$$Y(t) = Y(0) + \int_0^t \left[a(s) - \frac{1}{2}b(s)^2\right]ds + \int_0^t b(s)dW(s) \tag{2.93}$$

Replacing $X = \exp(Y)$, we get

$$X(t) = X(0)\exp\left(\int_0^t \left[a(s) - \frac{1}{2}b(s)^2\right]ds + \int_0^t b(s)dW(s)\right) \tag{2.94}$$

A case of importance in finance is when a and b are constant. In that case,

$$X(t) = X(0)\exp\left(\left(a - \frac{1}{2}b^2\right)t + bW(t)\right) \tag{2.95}$$

Moments of SDE Solutions

Often we are interested in computing the moments of the solutions of SDEs. One way to do this is to solve the SDE and then compute the moments. It turns out, however, that it is much easier to get ordinary differential equations for the moments that can then be solved either analytically or numerically.

For the process

$$dX(t) = a(X, t)dt + b(X, t)dW(t) \tag{2.96}$$

we can use Ito's lemma to get an SDE for the process $X(t)^n$:

$$dX^n(t) = \left[nX^{n-1}a(X, t) + \frac{1}{2}n(n-1)X^{n-2}b^2(X, t) \right]dt \tag{2.97}$$
$$+ nX^{n-1}b(X, t)dW(t)$$

We now have an ordinary differential equation for the expectation of X^n:

$$\frac{dE[X^n(t)]}{dt} = nE[X^{n-1}a(X, t)] \tag{2.98}$$
$$+ \frac{1}{2}n(n-1)E[X^{n-2}b^2(X, t)]$$

We can remark the following about this ordinary differential equation. Depending on the nature of $a(X, t)$ and $b(X, t)$, we can find two different situations.

- Equation 2.98 is part of a hierarchy, where the equations need to be solved in succession for $n = 1, 2, \ldots$ In this case, it may be possible to find analytical solutions or to solve for a number of moments numerically.
- Equation 2.98 is part of an open system of equations, where in order to find a particular moment you need to know higher order ones. In this case it is not possible to find exact analytical or numerical solutions of the exact equations for the moments. It is possible, however, to derive a sufficiently large set of equations and make assumptions about higher order moments. A practical implementation of this idea requires numerical solutions.

SDE Commonly Used in Finance

Stochastic differential equations are used primarily to model prices and interest rates. They can also be used to model other parameters, such as default intensities and volatilities.

Here we list a short sample of some of the most commonly used SDEs in finance. These models have become well established because they are analytically tractable and tend to represent the processes they are modeling fairly well. Perhaps the area where there has been the largest proliferation of models is in interest rates. Besides the first one, this short list refers to short rates models. For practical applications in computational finance, however, LIBOR models are of greater relevance. We will discuss those in detail in Chapter 4.

There are many variations beyond the simple models mentioned here. For a comprehensive discussion, see Duffie (1996).

Geometric Brownian Motion   This is the most commonly used process in continuous stock price modeling:

$$dS(t) = S(t)\mu dt + S(t)\sigma dW(t) \tag{2.99}$$

Earlier, we discussed this example in detail.

Ho and Lee Short Rate Model   This is one of the earliest Gaussian models for the short rate (Ho and Lee 1986). An important consideration in using this model is that it produces negative rates.

$$dr(t) = a(t)dt + \sigma dW(t) \tag{2.100}$$

Vasicek Interest Rate Model   This is a very common process for the short rate (Vasicek 1977). Like the Ho-Lee model, this model can produce negative rates. The innovation consists of the introduction of mean reversion in the drift:

$$dr(t) = [a - br(t)]dt + \sigma dW(t) \tag{2.101}$$

Hull and White Short Rate Model   This model has been used extensively in fixed income pricing (Hull and White 1990). It is also known as the *extended* or *generalized Vasicek model*:

$$dr(t) = [a(t) - br(t)]dt + \sigma dW(t) \tag{2.102}$$

Cox-Ingersoll-Ross Short Rate Model   This is the simplest model that prevents rates from being negative and also allows for analytical valuation of simple interest rate products (Cox 1985):

$$dr(t) = [a(t) - b(t)r(t)]dt + \sqrt{r(t)}\sigma dW(t) \tag{2.103}$$

The Markov Property of Solutions of SDE

A process $X(t)$ is said to satisfy the *Markov property*, or to be *Markovian*, if the random properties of the process at time $s \geq t$, conditional on information at time t, only depend on the value of the process at time t. This means that the process does not have a memory of events before the observation time that will influence its stochastic properties beyond the observation time. In other words, the behavior of the process beyond the observation time does not depend on the trajectory that the process followed up to the observation time.

Subject to technical conditions, the solution of the SDE,

$$dX(t) = a(X, t)dt + b(X, t)dW(t) \qquad (2.104)$$

is Markovian. Intuitively, the reason for this is that if the solution is known at a given time, t_0, all the properties at a later time, t_1, are uniquely determined by the value of the process at t_0, $X(t_0)$. This is the case because $X(t_0)$ is the initial condition of the solution that determines the behavior of the process at $t_1 \geq t_0$.

There are several ways to express the Markovian property of a stochastic process. In our case, we are interested in writing this property in terms of an expectation, because our immediate use for the Markovian property is the derivation of the Feynman-Kac theorem.

We use the following notation: $E_{(t,x)}$ means the expectation given t and x. Compare this with E_t, which means expectation conditional on information at time t.

For a Markovian process, the expectation of a function of the stochastic process $f(X)$ satisfies

$$E_t[f(X(s))] = E_{(t, X(t))}[f(X(s))], \ s \geq t \qquad (2.105)$$

This expression says that the process does not remember what happened before the observation time, t. In other words, the only relevant part of the information set at time t is the value of the process, $X(t)$.

The Feynman-Kac Theorem

The *Feynman-Kac theorem* states that we can find the (time-dependent) expectation of a function of a Markovian stochastic process by solving a partial differential equation, subject to appropriate boundary and end conditions.

Since, as we will see in the next chapter, we price derivatives by evaluating expectations of (properly discounted) cash flows, in many cases the Feynman-Kac theorem allows us to derive a PDE for the derivative's price.

The Feynman-Kac theorem states that given an SDE,

$$dX(t) = a(X, t)dt + b(X, t)dW(t) \qquad (2.106)$$

the expectation of a function of $X(T)$, for $0 \leq t \geq T$, given by

$$g(t, x) = E_{(t, X(t)=x)}[f(X(T))] \qquad (2.107)$$

satisfies the partial differential equation

$$\frac{\partial g}{\partial t} + a(x, t)\frac{\partial g}{\partial x} + \frac{1}{2}b^2(x, t)\frac{\partial^2 g}{\partial x^2} = 0 \tag{2.108}$$

subject to the end condition (EC):

$$g(t = T, x) = f(x) \tag{2.109}$$

Notice that $g(t, x)$ is not a random variable. If we replace x with $X(t)$ in $g(t, x)$, we have a stochastic process. We will show that this stochastic process is a martingale and then use this fact to show that $g(t, x)$ must satisfy the PDE above:

$$E_t[g(s, X(s))] = g(t, X(t)), \ s \geq t \tag{2.110}$$

Replacing the definition of g in $E_t[g(s, X(s))]$ we get

$$E_t[g(s, X(s))] = E_t\{E_{(s, X(s))}[f(X(T))]\} \tag{2.111}$$

Since we are assuming that the $X(t)$ is Markovian, we get

$$E_{(s, X(s))}[f(X(T))] = E_s[f(X(T))] \tag{2.112}$$

Replacing in Equation 2.111, we get

$$E_t[g(s, X(s))] = E_t\{E_s[f(X(T))]\} \tag{2.113}$$

From the properties of expectations, we get

$$E_t\{E_s[f(X(T))]\} = E_t[f(X(T))] \tag{2.114}$$

$$E_t[g(s, X(s))] = E_t[f(X(T))] \tag{2.115}$$

Invoking the Markovian property again, the result is

$$E_t[f(X(T))] = E_{(t, X(t))}[f(X(T))] \tag{2.116}$$

Replacing in Equation 2.115, we get

$$E_t[g(s, X(s))] = E_{(t, X(t))}[f(X(T))] \tag{2.117}$$

Finally, the result is

$$E_t[g(s, X(s))] = g(t, X(t)) \tag{2.118}$$

This shows that $g(t, X(t))$ is a martingale. Since g is a function of time and $X(t)$, we can use Ito's lemma to get the SDE that governs $g(t)$:

$$dg(t) = \left(\frac{\partial g}{\partial t} + a(X, t)\frac{\partial g}{\partial X} + \frac{1}{2}b^2(X, t)\frac{\partial^2 g}{\partial X^2} \right)dt$$
$$+ b(X, t)\frac{\partial g}{\partial X}dW(t)$$

(2.119)

Since g is a martingale, the drift of $dg(t)$ must be zero. This gives us the PDE satisfied by $g(t, x)$.

MEASURE CHANGES

The measure assigns probabilities to outcomes. Changing the measure means assigning different probabilities to the same outcomes. In our case, the outcomes are the paths or realizations of a stochastic process.

For example, a process may have a symmetrical distribution in one measure and an asymmetrical distribution in a different measure. Of particular importance in finance are so-called "equivalent" measures. We change from one measure to an equivalent measure if we distort the probability of outcomes such that those outcomes that have zero probability in the original measure also have zero probability in the new measure.

To illustrate the concept of measure change, consider the process

$$dS(t) = adt + bdW(t)$$

(2.120)

where a and b are constants and $W(t)$ is a Wiener process. Integrating this equation subject to the initial condition $S(0) = 0$, the process $S(t)$ is

$$S(t) = at + bW(t)$$

(2.121)

If we make a plot of the probability density of $S(t)$, we find that the probability density is a normal distribution of mean at and standard deviation $b\sqrt{t}$. This distribution results from the probabilities assigned to the outcomes of $W(t)$ by the measure under which $W(t)$ is a Wiener process.

Now we ask the question: Is it possible to distort the distribution of the outcomes of $S(t)$ in such a manner that this process can be written as

$$dS(t) = bd\hat{W}(t)$$

(2.122)

where $\hat{W}(t)$ is also a Wiener process? The answer is yes. (Notice that b is unchanged.) In fact, it is possible to express a measure such that $S(t)$ can be written as

$$dS(t) = \tilde{a}dt + bd\tilde{W}(t)$$

(2.123)

where $\tilde{a}$ is any (reasonable) drift we want, and $\tilde{W}(t)$ is a Wiener process under that measure.

Why is this important? To illustrate the implication of this statement, consider a case where we have two processes, $X(t)$ and $Y(t)$, and assume that we are interested in some computation that is only valid if process $Y(t)$ is a martingale. Originally, we are given processes

$$dX(t) = a_x dt + b_x dW(t) \tag{2.124}$$

$$dY(t) = a_y dt + b_y dW(t) \tag{2.125}$$

where $Y(t)$ is not a martingale. If we now transform the measure (distort the probability distribution) of process $Y(t)$ such that $dY(t) = b_y d\hat{W}(t)$, where $\hat{W}(t)$ is a Wiener process in this new measure, and then appropriately carry this distortion over to process $X(t)$, we will have both processes in the measure that makes $Y(t)$ a martingale. We can write this as

$$dX(t) = \hat{a}_x dt + b_x d\hat{W}(t) \tag{2.126}$$

$$dY(t) = b_y d\hat{W}(t) \tag{2.127}$$

where $\hat{a}_x$ is a new drift. This done, we can move on with our task that involved both $X(t)$ and $Y(t)$ and that required that $Y(t)$ should be a martingale.

It turns out that the measure change that causes $Y(t)$ to have the desired drift (zero in this case) *does not require* that we work with the *solution* of the SDE for $Y(t)$! All we do is change the SDE itself (in a very simple way, as we'll see shortly). In other words, getting $\hat{a}$ is very easy.

To see the implication of this, assume that our task consists of finding the expectation of the product $X(t)Y(t)$ in the new measure that makes $Y(t)$ a martingale. Using Ito's lemma, the process for $X(t)Y(t)$ in the new measure is

$$d(X(t)Y(t)) = (Y\hat{a}_x + b_x b_y)dt + (Yb_x + Xb_y)d\hat{W}(t) \tag{2.128}$$

and the result we were looking for is

$$E[X(t)Y(t)] = (Y(0)\hat{a}_x + b_x b_y)t \tag{2.129}$$

where this expectation is in the measure that makes $Y(t)$ a martingale. Since, as we will see, getting $\hat{a}$ is very easy and does not require solving any of the SDEs, we can accomplish what we want without actually implementing the distortion of probability density. All we need is reassurance that $\hat{W}(t)$ is indeed a Wiener process in the measure that made $Y(t)$ a martingale. The *Girsanov theorem* gives us this reassurance and the changes that need to be applied to the SDE.

The reason why the issue of changing the measure arises is that, as was suggested in the first chapter, in financial pricing we are interested in probabilities that are assigned by measures associated with assets or portfolios of assets. As it turns out, these probabilities are determined by the drift of the processes involved (not by their volatility).

Girsanov Theorem

The Girsanov theorem states that given a process $\theta(t)$, $0 \le t \le T$, adapted to the information generated by the Wiener process $W(t)$, the process

$$\hat{W}(t) = W(t) + \int_0^T \theta(t)dt \tag{2.130}$$

is a Wiener process in a measure defined by the relationship

$$d\hat{P} = Z(T)dP \tag{2.131}$$

where $Z(T)$ is called the *Radon-Nikodym derivative*. $Z(t)$ is a process given by

$$Z(t) = \exp\left(-\int_0^t \theta(s)dW(s) - \frac{1}{2}\int_0^t \theta^2(s)ds\right) \tag{2.132}$$

For any random variable Y, expectations in the two measures are related as follows:

$$Z(t)E_t^{\hat{P}}[Y] = E_t^P[Z(T)Y] \tag{2.133}$$

In the particular case of an expectation conditional on the initial information, we have

$$E_0^{\hat{P}}[Y] = E_0^P[Z(T)Y] \tag{2.134}$$

It now becomes clear the way we would handle the example in Equations 2.124 and 2.125. Rewrite these equations as

$$dX(t) = (a_x - a_y)dt + dW(t) + a_y dt \tag{2.135}$$
$$dY(t) = (a_y - a_y)dt + dW(t) + a_y dt \tag{2.136}$$

where $\theta(t) = a_y$. With the definitions

$$d\hat{W}(t) = dW(t) + a_y dt \tag{2.137}$$

$$\hat{a}_x = a_x - a_y \tag{2.138}$$

we recover Equations 2.126 and 2.127.

When applying the Girsanov theorem, we assume that a technical condition called the *Novikov condition* holds:

$$\mathrm{E}\left[\exp\left(\frac{1}{2}\int_0^T \theta(t)^2 dt\right)\right] < \infty \qquad (2.139)$$

It is also possible to derive a multidimensional version of the Girsanov theorem, in which case W and θ are vector processes. For a detailed derivation of the Girsanov theorem, refer to Oksendal (1995).

MARTINGALE REPRESENTATION THEOREM

We will use the martingale representation theorem in the next chapter to discuss the existence of a hedging process. This theorem is the converse of the Ito integral. The martingale representation theorem says that given a martingale $M(t)$, such that $M(0) = 0$, with respect to a measure P where $W(t)$ is a Wiener process, then there exists an adapted process $\eta(t)$ such that

$$M(t) = \int_0^t \eta(s)dW(s) \qquad (2.140)$$

For a proof of this theorem, see Oksendal (1995).

PROCESSES WITH JUMPS

In some instances, underlying processes may undergo changes that can be better modeled as unanticipated finite jumps.

When pricing financial derivatives, there are two occurrences of jumps we need to worry about. One occurrence is jumps in the underlying process of the derivative instrument. The other occurrence is jumps in the value of the instrument itself as a result of the jump in the underlying process.

There is an important mathematical difference brought about by the introduction of underlying processes with jumps. If we model the underlying processes as continuous drift-diffusion processes, Ito's lemma allows us to completely define the process of a function of the underlying processes. If we incorporate unanticipated finite jumps in the underlying processes, we can still use Ito's lemma, but we don't have enough information to completely define the jump of the derivative instrument as a result of the jump in the underlying process. We must supply this information as additional conditions that relate the two jumps. We discuss this more extensively in the next chapter.

How do we use Ito's lemma in the presence of jumps? To visualize this, consider that Ito's lemma gives us the process of a function of a drift-diffusion process.

So, as long as no jumps occur, Ito's lemma will apply. Ito's lemma applies without any changes in between jumps. However, we want to find a way to express Ito's lemma such that it applies across jumps as well, not only in between jumps.

The Poisson Jump Model

The Poisson model for jumps is commonly used in finance to model unanticipated changes such as stock price jumps or the occurrence of default. The Poisson model states that the probability of the occurrence of one jump in the interval Δt is $h\Delta t$ plus higher order terms, where h is called the *jump intensity*. Notice that the word *intensity* here refers to the probability of occurrence, not to the magnitude of the jump. In general, the jump intensity may itself be a stochastic process. For now we will assume that jump intensity is a deterministic function of time.

The probability of one jump over the infinitesimal interval dt is equal to $h(t)dt$. The probability that no jump has occurred in the interval $(0, t)$ is called the *survival probability* and is denoted by $p_s(t)$. The change in probability that no jump has occurred in the interval $(0, t)$ is given by

$$dp_s(t) = -p_s(t)h(t)dt \tag{2.141}$$

Integrating this equation gives us an expression for the survival probability:

$$p_s(t) = \exp\left(-\int_0^t h(s)ds\right) \tag{2.142}$$

The probability that at least one jump has occurred in the interval $0, t$ is simply $1 - p_s(t)$.

Defining a Pure Jump Process

Assume that the process $S(t)$ undergoes pure jumps. We will define the change of the process as a result of jumps by $d_j S(t)$, where the subscript indicates that in general this is not an infinitesimal quantity:

$$d_j S(t) = \lim_{\Delta t \to 0} (S(t + \Delta t) - S(t^-)) \tag{2.143}$$

Here $S(t^-)$ is the value of the process as it approaches t from the left. The value of $d_j S(t)$ is zero until a jump happens. The jump intensity, or the probability that the jump happens in the interval $t, t + dt$, may depend on S. If it does, it will be a function of the process immediately before the jump, $S(t^-)$.

If the jump happens, its magnitude, z, is drawn from a distribution $\eta(S(t^-), z)$. The expected magnitude of the pure jump is then

$$E[d_j S(t)] = h(S(t^-))dt \int_z z \eta(S(t^-), z)dz \tag{2.144}$$

We can now arrange Equation 2.143 as follows:

$$d_jS(t) = \mathrm{E}[d_jS(t)] + \underbrace{d_jS(t) - \mathrm{E}[d_jS(t)]}_{dJ_s(t)} \qquad (2.145)$$

The process $dJ_s(t)$ is called a *compensated process* and is a martingale. We can now write the pure jump process as

$$d_jS(t) = h(S(t^-))\int_z z\eta(S(t^-), z)dz + dJ_S(t) \qquad (2.146)$$

where

$$dJ_S(t) = S(t) - S(t^-) - \left[h(S(t^-))\int_z z\eta(S(t^-), z)dz\right]dt \qquad (2.147)$$

Defining a Jump-Diffusion Process

To define a jump-diffusion process, just add the jump component, $d_jS(t)$, to a drift-diffusion process.

If we add the jump component to the drift-diffusion process

$$dS(t) = \mu(t)dt + \sigma(t)dW(t) \qquad (2.148)$$

we get the jump-diffusion process

$$dS(t) = \left[\mu(t) + h(S(t^-))\int_z z\eta(S(t^-), z)dz\right]dt + \sigma(t)dW(t) + dJ_S(t) \quad (2.149)$$

Ito's Lemma in the Presence of Jumps

Since Ito's lemma is valid between jumps, the application of Ito's lemma to a function $g(S(t), t)$ of the process given by Equation 2.149 gives

$$dg(t) = \text{Ito's lemma applied to the drift-diffusion part of } S(t)$$
$$+ \underbrace{g(t) - g(t^-)}_{\text{Jump in } g \text{ due to jump in } S} \qquad (2.150)$$

If the jump in $S(t)$ happens, $g(t)$ jumps by an amount Δg. This amount is drawn from a distribution $\eta_g()$, which may depend on other variables such as $g(t^-)$, the jump magnitude of $S(t)$, and $S(t^-)$. As before, we can write

$$g(t) - g(t^-) = h(t)dt\int_{\Delta g} \Delta g\, \eta_g(.)d\Delta g + dJ_g(t) \qquad (2.151)$$

Replacing in the equation for $dg(t)$, we get

$$dg(t) = \left(\frac{\partial g}{\partial t} + \mu \frac{\partial g}{\partial S} + \frac{1}{2} \sigma^2 \frac{\partial g}{\partial S^2} + h(t) \int_{\Delta g} \Delta g \, \eta_g(.) d\Delta g \right) dt$$
$$+ \frac{\partial g}{\partial S} \sigma \, dW(t) + dJ_g(t)$$

(2.152)

In general, we may not have a way to specify the jump magnitude distribution of g as a function of the jump distribution of S. We will see examples of this in the next chapter when we discuss defaultable instruments.

CHAPTER 3

Pricing in Continuous Time

By formulating the pricing problem in continuous time we can bring to bear the analytical tools of stochastic calculus and partial differential equations. The basic formulation of the continuous time pricing problem consists of expressing the current value of a derivative security as an expectation of properly discounted future cash flows.

If $B(t)$ is the value of a traded asset that does not pay dividends, the basic relationship for computing the value of a European derivative security, $V(t)$, is of the form

$$\frac{V(t)}{B(t)} = \mathrm{E}_t^B \left[\frac{V(T)}{B(T)} \right] \qquad (3.1)$$

where the expectation is taken in a measure determined, or induced, by asset $B(t)$.

Asset $B(t)$ is called a *normalizing asset* or *numeraire*. This expression tells us that the value of a derivative, in units of B, is a martingale if the stochastic processes involved in $V(t)$ are expressed in a measure associated with $B(t)$. Equation 3.1 determines the measure under which other derivatives can be priced. For example, if $\tilde{V}(t)$ is the price of another European derivative,

$$\frac{\tilde{V}(t)}{B(t)} = \mathrm{E}_t^B \left[\frac{\tilde{V}(T)}{B(T)} \right] \qquad (3.2)$$

where the expectation is taken in the same measure as in Equation 3.1. Once we have formulated this expectation, we have at least three alternatives to compute its value. We can compute the expectation analytically (this is easy to do in the case of simple Black and Scholes European options), we can value the expectation through simulation, or we can express the expectation in terms of a partial differential equation. We can then solve the partial differential equation either analytically or numerically. With some significant changes, a similar picture carries over to the case of derivatives with early exercise features, such as Bermudan or American options. We will discuss European derivatives first and derivatives with early exercise later on.

The most commonly used normalizing asset in continuous time is the *money market account*, $\beta(t)$, defined as the value of a continuously reinvested unit of account.

$$\beta(t) = \exp\left(\int_0^t r(s)ds\right) \qquad (3.3)$$

The measure under which the value of a derivative normalized with the money market account is a martingale is called the *risk neutral measure*.

Risk neutral pricing, where the money market account is the normalizing asset, is the standard framework for pricing in continuous time. We will develop this framework in sufficient detail. Similar frameworks can also be set up for pricing with other normalizing assets.

We will start by pricing a derivative on a single asset in the risk neutral measure. We will then extend the same logic for the case where the normalizing asset is something other than the money market account. After that, we will consider the multidimensional case of risk neutral pricing.

ONE-DIMENSIONAL RISK NEUTRAL PRICING

We want to price a derivative, $V(t)$, whose payoff depends on the price process:

$$\frac{dS}{S} = \mu(t)dt + \sigma(t)dW(t) \qquad (3.4)$$

We assume that there is a money market account, Equation 3.3, whose process is

$$\frac{d\beta}{\beta} = r(t)dt \qquad (3.5)$$

We require that $\mu(t)$, $\sigma(t)$, and $r(t)$ be adapted to a filtration that contains the information generated by $W(t)$.

We now construct a portfolio, $Y(t)$, which consists of $\delta(t)$ units of $S(t)$ and an investment in $\beta(t)$.

Over an infinitesimal instant of time, the portfolio value will change for two reasons. The value invested in $S(t)$ will change in proportion to dS, causing capital gains or losses, and the value invested in the money market account will change in proportion to $\frac{d\beta}{\beta}$.

The change in value of this portfolio over an infinitesimal period of time, dt, is

$$dY(t) = \delta(t)dS(t) + [Y(t) - \delta(t)S(t)]\frac{d\beta(t)}{\beta(t)} \quad (3.6)$$

In the next few paragraphs we will show that if $W(t)$ is a Wiener process in the measure induced by $\beta(t)$, namely, the risk. neutral measure, the portfolio process $Y(t)$ normalized with $\beta(t)$ is a martingale, and there is a hedging process, $\delta(t)$, that allows us to match the values of $Y(T)$ with the payoff of the derivative at time T. Assuming for the moment that this is true, we get a pricing formula for the derivative as follows.

Since the normalized value of $Y(t)$ is a martingale,

$$\frac{Y(t)}{\beta(t)} = E_t^{\beta}\left[\frac{Y(T)}{\beta(T)}\right] \quad (3.7)$$

Since we are saying that there is a $\delta(t)$ that allows us to match $Y(T)$ with $V(T)$, the value of $Y(t)$ must be the value of the derivative at time t. This gives us the pricing formula:

$$\frac{V(t)}{\beta(t)} = E_t^{\beta}\left[\frac{V(T)}{\beta(T)}\right] \quad (3.8)$$

Since the portfolio $Y(t)$ can be made to track the derivative price by properly choosing $\delta(t)$, this portfolio is said to replicate the value of the derivative as a function of time. $Y(t)$ is called a *hedge portfolio* or a *replicating portfolio*.

The reader may infer that if instead of choosing the money market account as one of the components of $Y(t)$ we had chosen another asset, say, asset $B(t)$, we would arrive at a similar martingale expression, except that now the measure under which the Brownian motions in both $S(t)$ and $B(t)$ are expressed is determined, or induced, by $B(t)$ (we will show this later). Our pricing formula in this case would be

$$\frac{V(t)}{B(t)} = E_t^{B}\left[\frac{V(T)}{B(T)}\right] \quad (3.9)$$

We now prove the two necessary facts: The normalized replicating portfolio is a martingale, and the appropriate hedge ratio exists.

Using Ito's lemma, the process for $\frac{S(t)}{\beta(t)}$ is

$$\frac{d\frac{S}{\beta}}{\frac{S}{\beta}} = \frac{dS}{S} - \frac{d\beta}{\beta} - \frac{dS}{S}\frac{d\beta}{\beta} + \left(\frac{d\beta}{\beta}\right)^2 \quad (3.10)$$

Replacing $\frac{dS}{S}$ and $\frac{d\beta}{\beta}$ and keeping first-order terms yields

$$\frac{d\frac{S(t)}{\beta(t)}}{\frac{S(t)}{\beta(t)}} = (\mu(t) - r(t))dt + \sigma(t)dW \tag{3.11}$$

We can rewrite this expression as

$$\frac{d\frac{S(t)}{\beta(i)}}{\frac{S(t)}{\beta(t)}} = (\mu(t) - r(t))dt - (\mu(t) - r(t))dt + \sigma(t)dW + (\mu(t) - r(t))dt$$

$$= \sigma(t)\left(dW + \frac{\mu(t) - r(t)}{\sigma(t)}\right)dt \tag{3.12}$$

$$= \sigma(t)d\left(W(t) + \int_0^t \frac{\mu(s) - r(s)}{\sigma(s)}ds\right)$$

if we define

$$\theta(t) = \frac{\mu(s) - r(s)}{\sigma(s)}57 \qquad 0 \le t \le T \tag{3.13}$$

Girsanov theorem tells us that

$$W^\beta(t) = W(t) + \int_0^t \theta(s)ds$$

$$W^\beta(t) = W(t) + \int_0^t \frac{\mu(s) - r(s)}{\sigma(s)}ds \tag{3.14}$$

is a Wiener process in a world where the probability density of the outcomes of $W(t)$, dP, is distorted (or rescaled) in the following way,

$$dP^\beta = Z(T)dP \tag{3.15}$$

where $Z(t)$, known as the *Radon-Nikodym derivative*, is given by (see Equation 2.132)

$$Z(t) = \exp\left(-\int_0^t \theta(s)dW(s) - \frac{1}{2}\int_0^t \theta^2(s)ds\right) \tag{3.16}$$

Equation 3.12 becomes

$$\frac{d\frac{S(t)}{\beta(t)}}{\frac{S(t)}{\beta(t)}} = \sigma(t)dW^\beta(t) \tag{3.17}$$

This means that in the measure defined by Equation 3.15, the asset price normalized with the money market account is a martingale:

$$\frac{S(t)}{\beta(t)} = E_t^\beta\left[\frac{S(T)}{\beta(T)}\right] \qquad (3.18)$$

We can also express this result as follows: Equation 3.18 is a condition that changes the probability of outcomes of $W(t)$, $0 \le t \le T$, in a way that we can define a new Wiener process $W^\beta(t)$. In terms of this new Wiener process, the asset process becomes

$$
\begin{aligned}
\frac{dS}{S} &= \mu(t)dt + \sigma(t)dW(t) \\
&= \sigma(t)\left(dW^\beta(t) - \frac{\mu(s) - r(s)}{\sigma(s)}dt\right) \\
&= r(t)dt + dW^\beta \qquad (3.19)
\end{aligned}
$$

The process

$$\frac{dS}{S} = r(t)dt + dW^\beta \qquad (3.20)$$

is expressed in the risk neutral measure. The quantity

$$\eta(t) = \frac{\mu(t) - r(t)}{\sigma(t)} \qquad (3.21)$$

is called the *market price of risk*. The market price of risk is the amount by which the return of the asset exceeds the risk-free return per unit of volatility.

We will now show that the process for the normalized portfolio is also a martingale when expressed in the risk neutral measure. Replace $\frac{d\beta}{\beta}$ in Equation 3.6:

$$dY(t) = \delta(t)dS(t) + [Y(t) - \delta(t)S(t)]r(t)dt \qquad (3.22)$$

Replacing for $dS(t)$ and $Y(t)$, we get

$$
\begin{aligned}
d\frac{Y(t)}{\beta(t)} &= \frac{1}{\beta}dY - \frac{Y}{\beta}\frac{d\beta}{\beta} - \frac{1}{\beta}dY\frac{d\beta}{\beta} + \frac{Y}{\beta}\left(\frac{d\beta}{\beta}\right)^2 \\
&= \frac{1}{\beta}[\delta dS + (Y - \delta S)rdt] - \frac{Y}{\beta}rdt \\
&= \frac{1}{\beta}[\delta dS - \delta Srdt] \qquad (3.23) \\
&= \frac{1}{\beta}[\delta(rSdt + \sigma Sd W^\beta) - \delta Srdt] \\
&= \frac{\delta}{\beta}\sigma Sd W^\beta
\end{aligned}
$$

The process

$$d\frac{Y(t)}{\beta(t)} = \frac{\delta(t)}{\beta(t)}\sigma(t)S(t)dW^{\beta}(t) \tag{3.24}$$

is a martingale, since it has no drift. Integrating this equation, we rearrange the solution as follows:

$$\int_0^t \frac{\delta(s)}{\beta(s)}\sigma(s)S(s)dW^{\beta}(s) = \frac{Y(t)}{\beta(t)} - \frac{Y(0)}{\beta(0)} \tag{3.25}$$

The integral on the left-hand side is a martingale that starts at zero. Call this martingale $M(t)$:

$$M(t) = \int_0^t \frac{\delta(s)}{\beta(s)}\sigma(s)S(s)d\hat{W}(s) \tag{3.26}$$

The *martingale representation theorem* says that there exists an adapted process $f(t)$ such that

$$\begin{aligned} M(t) &= \int_0^t f(s)d\hat{W} \\ &= \int_0^t \frac{\delta(s)}{\beta(s)}\sigma(s)S(s)d\hat{W}(s) \end{aligned} \tag{3.27}$$

This says that there is the following hedge process:

$$\delta(t) = \frac{\beta(t)f(t)}{\sigma(t)S(t)} \tag{3.28}$$

In summary, we have accomplished the following:

- ■ We defined the risk neutral measure by the condition that the process of the ratio of the underlying asset price to the money market account should be a martingale.
- ■ We constructed a portfolio consisting of a certain amount of the underlying asset and the money market account.
- ■ We showed that this portfolio, normalized with the money market account, is also a martingale. If we assume that the terminal value of the portfolio equals the payoff of the derivative, this martingale gives us a pricing formula for the derivative.
- ■ We showed that the appropriate amount of the underlying asset in this portfolio can be found such that the portfolio value at maturity matches the value of the derivative at maturity.

The derivative security priced this way reflects absence of arbitrage. If portfolio $Y(t)$ did not track the value of the derivative, one could sell whichever is more expensive and purchase whichever is less expensive and realize a riskless profit at maturity (since both have the same payoff value).

We can view this one-dimensional analysis in two ways. We can think of a market that contains only one underlying asset (not a very interesting market), or we can think of a pricing exercise in a multidimensional market where we consider an underlying asset in isolation.

MULTIDIMENSIONAL MARKET MODEL

By a *multidimensional market* we mean a market where the sources of uncertainty are several correlated Wiener processes, or, equivalently, a market driven by a multidimensional Wiener process.

The standard model for a multidimensional market is to assume that the market has a fundamental set of N traded assets, plus a money market account. We assume that the price process of each traded asset, S_i, evolves according to a multidimensional Ito process as follows:

$$\frac{dS_i(t)}{S_i(t)} = \mu_i(t)dt + \sum_{j=1}^{j=M} \sigma_{i,j}(t)dW_j, \ i = 1,\ldots, N \qquad (3.29)$$

where $W = (W_1,\ldots, W_M)$ is an M-dimensional Wiener process, and where $\mu_i(t)$ and $\sigma_{i,j}(t)$ can be random, but are adapted to a filtration equal to or larger than the filtration generated by W.

In addition, we assume that there is a money market account process given by

$$\frac{d\beta(t)}{\beta(t)} = r(t)dt \qquad (3.30)$$

where $r(s)$ is the instantaneous return, which may be random.

To develop the pricing framework for a contingent claim, we will proceed in a similar way as in the one-dimensional case. However, unlike the one-dimensional case, where we are always able to get a pricing formula in the form of an expectation, in the multidimensional market this may not happen, or the expectation may not be unique (in which case it would not be very useful).

We summarize the steps:

■ Using the Girsanov theorem we show that the processes for assets, S_i, normalized with the money market account can be made driftless if we can compute so-called "market prices of risk." If we cannot compute market prices of risk, it is not possible to make these processes driftless, and we will not be able to express the price of a derivative as an expectation in the risk neutral measure.

■ We define a portfolio consisting of the assets, S_i, and the money market account. This portfolio is also a martingale in the risk neutral measure. We assume that this portfolio replicates the payoff of the derivative.

■ Using the martingale representation theorem we show that the quantities of assets needed to define the portfolio that replicates the payoff of the derivative can be found if the market prices of risk can be determined. This allows us to produce a meaningful formula for the derivative price in the form of an expectation.

Using Ito's lemma, Equation 3.29 gives

$$\frac{d\frac{S_i(t)}{\beta(i)}}{\frac{S_i(t)}{\beta(t)}} = (\mu_i(t) - r(t))dt + \sum_{j=1}^{j=M} \sigma_{i,j}(t)dW_j, \; i = 1,\dots, N \qquad (3.31)$$

We rewrite this as follows:

$$\frac{d\frac{S_i(t)}{\beta(i)}}{\frac{S_i(t)}{\beta(t)}} = (\mu_i(t) - r(t))dt - \sum_{j=1}^{j=M} \sigma_{i,j}(t)\eta_j(t)dt$$

$$+ \sum_{j=1}^{j=M} \sigma_{i,j}(t)d\left(W_j + \int_0^t \eta_j(s)ds \right), \; i = 1,\dots, N \qquad (3.32)$$

If we can determine a multidimensional market price of risk process, $\eta(t)$, by solving the linear system

$$\sum_{j=1}^{j=M} \sigma_{i,j}(t)\eta_j(t) = \mu_i(t) - r(t), \; i = 1,\dots, N \qquad (3.33)$$

then the discounted asset price can be written as follows:

$$\frac{d\frac{S_i(t)}{\beta(i)}}{\frac{S_i(t)}{\beta(t)}} = \sum_{j=1}^{j=M} \sigma_{i,j}(t)d\hat{W}_j, \; i = 1,\dots, N \qquad (3.34)$$

with

$$d\hat{W}_j(t) = dW_j(t) + d\left(\int_0^t \eta_j(s)ds\right) \tag{3.35}$$

where $\hat{W}_j(t), j = 1,..., M$ are Wiener processes in the risk neutral measure.

If we cannot solve Equation 3.33, there is no risk neutral measure. If Equation 3.33 has more than one solution, there is more than one risk neutral measure.

To price a claim that pays $V(T)$, we define a portfolio process, $Y(t)$, $0 \le t \le T$, whose end value at $t = T$ matches the payoff of the claim. It is straightforward to show that this process, normalized with the money market account, is a martingale under the risk neutral measure. The initial value of this process will then be equal to the value of the claim. The portfolio process is the value of an investment in the assets S_i and in a money market account that pays the risk-free rate $r(t)$. The investor holds the amount $\delta_i(t)$ of asset S_i over an infinitesimal time dt. During this interval, the investment changes in value for two reasons. There is a contribution due to change in the asset price equal to $\sum_{i=1}^{i=N}\delta_i(t)dS_i(t)$, and there is a contribution due to the return on the money market account equal to $r(t)[Y(t) - \sum_{i=1}^{i=N}\delta_i(t)S_i(t)]dt$. The portfolio process follows

$$dY(t) = \sum_{i=1}^{i=N} \delta_i(t)dS_i(t) + \left[Y(t) - \sum_{i=1}^{i=N} \delta_i(t)S_i(t)\right]r(t)dt \tag{3.36}$$

Using Equation 3.34 and a little algebra, we get

$$d\frac{Y(t)}{\beta(t)} = \sum_{i=1}^{i=N} \delta_i(t)\frac{S_i(t)}{\beta(t)} \sum_{j=1}^{j=M} \sigma_{ij}(t)d\hat{W}_j(t) \tag{3.37}$$

This shows that process $Y(t)$ normalized with the money market account is a martingale under the risk neutral measure. Since the portfolio process matches the payoff of the derivative, we have

$$\frac{Y(0)}{\beta(0)} = E^\beta\left[\frac{Y(T)}{\beta(T)}\right]$$

$$= E^\beta\left[\frac{V(T)}{\beta(T)}\right] \tag{3.38}$$

Since $\beta(0) = 1$, the value of the derivative is

$$V(0) = E^\beta\left[\frac{V(T)}{\beta(T)}\right] \tag{3.39}$$

Now we need to see under which conditions the processes $\delta_i(t)$ exist. We can prove that this process exists through the martingale representation theorem in the same way as the one-dimensional case.

The following is a martingale such that $M(0) = 0$:

$$M(t) = \sum_{i=1}^{i=N} \int_0^t \delta_i(s)\frac{S_i(s)}{\beta(s)} \sum_{j=1}^{j=M} \sigma_{ij}(s)d\hat{W}_j(s) \tag{3.40}$$

The multidimensional version of the martingale representation theorem says that there exist processes $f_i(t)$ such that

$$M(t) = \sum_{j=1}^{j=M} \int_0^t f_j(s)d\hat{W}_j(s) \tag{3.41}$$

This gives a system of equations for the hedging ratios:

$$\sum_{i=1}^{i=N} \delta_i(t)S_i(t)\sigma_{ij}(t) = f_j(t)\beta(t), \quad j = 1,..., M \tag{3.42}$$

The pricing and hedging problem is now defined in terms of two systems of equations: the market price of risk equations (3.33) and the hedging ratio equations (3.42).

We can make the following observations. If Equation 3.33 has a unique solution, namely, if there is a unique multidimensional process $\eta(t)$, then there is only one way to define the Radon-Nikodym derivative and, consequently, there is only one risk neutral measure.

If there is a unique solution for $\eta(t)$, there is a solution to the hedging Equation 3.42, and consequently, every derivative can be hedged. In this the market is said to be *complete*. Arbitrage is also ruled out because we can purchase or sell the replicating portfolio or the underlying assets in the right amounts and ensure a riskless profit.

If Equation 3.33 has multiple solutions for $\eta(t)$, the Radon-Nikodym derivative is not unique and we cannot use the equivalent martingale measure for pricing. In this case there is no arbitrage, but claims cannot be hedged. The market is said to be *incomplete*.

If Equation 3.33 does not have a solution for $\eta(t)$, there is arbitrage and the equivalent risk neutral measure does not exist.

To summarize,

- Complete market: Absence of arbitrage means that the equivalent risk neutral measure is unique and every derivative can be hedged.
- Incomplete market: Absence of arbitrage does not imply the equivalent risk neutral measure is unique and not every derivative can be hedged.
- No risk neutral measure: There are arbitrage opportunities.

Extension to Other Normalizing Assets

The approach followed here can be extended to consider assets other than the money market account as normalizing assets. This is important because it often happens that the pricing problem can be better formulated when a different normalizing asset is used. We will illustrate the derivation with a numeraire or normalizing asset that does not pay dividends. For simplicity of the derivation, this time we will use vector notation.

We consider an underlying asset, $S(t)$, and a normalizing asset, $B(t)$, with processes

$$\frac{dS(t)}{S(t)} = r(t)dt + \vec{\sigma}_S d\vec{W} \tag{3.43}$$

$$\frac{dB(t)}{B(t)} = r(t)dt + \vec{\sigma}_B d\vec{W} \tag{3.44}$$

where $\vec{W}$ is a multidimensional Wiener process. We assume that these are risk neutral processes and that these assets don't pay dividends. In order to operate with asset processes we must first make sure that all the Wiener processes involved are in a common measure. In this case it is just a matter of convenience to choose the risk neutral measure.

The process for the underlying asset, normalized with asset $B(t)$ is

$$\frac{d\frac{S}{B}}{\frac{S}{B}} = \frac{dS}{S} - \frac{dB}{B} - \frac{dS}{S}\frac{dB}{B} + \left(\frac{dB}{B}\right)^2$$

$$= r(t)dt + \vec{\sigma}_S d\vec{W} - r(t)dt - \vec{\sigma}_B d\vec{W}$$
$$- \vec{\sigma}_S \vec{\sigma}_B dt + \vec{\sigma}_B \vec{\sigma}_B dt \tag{3.45}$$

We can rewrite this as follows:

$$
\frac{d\frac{S}{B}}{\frac{S}{B}} = -\vec{\sigma}_B(\vec{\sigma}_S - \vec{\sigma}_B)dt + (\vec{\sigma}_S - \vec{\sigma}_B)d\vec{W}
$$

$$
= -\vec{\sigma}_B(\vec{\sigma}_S - \vec{\sigma}_B)dt + \vec{\sigma}_B(\vec{\sigma}_S - \vec{\sigma}_B)dt
$$
$$
+ (\vec{\sigma}_S - \vec{\sigma}_B)d(\vec{W} - \int_0^t \vec{\sigma}_B(s)ds)
$$

(3.46)

The Girsanov theorem tells us that the process

$$
\vec{W}^B = \vec{W} - \int_0^t \vec{\sigma}_B(s)ds
$$

(3.47)

is a Wiener process in a measure defined through the appropriate Radon-Nykodim derivative. We refer to the measure under which $\vec{W}^B(t)$ is a Wiener process as the measure *induced* by $B(t)$. In order to obtain useful pricing formulas or pricing equations, we usually don't need to compute this new measure transformation explicitly. All we need is the knowledge that in this new measure, $\vec{W}^B(t)$ is a Wiener process.

In the measure induced by $B(t)$, the normalized asset process is

$$
\frac{d\frac{S}{B}}{\frac{S}{B}} = (\vec{\sigma}_S - \vec{\sigma}_B)d\vec{W}^B
$$

(3.48)

We now consider a replicating portfolio consisting of the underlying asset, $S(t)$, and the normalizing asset, $B(t)$. Following the same line of thought as in the previous section, we consider a portfolio $Y(t)$ consisting of a hedge amount $\delta(t)$ invested in asset $S(t)$, and the difference between the value of the portfolio and the value invested in the underlying asset is invested in the normalizing asset. The portfolio process is

$$
dY(t) = \delta(t)dS(t) + [Y(t) - \delta(t)S(t)]\frac{dB(t)}{B(t)}
$$

(3.49)

The fundamental difference between this portfolio and the one created with the money market account is that now the component of return due to asset $B(t)$ is stochastic. Before, this component was $r(t)dt$, which is deterministic conditional on information at time t. As before, we now use Ito's lemma to get a process for $\frac{Y}{B}$:

$$
\begin{aligned}
d\frac{Y}{B} &= \frac{1}{B}dY - \frac{Y}{B}\frac{dB}{B} - \frac{1}{B}dY\frac{dB}{B} + \frac{Y}{B}\left(\frac{dB}{B}\right)^2 \\
&= \frac{1}{B}\left[\delta(t)dS + (Y - \delta(t)S)\frac{dB}{B}\right] - \frac{Y}{B}\frac{dB}{B} \\
&\quad - \left[\delta(t)dS + (Y - \delta(t)S)\frac{dB}{B}\right]\frac{1}{B}\frac{dB}{B} + \frac{Y}{B}\left(\frac{dB}{B}\right)^2 \\
&= \delta(t)\frac{S}{B}[(\vec{\sigma}_S - \vec{\sigma}_B)d\vec{W} - (\vec{\sigma}_S - \vec{\sigma}_B)\vec{\sigma}_B dt] \\
&= \delta(t)\frac{S(t)}{B(t)}(\vec{\sigma}_S - \vec{\sigma}_B)(d\vec{W} - \vec{\sigma}_B dt)
\end{aligned}
\tag{3.50}
$$

Using Equation 3.47, the process for the normalized replicating portfolio is

$$
d\frac{Y}{B} = \delta(t)\frac{S(t)}{B(t)}(\vec{\sigma}_S(t) - \vec{\sigma}_B(t))dW^B
\tag{3.51}
$$

This says that the portfolio price normalized with asset $B(t)$ is a martingale. If we now consider a portfolio that matches the payoff of the derivative, we get a pricing equation in the form of an expectation taken with respect to the measure induced by $B(t)$:

$$
\frac{Y(0)}{B(0)} = E_0^B\left[\frac{Y(T)}{B(T)}\right]
\tag{3.52}
$$

Since $Y(T) = V(T)$, the pricing formula is

$$
V(0) = B(0)E_0^B\left[\frac{V(T)}{B(T)}\right]
\tag{3.53}
$$

Deriving Risk-Neutralized Processes

As we will see in the next chapter, one of the main tasks in pricing is to transform all the processes involved to the measure where the pricing is done. In many cases this is the risk neutral measure. In other cases this measure is induced by an asset price other than the money market account. In most cases the first step for getting the process in the desired measure is getting the processes in the risk neutral measure.

If the underlying assets S_i don't pay dividends, it is straightforward to get the risk-neutralized process for the assets. All we need to do is replace the Wiener process in the market measure with the Wiener process in the risk neutral measure. For example, for the case of a one-dimensional asset we have

$$dS(t) = \mu S(t)dt + \sigma(t)S(t)dW(t) \qquad (3.54)$$

$$= \mu S(t)dt + \sigma(t)S(t)(d\hat{W}(t) - \eta dt) \qquad (3.55)$$

$$= \mu S(t)dt + \sigma(t)S(t)\left(d\hat{W}(t) - \frac{\mu - r}{\sigma}dt\right) \qquad (3.56)$$

$$= rS(t)dt + \sigma(t)S(t)d\hat{W}(t) \qquad (3.57)$$

The risk-neutralized process for asset S is then

$$dS(t) = r(t)Sdt + \sigma(t)S(t)d\hat{W}(t) \qquad (3.58)$$

If the asset pays a dividend rate y, however, the asset process in the market measure must reflect the dividend payments as a drop in value:

$$dS(t) = (\mu(t) - y)S(t)dt + \sigma(t)S(t)dW(t) \qquad (3.59)$$

In this case, the process that must be driftless is

$$d\frac{S(t)}{\beta(t)} + \frac{yS(t)}{\beta(t)}dt \qquad (3.60)$$

This is consistent with requiring that

$$\frac{S(t)}{\beta(t)} + \int_0^t \frac{yS(s)}{\beta(s)}ds \qquad (3.61)$$

should be driftless. This equation results from regarding each infinitesimal dividend payment $yS(t)dt$ as a payoff.

Equation 3.60 leads to the following expression for the risk-neutralized asset process:

$$dS(t) = (r(t) - y)S(t)dt + \sigma(t)S(t)d\hat{W}(t) \qquad (3.62)$$

This last equation is also consistent with a martingale for the portfolio process $Y(t)$.

Another simple example is the derivation of the risk neutral process for the foreign exchange rate, $X(t)$, which represents the units of domestic currency needed to purchase one unit of foreign currency (notice that this definition is typically the inverse of the quoted foreign exchange rates, with the exception of the British Pound). We assume that the process for $X(t)$ is of the form

$$\frac{dX(t)}{X(t)} = \mu_x dt + \vec{\sigma}_x d\vec{W} \tag{3.63}$$

where $\vec{W}$ is a multidimensional Wiener process. In order to derive the process for the foreign exchange, we must take into account that a Wiener process in the risk neutral measure in the foreign market (the one relevant to the exchange rate $X(t)$) is not in general a Wiener process in the risk neutral measure in the domestic market. In order to obtain a relationship for the drift we may consider the price process of a foreign asset, $S_f(t)$, translated into the domestic currency, namely, $d(X(t)S_f(t))$. If we did this for an arbitrary asset S_f, we would introduce the Wiener process of S_f, whose risk neutral drift in the domestic currency is not known. If, however, we select the foreign money market account as the foreign asset, we don't introduce any additional Brownian motions and we get

$$\frac{d(X(t)\beta_f(t))}{X(t)\beta_f(t)} = (\mu_x + r_f)dt + \vec{\sigma}_x d\vec{W} \tag{3.64}$$

The drift of the foreign exchange rate is obtained by requiring that the drift of the translated foreign money market account should be the risk-free rate. This gives us

$$\mu_x = r - r_f \tag{3.65}$$

This says that in the domestic measure, the foreign exchange rate behaves like an asset that pays a dividend yield equal to the instantaneous foreign risk-free rate.

As a second example, we consider the relationship between Wiener processes in the foreign risk-free measure and Wiener processes in the domestic risk-free measure. Consider a foreign asset that in the foreign risk-free measure has the process

$$\frac{dS_f(t)}{S_f(t)} = r_f dt + \vec{\sigma}_f d\vec{W}_f \tag{3.66}$$

The process for the foreign asset translated into the domestic currency is

$$\frac{d(X(t)S_f(t))}{X(t)S_f(t)} = (r - r_f)dt + r_f dt + \vec{\sigma}_x d\vec{W} + \vec{\sigma}_f d\vec{W}_f + \vec{\sigma}_x \vec{\sigma}_f dt \tag{3.67}$$

where $\vec{\sigma}_x \vec{\sigma}_f dt$ stands for $\text{cov}(\frac{dX}{X}, \frac{dS_f}{S_f})$. This expression will produce the correct domestic risk neutral drift if the following relationship is satisfied:

$$\vec{\sigma}_f d\vec{W}_f^* = \vec{\sigma}_f d\vec{W}_f - \vec{\sigma}_x \vec{\sigma}_f dt \tag{3.68}$$

where $\vec{W}_f^*$ is a Wiener process in the domestic measure. This is the fundamental relationship that connects the two Wiener processes.

THE PRICING EQUATION

When pricing a European derivative the task is to compute an expectation of the form

$$\frac{V(0)}{B(0)} = \mathrm{E}_0^B\left[\frac{V(T)}{B(T)}\right] \tag{3.69}$$

where $B(.)$ is the value of the normalizing or numeraire asset and $V(T)$ is the (known) value of the derivative at maturity. Computationally, there are two ways to evaluate this expectation.

■ Solve the problem by simulation and get an approximate value for the expectation. We will see this in detail in Chapter 5.
■ Recast the expectation in the form of a partial differential equation. Solve the PDE with a numerical technique. In Chapter 7 we discuss the use of finite differences to accomplish this.

When pricing an American derivative or a derivative with early exercise, our objective is to compute an expectation of the form

$$\frac{V(0)}{B(0)} = \sup_{0 \le \tau \le T} \mathrm{E}_0^B\left[\frac{F(\tau)}{B(\tau)}\right] \tag{3.70}$$

where $t = \tau$ are exercise times and $F(\tau)$ is the (known) exercise value, or payoff, of the derivative at $t = \tau$. Computationally, we will also discuss two ways to evaluate this expectation.

■ Solve the problem by simulation using an adaptation of Monte Carlo simulation to deal with early exercise. We will see this in detail in Chapter 6. This extension to early exercise is *not* an easy modification of the techniques for European pricing.
■ Recast the expectation as a set of partial differential inequalities. These inequalities are called a *partial differential complementarity problem*. This problem can be solved with the finite difference techniques of Chapter 7. The numerical implementation of the partial differential

complementarity problem with finite differences is a straightforward modification (quite trivial in most cases) of the finite difference formulation for European pricing.

European Derivatives

Although we often refer to the pricing equation of European derivatives as a *partial differential equation* (PDE), in general the equation is a *partial-integro differential equation* (PIDE). The difference is significant mathematically, but it is not a substantial complication numerically.

The derivation of a PDE as the pricing equation for a European derivative is possible if the underlying processes are Markovian. Difficulties arise if the underlying process is not Markovian; that is, if the underlying process depends on the path of the Wiener processes involved. The best-known example is the case of the short rate process in the Heath-Jarrow-Morton model (Heath, Jarrow, and Morton, 1992). Some of the well-known models for the short rate are ways of getting around this problem. Such models are designed with features that make the short rate Markovian (Bhar and Chiarella, 1997).

The typical pricing equation looks as follows:

$$
\underbrace{\frac{\partial V}{\partial t} + a\frac{\partial V}{\partial S} + b\frac{\partial V}{\partial r} + c\frac{\partial V}{\partial I}}_{\text{Convection}} + \underbrace{d\frac{\partial^2 V}{\partial S^2} + e\rho\frac{\partial^2 V}{\partial S \partial r} + f\frac{\partial^2 V}{\partial r^2}}_{\text{Diffusion}}
$$

$$
= \underbrace{rV - h\left(\underbrace{\int \eta(\xi)V(\xi)d\xi}_{\text{Convolution}} - V\right)}_{\text{Jump}} \tag{3.71}
$$

where S and r are Ito processes, a, b, c, d, e, and f are functions of S, r, and t, I is a coordinate that does not have a corresponding diffusion term, h is a Poisson jump intensity (this could also be a stochastic process), and $\eta(.)$ is the jump density.

The classical Black-Scholes equation lacks the I coordinate and the jump term. The convolution integral does not add significant difficulties to the numerical task of solving this equation. We now describe the two main approaches for deriving the pricing equation.

In the absence of jumps in the underlying processes, there are two fundamental approaches for deriving the pricing equations for European derivatives. The first approach consists in constructing a hedging portfolio whose value tracks the value of the derivative as a function of time. The second approach is based on the *Feynman-Kac theorem*, which states that the conditional expectation of a stochastic process obeys a partial differential equation. If there are jumps in the underlying processes, we need to introduce additional assumptions about the effect of the jumps. We devote a separate section to the derivation of the pricing equation in the presence of jumps.

Hedging Portfolio Approach

Consider an option on an underlying process $S(t)$, $t \in [0, T]$, with a payoff $V(S(T), T) = g(S(T))$. We want to obtain the equation describing the value of the option at time $t \in [0, T]$, $V(S(t), t)$. Assume that the underlying process is as follows, where $\mu(S(t), t)$ and $\sigma(S(t), t)$ are known given the information available at time t:

$$\frac{dS(t)}{S(t)} = \mu(S(t), t)dt + \sigma(S(t), t)dW(t) \qquad (3.72)$$

For notational convenience, we will from now on omit the arguments in V and its derivatives, μ, σ, and W unless there is need for additional clarity. Applying Ito's lemma to $V(S(t), t)$, we get

$$dV(S(t), t) = \left(\frac{\partial V}{\partial t} + \mu S \frac{\partial V}{\partial S} + \frac{1}{2}\sigma^2 S^2 \frac{\partial^2 V}{\partial S^2} \right)dt + \sigma S \frac{\partial V}{\partial S}dW \qquad (3.73)$$

Assume now a hedging portfolio, $Y(t)$, designed to track the evolution of the value of the derivative from time 0 to T, as we did earlier in the chapter. The portfolio will consist of $\delta(t)$ units of $S(t)$, plus borrowing or lending. Over an infinitesimal interval of time, the portfolio value will change as described by Equation 3.6. Denoting the instantaneous borrowing or lending rate by $r(t)$, the change in the replicating portfolio value is

$$dY = \delta(t)dS + (Y(t) - \delta(t)S(t))r(t)dt \qquad (3.74)$$

Substituting dS from Equation 3.72 into Equation 3.74, the replicating portfolio process is

$$dY = [Y(t)r(t) + \delta(t)S(t)(\mu(t) - r(t))]dt + \delta(t)S(t)\sigma dW \qquad (3.75)$$

In order for the portfolio to hedge the option, $V(S(t), t)$ and $Y(t)$ must have the same drift and the same volatility. Equating the drifts in Equations 3.73 and 3.75, we find the following equation for the value of the option:

$$\frac{\partial V}{\partial t} + \mu S \frac{\partial V}{\partial S} + \frac{1}{2}\sigma^2 S^2 \frac{\partial^2 V}{\partial S^2} = rY + n(\mu - r)S \qquad (3.76)$$

Equating the volatilities, we find the number of units of S must satisfy the relationship

$$\delta(t) = \frac{\partial V}{\partial S} \qquad (3.77)$$

Since we require that the hedging portfolio should replicate the option for any $t \in [0, T]$, we set $Y(t) = V(S(t), t)$ in Equation 3.76. Replacing for n in Equation 3.76, we get the following pricing equation,

$$\frac{\partial V}{\partial t} + rS \frac{\partial V}{\partial S} + \frac{1}{2}\sigma^2 S^2 \frac{\partial^2 V}{\partial S^2} = rV \qquad (3.78)$$

with the end condition

$$V(T, S(T)) = g(S(T)) \qquad (3.79)$$

This is the Black-Scholes partial differential equation of option pricing. Notice that the drift $\mu(S(t), t)$ of the underlying process does not appear in this expression.

Equation 3.78 applies if r is a deterministic function of time. If r itself were governed by a stochastic process, this should be reflected in the derivation and additional terms would appear. Notice also that if we set $\mu = r$ and $Y = V$ in Equation 3.76, we obtain the Black and Scholes equation. However, Equation 3.76 only enforces the drifts of dV and dY to be the same, not their unanticipated changes. In other words, assuming that $\mu = r$ has the same effect as requiring that the volatility component of the option price process and the volatility component of the replicating portfolio process should be the same. As we saw earlier, if $r(t)$ is the instantaneous risk-free rate, a situation where we assume that the rate of growth of any non-dividend paying asset is equal to $r(t)$ is equivalent to expressing the process for the asset in the risk neutral measure. As a result, the invocation of risk neutrality allows us, in the absence of cash flows associated with the underlying processes, to determine the pricing equation by simply enforcing the equality $E_t[dV(S(t), t)] = r(t)V(S(t), t)$, where $dV(S(t), t)$ is the increment of V obtained through the application of Ito's lemma. Invoking risk neutrality means that the drifts of the underlying processes must be consistent with risk neutral returns of traded assets. If the underlying process is the price of a stock that does not pay dividends, this consistency with risk neutrality simply means that $E_t[dS(t)] = r(t)S(t)$. In more complex cases, obtaining the appropriate risk neutral drift may require significant elaboration, as we discussed earlier in the chapter.

Feynman-Kac Approach

The Feynman-Kac theorem establishes a relationship between stochastic differential equations and partial differential equations. Given the stochastic differential equation

$$dy(t) = \mu(y(t), t)dt + \sigma(y(t), t)dW(t) \qquad (3.80)$$

the Feynman-Kac theorem states that the expectation

$$f(y, t) = E_{y,t}[g(y(T))] \qquad (3.81)$$

is the solution to the following partial differential equation,

$$\frac{\partial f}{\partial t} + \mu \frac{\partial f}{\partial y} + \frac{1}{2}\sigma^2 \frac{\partial^2 f}{\partial y^2} = 0 \qquad (3.82)$$

subject to the end condition

$$f(y, T) = g(y) \qquad (3.83)$$

In the case of several underlying processes, $y_1(t), y_2(t),..., y_n(t)$, following the stochastic differential equations,

$$dy_i = \mu_i(y_1, y_2,..., y_n, t)dt + \sigma_i(y_1, y_2,..., y_n, t)dW_i \qquad (3.84)$$

the function

$$f(y_1, y_2,..., y_n, t) = E_{y_1,y_2,...,y_n,t}[g(y_1(T), y_2(T),..., y_n(T))] \qquad (3.85)$$

is given by the solution of the differential equation:

$$\frac{\partial f}{\partial t} + \sum_{i=0}^{i=n} \mu_i \frac{\partial f}{\partial y_i} + \frac{1}{2}\sum_{i,j=0}^{i,j=n} \rho_{ij}\sigma_i\sigma_j \frac{\partial f}{\partial y_i y_j} = 0 \qquad (3.86)$$

subject to

$$f(y_1, y_2,..., y_n, T) = g(y_1, y_2,..., y_n) \qquad (3.87)$$

where $\rho_{ij} = \text{cov}(dW_i, dW_j)/dt$.

As an example of the Feynman-Kac approach, consider the derivation of the pricing equation for a claim in the case where the interest rate is described by the Hull and White model (Equation 2.102). In the risk neutral measure, the price of a claim on $S(t)$ paying $g(S(T))$ at maturity is given by

$$V(r(t), S(t), t) = E_{r,S,t}\left(g(T)e^{-\int_t^T r(\xi)d\xi}\right) \tag{3.88}$$

Assume that the processes for $S(t)$ and $r(t)$ are given by

$$dS = rS dt + \sigma_s S dW_s \tag{3.89}$$

and

$$dr = (a(t) - br)dt + \sigma_r dW_r \tag{3.90}$$

where σ_S and σ_r may be functions of the state variables r and S and time. Notice that the argument in the expectation in Equation 3.88 is not simply a function of T, but it depends on the trajectories of r. In order to apply the Feynman-Kac formula, we need to transform the argument of the expectation, so that it depends on the values of processes at time T only. We can accomplish this at the expense of temporarily increasing the dimensionality of the problem by defining an auxiliary process of the form

$$dz = -r(t)dt \tag{3.91}$$

With this, the value of the claim is (notice the conditions required of the expectation)

$$V(r, S, t) = e^{-z}E_{r,S,z,t}[g(T)e^{z(T)}] \tag{3.92}$$

We now define

$$V(r, S, t) = e^{-z}U(r, S, z, t) \tag{3.93}$$

and apply the three-dimensional Feynman-Kac formula to $U(r, S, z, t)$:

$$\frac{\partial U}{\partial t} + rS\frac{\partial U}{\partial S} + (a(t) - br)\frac{\partial U}{\partial r} - r\frac{\partial U}{\partial z} + \frac{1}{2}\sigma_s^2 S^2\frac{\partial^2 U}{\partial S^2}$$
$$+ S\sigma_s\sigma_r\rho_{s,r}\frac{\partial^2 U}{\partial S\partial r} + \frac{1}{2}\sigma_r^2\frac{\partial^2 U}{\partial r^2} = 0 \tag{3.94}$$

We can now eliminate the additional dimension, z, by replacing $U(r, S, z, t) = e^z V(r, S, t)$ in Equation 3.95. This gives the two-dimensional pricing equation

$$
\frac{\partial V}{\partial t} + rS \frac{\partial V}{\partial S} + (a(t) - br) \frac{\partial V}{\partial r} - rV + \frac{1}{2} \sigma_s^2 S^2 \frac{\partial^2 V}{\partial S^2}
$$
$$
+ \rho_{S,r} \sigma_s \sigma_r S \frac{\partial^2 V}{\partial S \partial r} + \frac{1}{2} \sigma_r^2 \frac{\partial^2 V}{\partial r^2} = 0
$$

(3.95)

with the end condition

$$
V(r, S, T) = g(S(T)), \; r \in [-\infty, +\infty], \; S \in [0, +\infty]
$$

(3.96)

THE PRICING EQUATION IN THE PRESENCE OF JUMPS

Jump processes are frequently used to produce a more realistic description of the underlying processes, such as in the case of jump diffusion models for stock price movements (Merton, 1976). In other instances, the introduction of jumps is an essential component of a pricing framework, such as in the case of credit derivatives (Duffie and Singleton, 1999).

If one or more of the underlying processes are discontinuous, the derivation of a pricing equation becomes somewhat more involved. As we saw in the previous section, the argument that we can construct a hedging portfolio containing a given amount of the underlying security leads to the pricing equation and to the conclusion that the derivative should grow at the risk-free rate. If, instead of invoking the argument of a hedging portfolio, we take the expectation of the derivative process in a risk neutral world, we arrive at the same pricing equation. In the case of jumps, the pricing equation that we can get by invoking the hedging portfolio argument may depend on a criterion for the risk of the hedged portfolio. A common criterion is to state that the hedged portfolio should have minimum variance (Wilmott, 1998). This criterion leads to a particular pricing equation. We may justifiably ask, however, whether the equation obtained in this way is the one followed by market prices of the derivative (Tavella and Randall, 2000). An alternative approach to derive a pricing equation is to invoke the idea that changes in prices due to jumps are diversified away in the marketplace. This argument allows us to obtain a pricing equation by requiring that the risk neutral expectation of the derivative price change should be proportional to the risk-free rate. This is the approach we take in the next two examples.

An Application of Jump Processes: Credit Derivatives

The purpose of this section is to illustrate issues in the derivation of pricing equations when jumps are involved. The reader interested in gaining a broader understanding of credit derivatives may consult some of the numerous articles in the literature (e.g., Duffie and Singleton, 1999; Schoenbucher, 1997).

Credit derivatives are instruments sensitive to changes in either the credit quality of the issuer of an underlying security, or to so-called "credit events" affecting the issuer of the underlying security. Among the credit events that affect the quality of the issuer are defaults and changes in credit rating. In principle, a corporate bond can be viewed as a credit derivative much the same way a nondefaultable bond can be viewed as an interest rate derivative. The market has agreed to call credit derivatives instruments specifically designed to manage credit risk, either by mitigating the risk or by gaining exposure to credit risk.

The two main approaches for pricing credit derivatives are *structural methods*, which attempt to establish relationships between the capital structure of the issuer of securities underlying the credit derivative, and *reduced methods*, where pricing is done by postulating models for the stochastic processes involved, without particular regard for capital structure considerations.

We will concentrate on the applications to reduced models. We will illustrate the derivation of the pricing equations by considering a derivative that depends on a credit event such as default or credit change. We will assume that the credit event can be characterized as a pure jump process. If the credit event is a default, the value of the jump process at time t is an integer number that indicates the number of defaults that have occurred up to time t.

The process for the value of the derivative will be a function of the stochastic process that represents the credit event, as well as a function of any other relevant diffusion processes, such as the short rate.

In Chapter 2 we discussed the application of Ito's lemma to the case of processes with jumps. Consider the combined jump-diffusion process x (for additional details, please refer to Chapter 2):

$$dx(t) = \left(\mu + h(x(t), t)\int z\eta(x(t), z)dz\right)dt + \sigma dW(t) + dJ_x \qquad (3.97)$$

If we now set $\mu = 0$ and $\sigma = 0$, we obtain a pure jump process with jumps at time t of magnitude z, distributed according to $\eta(x(t), z)$

$$dx(t) = \left(h(x(t),\, t) \int z\eta(x(t),\, z)dz \right)dt + dJ_x(t) \qquad (3.98)$$

If in addition, we also assume that $\eta(x(s),\, z) = \delta(z - 1)$, where $\delta(.)$ is the Dirac delta function, we obtain a jump process that can jump by one at time t. We will assume that this is a useful representation of the process of credit events we are interested in. Notice that at this stage we are not precisely specifying what the credit event is. The event intensity, h, can depend on both the event count, $x(t)$, and time. If the credit event were a default and we restricted our attention to the first event of default, the intensity would be only a function of time. The process for the credit event becomes

$$dx(t) = h\,dt + dJ_x \qquad (3.99)$$

Additionally, we may assume that the intensity of occurrence of the credit event follows a diffusion process

$$dh(t) = \mu_h dt + \sigma_h dW_h \qquad (3.100)$$

where μ_h and σ_h can be functions of time and the other continuous processes in the problem. To illustrate the derivation of the pricing equation for credit derivatives, let's also assume that the short rate is described by a diffusion process

$$dr = \mu_r dt + \sigma_r dW_r \qquad (3.101)$$

where the drift and the volatility can be functions of time and the other continuous processes in the problem. Using Ito's lemma with jumps, the value of the derivative, $V(t)$, is governed by the following jump-diffusion process:

$$
\begin{aligned}
dV(t) = & \left(\frac{\partial V}{\partial t} + \mu_r \frac{\partial V}{\partial r} + \mu_h \frac{\partial V}{\partial h} + \frac{\sigma_r^2}{2}\frac{\partial^2 V}{\partial r^2} + \sigma_r \sigma_h \rho_{r,h}\frac{\partial^2 V}{\partial r \partial h} + \frac{\sigma_h^2}{2}\frac{\partial^2 V}{\partial h^2} \right)dt \\
& + \left(h(\overline{x(t)},\, t)\int [V(x(t)+z,\, r,\, t) - V(x(t),\, r,\, t)]\delta(z - 1)dz \right)dt \\
& + \frac{\partial V}{\partial r}\sigma_r dW_r + \frac{\partial V}{\partial h}\sigma_h dW_h + dJ_V
\end{aligned}
$$

$$\qquad (3.102)$$

where the last term represents the random shocks undergone by the derivative's price as a result of the jumps in default process x. Carrying out the integral in Equation 3.102, we get

$$dV(t) = \left(\frac{\partial V}{\partial t} + \mu_r \frac{\partial V}{\partial r} + \mu_h \frac{\partial V}{\partial h} + \frac{\sigma_r^2}{2} \frac{\partial^2 V}{\partial r^2} + \sigma_r \sigma_h \rho_{r,h} \frac{\partial^2 V}{\partial r \partial h} + \frac{\sigma_h^2}{2} \frac{\partial^2 V}{\partial h^2} \right) dt$$

$$+ h[V(x(t) + 1, r, t) - V(x(t), r, t)] \, dt$$

$$+ \frac{\partial V}{\partial r} \sigma_r d W_r + \frac{\partial V}{\partial h} \sigma_h d W_h + dJ_V$$

(3.103)

Assume now that the market fully diversifies the shocks due to default. This means that the risk neutral expectation of $dV(t)$ must be equal to $rV(t)$. If we assume that the processes for h, r, and x are in the risk neutral measure, this expectation gives us the partial differential equation governing the derivative price. Taking the expectation of Equation 3.103,

$$\frac{\partial V}{\partial t} + \mu_r \frac{\partial V}{\partial r} + \mu_h \frac{\partial V}{\partial h} + \frac{\sigma_r^2}{2} \frac{\partial^2 V}{\partial r^2} + \sigma_r \sigma_h \rho_{r,h} \frac{\partial^2 V}{\partial r \partial h} + \frac{\sigma_h^2}{2} \frac{\partial^2 V}{\partial h^2}$$

$$= (V(x(t))r - h[V(x(t) + 1) - V(x(t))])$$

(3.104)

where we used the fact that W_r, W_h, and J_V are martingales.

For clarity of the discussion, assume now that the credit event characterized by $x(t)$ is the default process. Notice that x does not contribute to the dimensionality of the problem because it does not appear on the left-hand side of the pricing equation. It is convenient to rewrite the pricing equation as follows:

$$\frac{\partial V}{\partial t} + \mu_r \frac{\partial V}{\partial r} + \mu_h \frac{\partial V}{\partial h} + \frac{\sigma_r^2}{2} \frac{\partial^2 V}{\partial r^2} + \sigma_r \sigma_h \rho_{r,h} \frac{\partial^2 V}{\partial r \partial h} + \frac{\sigma_h^2}{2} \frac{\partial^2 V}{\partial h^2}$$

$$= Vr - h \delta V$$

(3.105)

where δV is the known change in value of the derivative if default occurs. We will next discuss two simple examples of application of the pricing equation.

Defaultable Bonds

In the event of default of the issuer of a bond, the bond drops in value to a level called the *recovery value* of the bond. The way the recovery value of the bond is characterized can have a significant influence on the pricing of the bond. Let's assume that upon default, the holder of the bond receives a given fraction, $R(t)$, of the contemporaneous market value of the bond. In that case, the right-hand side of Equation 3.105 can be written as

$$Vr - h \delta V = Vr - h(RV - V) = Vr + hLV = V(r + Lh)$$

(3.106)

where L is the loss fraction in the event of default. Of course, $R(t)$ can be a stochastic process. This assumption about recovery is known as *recovery of market value* (Duffie and Singleton, 1999). The pricing equation is now

$$
\frac{\partial V}{\partial t} + \mu_r \frac{\partial V}{\partial r} + \mu_h \frac{\partial V}{\partial h} + \frac{\sigma_r^2}{2}\frac{\partial^2 V}{\partial r^2} + \sigma_r \sigma_h \rho_{r,h}\frac{\partial^2 V}{\partial r \partial h} + \frac{\sigma_h^2}{2}\frac{\partial^2 V}{\partial h^2} \tag{3.107}
$$
$$
= V(r + Lh)
$$

In addition, we need an end condition at maturity and boundary conditions for $r = 0$, $r = \infty$, $h = 0$, $h = \infty$. If we view the bond as a contract that terminates upon default, the end condition will be equal to a known payment equal to the notional amount. Although the boundary conditions will be discussed in greater detail in Chapter 7, here we can make an observation that brings up the significance of assuming the recovery to be a given fraction of market value as opposed to a given amount. If we ask ourselves what the value of the bond is as $h \to \infty$, it appears intuitively clear that if the recovery is equal to a given amount to be paid in case of default, the value of the bond should be precisely this amount. The reason for this is that if the intensity of default is infinitely large, the bond will default immediately and the holder will receive the known amount immediately. If, on the other hand, recovery is given in terms of market value, the pricing equation will contain a source term of the form LVh, which cannot be balanced by the finite terms on the left-hand side if $V \neq 0$. The only way for the equation to make sense as $h \to \infty$ (assuming V remains smooth) is for $V \to 0$ as $h \to \infty$.

The suitable boundary condition for $h = 0$ is the solution to the PDE describing a default-free bond.

Full Protection Credit Put

A *credit put* compensates the holder for the loss of value of defaultable bonds as a result of default, credit degradation, or both. Here we formulate a simple example as follows. Consider a derivative that pays the holder the following amount if default occurs at time t, where $0 < t < T$,

$$
KB(t, T_B) - R(t)B_d(t, T_D) \tag{3.108}
$$

where $R(t)$ is the recovery rate, $B(t, T_B)$ is a risk-free bond maturing at time T_B, $B_d(t, T_D)$ is a defaultable bond maturing at time T_D, and K is a constant. We will assume that the occurrence of a default is enough to trigger the payment. In such a case, the contract terminates. If no payments triggered by default have occurred until maturity, at maturity the derivative pays the following:

$$
\max[0, KB(T, T_B) - B_d(T, T_D)] \tag{3.109}
$$

This is a full-protection credit put because it protects both against defaults and drop of value as a result of increased yields.

The right-hand side of Equation 3.105 in this case is

$$
\begin{aligned}
Vr - h\delta V &= Vr - [KB(t, T_B) - R(t)B_d(t, T_D) - V] \\
&= V(r + h) - h[KB(t, T_B) - R(t)B(t, T_D)]
\end{aligned}
\tag{3.110}
$$

The pricing equation of the credit put can be written as

$$
\frac{\partial V}{\partial t} + \mu_r \frac{\partial V}{\partial r} + \mu_h \frac{\partial V}{\partial h} + \frac{\sigma_r^2}{2} \frac{\partial^2 V}{\partial r^2} + \sigma_r \sigma_h \rho_{r,h} \frac{\partial^2 V}{\partial r \partial h} + \frac{\sigma_h^2}{2} \frac{\partial^2 V}{\partial h^2} \tag{3.111}
$$
$$
= V(r + h) - h[KB(t, T_B) - R(t)B(t, T_D)]
$$

with the end condition

$$
V(T) = \max[0, KB(T, T_B) - B_d(T, T_D)] \tag{3.112}
$$

and suitable boundary conditions.

Notice that in order to solve Equation 3.111 we need to know $B(t, T_B)$ and $B_d(t, T_D)$ at every point in the solution space. This means that in addition to this PDE, we need to solve the two additional ones representing the values of the riskless and defaultable bonds. For the riskless bond we have

$$
\frac{\partial B}{\partial t} + \mu_r \frac{\partial B}{\partial r} + \frac{\sigma_r^2}{2} \frac{\partial^2 B}{\partial r^2} = Br \tag{3.113}
$$

and for the defaultable bond,

$$
\frac{\partial B_d}{\partial t} + \mu_r \frac{\partial B_d}{\partial r} + \mu_h \frac{\partial B_d}{\partial h} + \frac{\sigma_r^2}{2} \frac{\partial^2 B_d}{\partial r^2} + \sigma_r \sigma_h \rho_{r,h} \frac{\partial^2 B_d}{\partial r \partial h} + \frac{\sigma_r^2}{2} \frac{\partial^2 B_d}{\partial h^2} \tag{3.114}
$$
$$
= B_d(r + Lh)
$$

In addition, we need suitable boundary conditions. The issue of boundary conditions will be discussed in detail in Chapter 7. The pricing problem is then the solution of a system of the three partial differential Equations 3.111, 3.113, and 3.114.

AMERICAN DERIVATIVES

An American style derivative is a contract whose cash flows can be influenced by the holder. The holder affects the cash flows of the contract through an exercise strategy. In its simplest form, the exercise strategy may simply consist of the decision to exercise or not exercise at any given time between the inception of the contract and its maturity date. In general, however, the exercise policy can consist of complex rules stipulated in the contract. The market has evolved specialized names for specific types of exercise policies. Here, however, we call an *American derivative* any derivative whose cash flows can be affected by the holder in a nontrivial manner (the trivial manner to affect the cash flows is to sell the contract).

Relationship between European and American Derivatives

For simplicity of exposition, we will consider the case of a single underlying process, $S(t)$. We denote the set of exercise strategies by $c(.)$, whose arguments may include items such as the underlying process, properties of the past history of the underlying processes, time, and so on. In the simple case of an American put, $c(S, t)$ is a binary variable representing the *exercise* or *don't exercise* decisions.

If markets are complete, there is a straightforward conceptual relationship between European and American derivatives. If the market is complete, the cash flows generated by any derivative security can be replicated through a dynamic trading strategy with other securities. Fixing an exercise strategy means that the holder of the security will not be able to influence the cash flows. This means that for every exercise strategy of an American security there is a corresponding European security. Consider a derivative whose price, V, depends on an exercise strategy, c. Consider now a particular exercise strategy $\hat{c}$, such that

$$V(\hat{c}) = \max_c V(c) \tag{3.115}$$

The exercise strategy $\hat{c}$ is called an *optimal exercise strategy*. It is easy to see that in order to prevent arbitrage, the value of the American security must equal $V(\hat{c})$. Assume that the American security's price is less than $V(\hat{c})$. In this case, we sell the portfolio that replicates $V(\hat{c})$ and we purchase the American derivative. We now follow an optimal exercise strategy, thereby matching the cash flows between the American security and $V(\hat{c})$, and we keep the initial risk-free profit. If, on the other hand, the price of the American security were greater than $V(\hat{c})$, we can buy the portfolio that replicates $V(\hat{c})$ and sell the American derivative. The holder of the American security will follow an optimal exercise strategy, thus causing the cash flows between the American security and $V(\hat{c})$ to be matched. Again, we keep the initial risk-free profit. Notice that because we assume that markets are complete, there is no problem in replicating $V(\hat{c})$.

We see that the valuation of American options is no different than the valuation of European options, *provided we know the optimal exercise strategy* $\hat{c}$. Of course, we don't know ahead of time what the optimal exercise strategy is. In practice, the optimal exercise strategy is found simultaneously with the price.

In derivatives pricing, optimal exercise strategies are associated with the concept of *free boundaries*. For illustration, consider the case of the simple *exercise–don't exercise* version of exercise strategy. The free boundary separates the region in (S, t) where it is optimal to exercise the option from the region where it is optimal to hold the option. The free boundary is also referred to as the *exercise boundary*. The argument in the previous paragraph indicates that the price of the American security will have the same description as a European security on the side of the free boundary where it is optimal to hold the security, and it will be equal to the exercise value on the side where it is optimal to exercise. Since the European pricing problem is described by a partial differential equation, the presence of the exercise boundary poses the question of suitable conditions at those boundaries. In the approaches that we follow in this book, it is not necessary to be concerned about the details of what happens at the exercise boundaries. The reason is that in the least squares Monte Carlo method and in the linear complementarity implementation of finite differences, our methods of choice for dealing with early exercise, the exercise boundary is resolved as part of the solution. In order to better understand the behavior of the solution, however, the next two sections discuss the conditions that must be satisfied at the exercise boundaries. It is possible to pose the problem such that the exercise boundary is also a boundary of the computational domain. This is easy to do if the problem has one space variable. The resolution of the boundary as an integral part of the solution, however, is a much more practical approach, especially in several dimensions (this is true of simulation and finite differences).

For the purpose of clarifying the conditions at the exercise boundaries, the next two sections address the American pricing problem in the context of dynamic optimization.

American Options as Dynamic Optimization Problems

This discussion is not intended as a real solution strategy, but as a device to derive the continuity conditions at the exercise boundaries. For the purpose of illustration, consider an American derivative with an *exercise–don't exercise* strategy that applies in the interval $0 \leq t \leq T$. Here, at every time t the decision must be made whether to exercise the option or to continue to hold it. Notice that direct optimization of the option value over the space of exercise strategies will in general lead to a problem with a very large number of dimensions, since the number of possible exercise strategies is very large. We can, in principle, parameterize the problem by a suitable description of the free boundaries and solve an optimization problem over a reduced number of dimensions. Although this is often done in practice (Ingersoll, 1998), it requires a priori knowledge of the features and location of the free boundaries.

In the case when the optimal exercise strategy depends only on the current value of the underlying processes and time, there is a powerful alternative for determining the optimal strategy and thereby the option value, known as the *Bellman principle of dynamic programming* (Dixit and Pindyck, 1994).

The Bellman principle leads to a recursive argument that states the optimal strategy in terms of two components. In the case of an American option with an *exercise–don't exercise* strategy, the Bellman principle in continuous time can be phrased as follows. *At a given time, the optimal strategy corresponds to the maximum of either the exercise value or the value associated with selecting an optimal strategy an instant later.* This idea can be expressed in what is known as the *Bellman equation of dynamic programming*. For simplicity, consider only one underlying price process, $S(t)$, and an exercise value, $F(S(t))$, that depends only on $S(t)$. Notice that we assume the exercise value itself does not depend on the exercise strategy. The Bellman equation is

$$V(S(t), t) = \max\{F(S(t)), \text{PV}_t[V(S(t) + dS(t), t + dt)]\} \qquad (3.116)$$

where PV_t stands for present value at time t.

Notice that the recursive structure of Equation 3.116 allows us to solve for both the optimal strategy and the value of the security if we know end conditions and work backward in time. *The commonly used backward induction techniques implemented through trees for American option pricing are particular implementations of solutions of the Bellman equation.* We will use the Bellman equation to discuss the boundary conditions at exercise boundaries.

Conditions at Exercise Boundaries

The purpose of this section is to better understand the way the solution behaves near exercise boundaries. In practice, we don't need to concern ourselves with the properties of the exercise boundary, since the exercise boundary is automatically captured by simulation or by the linear complementarity formulation. There are two conditions that must be satisfied at exercise boundaries. The first condition is that the exercise value and the continuation value of the option must be the same at the exercise boundary.

This is a way of characterizing the exercise boundary as a region of indifference between exercising and not exercising the option.

The second condition is that the gradient of the option value with respect to the underlying variables must be continuous at the exercise boundary. This condition is known as *smooth pasting* and it states that the gradient of the exercise value of the option must be equal to the gradient of the continuation value.

To prove the condition of smooth pasting, consider the implications of Equation 3.116 when we are at the exercise boundary. If we are at the exercise boundary, we must have $V(S, t) = F(S)$. Assume that an upward movement in S would place us in the exercise region, while a downward movement would place us in the continuation region (this only requires continuity of $V(S, t)$ at the exercise boundary). If there is an upward movement in S, the option payoff will be

$$F(S + dS) \qquad (3.117)$$

If there is a downward movement, the option value will be

$$V(S + dS, t + dt) + \mathrm{E}_{t+dt} dV \qquad (3.118)$$

Assume now that the probability of an upward movement is equal to p. The option value can be written as

$$V(S, t) = \mathrm{PV}[F(S + dS)p + (V(S + dS, t + dt) + \mathrm{E}_{t+dt}dV)(1-p)] \quad (3.119)$$

where PV(.) denotes present value. Since at the exercise boundary we are indifferent between exercising and waiting, $V(S, t)$ must equal the discounted expectation of $V(S + dS, t + dt)$. Replacing this in Equation 3.119, we get

$$\mathrm{PV}[\, V(S + dS, t + dt) - F(S + dS)p \\ - (V(S + dS, t + dt)(1-p) - \mathrm{E}_{t+dt}dV)(1-p)] = 0 \qquad (3.120)$$

Expanding in Taylor series and replacing $F = V$, we get

$$\mathrm{PV}\left[\left(\frac{\partial F}{\partial S}dS - \frac{\partial V}{\partial S}dS - \frac{\partial V}{\partial t}dt\right)p + (\mathrm{E}_{t+dt}dV)(1-p)\right] = 0 \qquad (3.121)$$

If the underlying process is a diffusion process of the form $dS = \mu dt + \sigma dW$, then infinitesimal changes in S are proportional to $\sqrt{dt}$. In addition, the probability of upward or downward movements also deviates from one proportionally to $\sqrt{dt}$. This means that the last equation can be written as follows:

$$PV\left[\left(\frac{\partial F}{\partial S}\mathcal{O}(\sqrt{dt}) - \frac{\partial V}{\partial S}\mathcal{O}(\sqrt{dt}) - \frac{\partial V}{\partial t}dt\right)p + (E_{t+dt}dV)\mathcal{O}\sqrt{dt}\right] = 0 \quad (3.122)$$

Neglecting higher order terms, we get the following relationship that must be satisfied at the exercise boundary:

$$\frac{\partial V}{\partial S} = \frac{\partial F}{\partial S} \quad (3.123)$$

This condition is known as *smooth pasting*.

Linear Complementarity Formulation of American Option Pricing

The value at time t of an option that can be exercised at times τ is given by the following expectation:

$$V(r, S, t) = \sup_{\tau} E_{r,S,t}\left[e^{-\int_t^\tau r(\xi)d\xi}F(s(\tau))\right] \int \quad (3.124)$$

where τ are stopping times conditional on information at time t, and $F(.)$ is the payoff if the option is exercised at time equal to the stopping time τ (Lamberton and Lapeyre, 1996).

It can be shown that Equation 3.124 will hold if the following system of partial differential inequalities is satisfied (Lamberton and Lapeyre, 1996):

$$V \geq F$$
$$\frac{\partial V}{\partial t} + rS\frac{\partial V}{\partial S} + \frac{1}{2}\sigma^2 S^2\frac{\partial^2 V}{\partial S^2} \leq rV$$
$$\left(\frac{\partial V}{\partial t} + rS\frac{\partial V}{\partial S} + \frac{1}{2}\sigma^2 S^2\frac{\partial^2 V}{\partial S^2} - rV\right)(V - F) = 0 \quad (3.125)$$
$$V(S, T) = F(S)$$

Intuitively, this system can be understood in the following manner. The first inequality expresses the fact that at all times the value of the option cannot fall below its intrinsic value. The second inequality reflects the fact that if the value of the option grows more slowly than that of a riskless bond, the option is exercised. The third condition enforces the fact that if the value of the option is above its intrinsic value, the price of the option is described by the same partial differential equation that describes the corresponding European option. The last condition indicates that the option value at maturity equals its intrinsic value. In Chapter 7 we will describe in some detail a standard method for solving Equation 3.125.

PATH DEPENDENCY

In this section, *path dependency* refers to the dependency of the payoff of the derivative on the trajectory followed by one or more of the underlying processes. Another notion of path dependency refers to the underlying processes themselves being a function of the trajectory. There is a distinction between these two notions of path dependency. If the underlying processes themselves are path dependent, we may not be able to obtain, without further assumptions (Bhar and Chiarella, 1997), a pricing equation in the form of a partial differential equation. Our case of interest is when the value of the derivative depends on the trajectory but the underlying processes are Markovian.

There are two primary reasons why path dependency is a concern in the context of numerical solutions. One reason is that if the cash flows of the derivative depend on some function of the trajectory of the underlying processes, this dependency will result in a larger number of dimensions in the pricing equation. Another reason is that it may cause the resulting pricing equation to be significantly more difficult to solve. The reason is the additional difficulty imposed by absence of diffusion in the additional dimension. In order to illustrate the second point, consider a simple case of a single underlying process, $S(t)$, where the derivative price depends on the time integral of some function of the underlying process, $g(t)$, defined as follows:

$$g(t) = \int_0^t f(S(t))dt \qquad (3.126)$$

The derivative price will be a function of S, g, and t. Assume that S follows the log-normal process $dS = S\mu dt + S\sigma dW$. The application of Ito's lemma to $g(t)$ gives us

$$dg(t) = f(S(t))dt \qquad (3.127)$$

This means that the increment of g at time t is known if the information set at time t is known. The fact that g was given by an integral of a function of the underlying process means that dg does not have a diffusion component. We can now apply Ito's lemma to $dV(S, g, t)$ and use the procedures described earlier to derive the pricing equation:

$$\frac{\partial V}{\partial t} + rS\frac{\partial V}{\partial S} + f(S)\frac{\partial V}{\partial g} + \frac{1}{2}\sigma^2 S^2\frac{\partial^2 V}{\partial S^2} - rV = 0 \qquad (3.128)$$

There are two observations we can make about the effect of the g dimension. The most obvious one is that there is no corresponding diffusion in the g dimension. This alone can be a reason for concern, since, as will be established in Chapter 7, it is the diffusion term that contributes to the stability of the numerical schemes used to solve the pricing equation. A more subtle observation, however, is that the coefficient in front of $\frac{\partial V}{\partial g}$ can in principle be of a very different magnitude than the other coefficients in the equation, depending on the definition of $f(S)$. This may also significantly add to the numerical difficulty (Zvan et al., 1997–1998).

In practice, the additional convective term turns out not to be a significant difficulty if one considers the case of *discrete sampling*. Discrete sampling will be the main approach to path dependency in this book. The interested reader is referred to reference Zvan et al., 1997–1998, as a good example of work on the development of robust algorithms for the continuous case. An alternative approach to getting around the problem of absent diffusion in a particular coordinate is to introduce artificial diffusion in that direction and then obtain the limit as the artificial diffusion vanishes. This can be done numerically quite efficiently.

Discrete Sampling of Path Dependency

Discrete sampling of path dependency is of course a better approximation of what really happens, since the movement of the underlying processes can only be observed at discrete points in time. Discrete sampling, however, can also be viewed as a means of dealing with the problem introduced by the additional convective term and the absence of corresponding diffusion. The key observation is that the value of the option immediately before the sampling time and immediately after the sampling time must be the same. This will be the case as long as sampling itself does not trigger cash flows. Denoting the sampling times by t_i, $i = 1, 2, \ldots$, and the times immediately preceeding the sampling time by t_i^-, $i = 1, 2, \ldots$, this continuity condition is expressed as

$$V(S(t_i), g(t_i, t_i), t_i) = VS(t_i^-),(g(t_i^-, t_i^-), t_i^-), i = 1, 2, \ldots \qquad (3.129)$$

In Chapter 7 we will refer to this condition as *displacement shock*. The pricing equation between sampling times is obtained by applying Ito's lemma to the relevant underlying processes. Since $g(S, t)$ is constant between sampling times $g(S, t)$ does not appear in the pricing equation. Between sampling times we must solve

$$\frac{\partial V}{\partial t} + rS\frac{\partial V}{\partial S} + \frac{1}{2}\sigma^2 S^2 \frac{\partial^2 V}{\partial S^2} = rV \qquad (3.130)$$

where the term $f(S)\frac{\partial V}{\partial g}$ does not enter. This equation must be solved within each sampling interval subject to initial conditions derived from the continuity condition above.

The initial condition at the beginning of each sampling interval must be extracted from the solution at the end of the previous sampling interval such that the continuity conditions are satisfied. Notice that although the g dimension has dropped from the PDE, the solution itself still has the g dimension. What has happened is that the changes in the g dimension, which in the continuous sampling case occur through the differential equation, here occur through the initial conditions in each sampling interval. The application of the continuity condition given by Equation 3.129 has the effect of concentrating the convection at the boundaries of sampling intervals.

The practical implementation of the continuity condition or displacement shock will be discussed in greater detail in Chapter 7. The continuity condition is also referred to as a *jump condition* in the literature (Wilmott, DeWynne, and Howison, 1993).

CHAPTER 4

Scenario Generation

Generating scenarios of the underlying processes that determine the derivative's price is an essential and delicate task from an analytical perspective as well as from a system design viewpoint. This chapter sets up the nomenclature we will use in the remaining chapters to refer to scenarios and describes the main issues and methods for generating scenarios for pricing.

The two main applications of scenarios are *risk management* and *pricing*. The objectives of using scenarios in risk management are to obtain distributions of possible gains and losses as a function of future time and to determine the concentration of risk among various components of a portfolio of instruments. The main objective of scenarios in pricing is to compute the expectation that gives us the value of the financial instrument. Scenarios are used when this is done by simulation, the topic of the next two chapters.

These two applications have different implications in the methods used to generate scenarios. The most obvious difference is that if we are interested in determining probabilities of future gains and losses, we would expect our scenarios to be based on real world probabilities. If we are using the scenarios for pricing, on the other hand, the scenarios must be based on the probabilities associated with the measure induced by the numeraire asset, as we discussed extensively in last two chapters. If we don't do this, our expectation will give us the wrong price. When generating scenarios for pricing, using the right measure is essential. When generating scenarios for risk management, however, which probability measure we use to produce the scenarios is a much less significant issue. This is the case because the dispersion of values, especially over short time horizons, is primarily dominated by the volatility and correlation of the underlying processes, rather than by their drifts. Since the difference in probability measure is determined by the drift of the underlying processes, as long as the time horizon is not large it may not matter whether we do value-at-risk analysis using scenarios meant for pricing. It must be clear, however, that doing pricing with scenarios meant for risk management is not possible in general.

This distinction between scenarios for pricing and scenarios for risk management has a bearing on the design of pricing and risk management systems.

We can visualize a situation where value-at-risk analysis is conducted on a portfolio of instruments where some of the instruments are priced by simulation. In designing a system it is important to have an architecture that allows for proper separation between pricing and risk management scenarios.

In this chapter we will discuss issues pertaining to scenarios for pricing through simulation.

SCENARIO NOMENCLATURE

As we saw in the last chapter, the value of a derivative security with payoffs at a known time T is given by the expectation of its payoff, normalized with the numeraire asset. The value of a European derivative whose payoff depends on a single underlying process, $S(t)$, is given by the expectation

$$V(S(0),0) = B(0)E_0^B\left[\frac{V(S(T),T)}{B(T)}\right] \tag{4.1}$$

where all stochastic processes in this expectation are consistent with the measure induced by the numeraire asset $B(t)$.

If we wish to construct scenarios for computing this expectation numerically, we can raise the following questions.

■ Should we generate scenarios for $S(t)$ and $B(t)$ separately and then compute the argument in the expectation operator?
■ Should we generate scenarios for $V(S(t), t)$ and $B(t)$ separately?
■ Should we instead generate scenarios for the ratio $\frac{V(S(t), t)}{B(t)}$?

All of these alternatives are possible. The last alternative, in particular, can lead to extremely fast computations. From a system's design perspective and code reusability, the preferred approach is the first one, which we will focus on for the remainder of the chapter.

Another important question is: Are the scenarios for pricing European derivatives and derivatives with early exercise the same? This question is relevant because the expectation for early exercise derivatives (such as American and Bermudan) is taken at an unknown exercise time, τ, that maximizes the expectation:

$$V(S(0), 0) = B(0) \sup_{0 \le \tau \le T} E_0^B\left[\frac{V(S(\tau), \tau)}{B(\tau)}\right] \tag{4.2}$$

For the particular approach for computing early exercise options with simulation that we will emphasize in this book, the answer is *yes*. The same scenarios used in European pricing can be used in early exercise pricing.

This is not true in general, but it is true in our case. We are now ready to introduce the scenario nomenclature.

We consider an underlying process $S(t)$, described by the stochastic differential equation

$$dS(t) = a(S, t)dt + b(S, t)dW \qquad (4.3)$$

A scenario is a set of values $\hat{S}^j(t_i)$, $i = 1,...,$ that are an approximation to the jth realization, $S^j(t_i)$, of the solution of Equation 5.112, evaluated at times $0 \le t_i \le T, i = 1,..., I$. A scenario is also called a *trajectory*. For the next several sections we will be talking about *spot* trajectories. A spot trajectory can be visualized as a line in the state-versus-time plane, describing the path followed by a realization of the stochastic process (actually, by an approximation to the stochastic process). Later, we will discuss *LIBOR rate trajectories*. A LIBOR rate trajectory is not a single line in the state-versus-time space, because the state itself is now a collection of rates (an interest rate curve). The methodology we discuss here, however, applies to both types of trajectories.

A *scenario set* is a collection of scenarios or trajectories, $\hat{S}^j(t_i), j = 1,..., J$, $1,..., i = I$. If we consider a multidimensional process, $\vec{S}(t)$, instead of a scalar process, S, the same definitions apply. In this case, a scenario consists of a vector $\vec{s}^j(t_i), i = 1,..., I$.

Notice that because our scenarios are usually approximations to the paths followed by the solution of the stochastic differential equation, we differentiate between scenarios and exact paths by the use of a ^. Since this notation is cumbersome, we will drop the ^ when there is no issue of confusion.

SCENARIO CONSTRUCTION

There are several ways to construct scenarios for pricing. We now give a summary and then discuss the various procedures in detail.

- Constructing a path of the solution to Equation 5.112 at times t_i, $i = 1,..., I$ by exact advancement of the solution: This method is only possible if we have an analytical expression for the solution of the stochastic differential equation.
- Sampling from the joint distribution of $S(t_i)$, $i = 1,..., I$: This approach requires that we have an analytical solution for the SDE and that we be able to derive the joint distribution of $S(t_i)$.
- Approximate numerical solution of the stochastic differential equation: This is the method of choice if we cannot use any of the previous ones. Just as in the case of ordinary differential equations, there are numerical techniques for discretizing and solving stochastic differential equations.

Exact Solution Advancement

This approach is best illustrated with a simple example. Consider a lognormal process with constant drift and volatility,

$$\frac{dS}{S} = \mu dt + \sigma dW(t) \qquad (4.4)$$

with solution

$$S(t) = S(0)\exp\left(\left(\mu - \frac{1}{2}\sigma^2\right)t + \sigma W(t)\right) \qquad (4.5)$$

Using this expression, we can construct our trajectories as follows:

$$S(t_i) = S(t_{i-1})\exp\left(\left(\mu - \frac{1}{2}\sigma^2\right)(t_i - t_{i-1}) + \sigma(W(t_i) - W(t_{i-1}))\right) \quad i = 1,...,I \qquad (4.6)$$

Our problem now is to obtain a sequence of Wiener processes $W(t_i)$ to use in Equation 4.6. There is more than one way to accomplish this. We discuss the simplest way now and elaborate on other alternatives later. The increment of the Wiener process can be generated by

$$W(t_i) - W(t_{i-1}) = \sqrt{t_i - t_{i-1}}Z \qquad (4.7)$$

where Z is a standard normal random variable. Notice that if the time spacing is uniform, all the increments we add to construct the Wiener path have the same variance. We will elaborate on this later, but at this stage we should realize that building the path this way means that we are sampling from a multidimensional distribution (each $W(t_i)$ represents one dimension), where all the dimensions have the same variance. This is fine in some cases but is not fine in others. More on this later.

Replacing this increment in Equation 4.6 we get

$$S(t_i) = S(t_{i-1})\exp\left(\left(\mu - \frac{1}{2}\sigma^2\right)(t_i - t_{i-1}) + \sigma\sqrt{t_i - t_{i-1}}Z\right) \quad i = 1,...,I \quad (4.8)$$

Defining the outcomes of successive drawings of the random variable Z corresponding to the jth trajectory by Z_i^j, we finally get the following recursive expression for the jth trajectory of $S(t)$:

$$S^j(t_i) = S^j(t_{i-1})\exp\left(\left(\mu - \frac{1}{2}\sigma^2\right)(t_i - t_{i-1}) + \sigma\sqrt{t_i - t_{i-1}}Z_i^j\right) \quad i = 1,...,I \quad (4.9)$$

In this particular case, constructing trajectories is very simple if we have a way to generate independent standard normal random variables. However, some observations are in order. Although the process $W(t)$ is one dimensional in the sense that it represents a single source of uncertainty driving $S(t)$ in the stochastic differential Equation 4.4, the set $\{W(t_i),\ i = 1, \ldots,\ I\}$ must be viewed as the components of a vector of random variables with a multidimensional distribution. This also means that for a fixed j, the Z_i^j are realizations of a multidimensional standard normal random variable, which happen to be independent. Whether we view the Z_i^j as coming from a multidimensional distribution of independent normals or as drawings from a single one-dimensional distribution does not affect the outcome (that is, the statistical properties of the scenarios), as long as the Z_i^j are generated from *pseudorandom numbers*. Pseudorandom numbers are produced by algorithms that try to approximate the properties of true random numbers. This distinction, however, is conceptually important and it becomes essential if we generate the Z_i^j not from pseudorandom numbers, but from *quasi-random sequences*. Quasi-random sequences approximate some, but not all, of the properties of true random numbers. This will become much clearer soon.

Sampling from the Joint Distribution of the Random Process

If the solution of Equation 4.3 is Gaussian (or it can be transformed into a Gaussian) and we know it explicitly, we may be able to construct the joint distribution of $S(t_i)$. We can then sample from this joint distribution extremely efficiently and construct the entire trajectory $S^j(t_i)$ at once (if we do this we get an exact solution; this is the reason for not having a ˆ on the S). In doing this we don't have to advance from one time step to another. As a result, the computation can be very fast.

The simplest example is the construction of a standard Wiener process trajectory, $W^j(t_i),\ i = 1, \ldots,\ I$. The covariance matrix of the $W(t_i)$ is

$$
\begin{aligned}
\operatorname{cov}\left(W(t_i), W(t_{i-1})\right) &= \mathrm{E}[\,W(t_i)\,W(t_{i-1})\,] - \underbrace{\mathrm{E}[\,W(t_i)\,]}_{=0}\ \underbrace{\mathrm{E}[\,W(t_{i-1})\,]}_{=0} \\
&= \mathrm{E}[\,W(t_i) - W(t_{i-1}) + W(t_{i-1}), W(t_{i-1})\,] \\
&= \underbrace{\mathrm{E}[\,W(t_i) - (W(t_{i-1})), W(t_{i-1})\,]}_{=0} \qquad (4.10) \\
&\quad + \mathrm{E}[\,W(t_{i-1}), W(t_{i-1})\,] \\
&= \mathrm{E}[\,W(t_{i-1}), W(t_{i-1})\,] \\
&= \operatorname{var}[\,W(t_{i-1}), W(t_{i-1})\,] \\
&= t_{i-1}
\end{aligned}
$$

This means

$$\text{cov}\,(W(t_k), W(t_l)) = \min\,[t_k,\,t_l] \tag{4.11}$$

and the correlation coefficient is

$$\rho_{W_k, W_l} = \frac{\min\,[t_k, t_l]}{\sqrt{t_l t_k}} \tag{4.12}$$

Remember that $W(t_i)$ is related to a standard normal, Z, through the relationship

$$W(t_i) = \sqrt{t_i}\,Z \tag{4.13}$$

This means

$$\begin{aligned}
\text{cov}\,(W(t_k), W(t_l)) &= \min\,[t_k,\,t_l] \\
&= \text{cov}\,(\sqrt{t_k}\,Z_k,\,\sqrt{t_l}\,Z_l) \\
&= \sqrt{t_k t_l}\,\text{cov}\,(Z_k,\,Z_l) \\
&= \sqrt{t_k t_l}\,\rho_{Z_k, Z_l}
\end{aligned} \tag{4.14}$$

This means that given t_i, $i = 1, \ldots, I$, if we sample from a standard joint normal distribution with correlation matrix

$$\rho_{Z_k, Z_l} = \frac{\min\,[t_k, t_l]}{\sqrt{t_l t_k}} \tag{4.15}$$

we get the desired $W^j(t_i)$ by replacing the jth realization of Z_i in Equation 4.13

$$W^j(t_i) = \sqrt{t_i}\,Z_i^j \tag{4.16}$$

The standard procedure for sampling from a joint normal distribution is to create correlated standard normal random variables from linear combinations of uncorrelated standard normals. This is known as the *Choleski decomposition* and is explained in detail later in the chapter.

Another simple example is the case of a log-normal process with constant drift and volatility. Using Ito's lemma on

$$\frac{dS}{S} = \mu dt + \sigma dW \tag{4.17}$$

we have

$$d\log S = \left(\mu - \frac{1}{2}\sigma^2\right)dt + \sigma dW \tag{4.18}$$

and

$$\log S(t_k) = \left(\mu - \frac{1}{2}\sigma^2\right)t_k + \sigma W(t_k) \tag{4.19}$$

The covariance between $\log S(t_k)$ and $\log S(t_l)$ is

$$
\begin{aligned}
\operatorname{cov}\left(\log S(t_k), \log S(t_l)\right) &= \operatorname{cov}\left(\left(\mu - \frac{1}{2}\sigma^2\right)t_k + \sigma W(t_k), \left(\mu - \frac{1}{2}\sigma^2\right)t_l + \sigma W(t_l)\right) \\
&= \operatorname{cov}(\sigma W(t_k), \sigma W(t_l)) \tag{4.20} \\
&= \sigma^2 \operatorname{cov}(W(t_k), W(t_l)) \\
&= \sigma^2 \min\,[t_k, t_l]
\end{aligned}
$$

The correlation coefficient is

$$\rho_{\log S_k, \log S_l} = \frac{\min\,[t_k, t_l]}{\sqrt{t_l t_k}} \tag{4.21}$$

If we sample from a joint normal distribution with a correlation matrix whose entries are given by the last equation and call the drawings of the jth trajectory Z_i^j, we get the trajectories of $\log S$ by rescaling Z_i^j with the volatility of $\log S$ and displacing Z_i^j with the expectation of $\log S$:

$$\log S^j(t_i) = \left(\mu t_i - \frac{1}{2}\sigma^2\right)t_i + \sigma \sqrt{t_i}\, Z_i^j \tag{4.22}$$

or, equivalently,

$$S^j(t_i) = \exp\left(\left(\mu t_i - \frac{1}{2}\sigma^2\right)t_i + \sigma \sqrt{t_i}\, Z_i^j\right) \tag{4.23}$$

In this simple case we could have replaced the results from Equation 4.16 in the analytical solution of the log-normal SDE,

$$S(t_k) = S(0)\exp\left(\left(\mu - \frac{1}{2}\sigma^2\right)t_k + \sigma W(t_k)\right) \tag{4.24}$$

because the variance of $S(t)$ and the correlation of $\log S(t_k)$, $S(t_l)$ are the same as the variance of $\sigma W(t)$ and the correlation of $\sigma W(t_k)$, $\sigma W(t_l)$.

In general, however, this is not so simple, and to get the correlation matrix of the random variables that make up the trajectory, there may be a significant amount of algebra. A powerful and fairly general procedure for getting the correlation matrix is by solving the evolution equation of the covariance of the stochastic process at two points in time.

Time Evolution of the Covariance of $S(t_k)$ and $S(t_l)$ In Chapter 2 we derived ordinary differential equations for the time evolution of the moments of a stochastic process. Here we do something similar for the covariance.

We would like to get an ordinary differential equation of the form:

$$\frac{d\mathrm{cov}(S(t_k), S(t))}{dt} = f(S(t_k), t_k, S(t), t) \tag{4.25}$$

If we can integrate this equation from $t = t_k$ to $t = t_l$, subject to the initial condition $\mathrm{cov}(S(t_k), S(t_k)) = \mathrm{var}(S(t_k))$, we get an analytical expression for the covariance of the process at two points in time.

To derive the evolution equation, we start from the definition of covariance:

$$\mathrm{cov}(S(t_k), S(t)) = E[S(t_k), S(t)] - E[S(t_k)]E[S(t)] \tag{4.26}$$

This gives

$$\frac{d\mathrm{cov}(S(t_k), S(t))}{dt} = \frac{dE[S(t_k)S(t)]}{dt} - E[S(t_k)]\frac{dE[S(t)]}{dt} \tag{4.27}$$

To get $\frac{dE[S(t)]}{dt}$, use

$$\begin{aligned}
\frac{dE[S(t)]}{dt} &= \left(\frac{dE[S(t+dt)] - E[S(t)]}{dt}\right) \\
&= \left(\frac{E[S(t) + dS] - E[S(t)]}{dt}\right) \\
&= \left(\frac{E[S(t) + a(S(t), t)dt + b(S(t), t)dW(t)] - E[S(t)]}{dt}\right) \\
&= \left(\frac{E[a(S(t), t)dt + b(S(t), t)dW(t)]}{dt}\right) \\
&= \left(\frac{E[a(S(t), t)dt]}{dt} + \overbrace{\frac{E[b(S(t), t)dW(t)]}{dt}}^{=0}\right) \\
&= E[a(S(t), t)]
\end{aligned} \tag{4.28}$$

To get $\frac{dE[S(t_k)S(t)]}{dt}$, use

$$\begin{aligned}
\frac{dE[S(t_k)S(t)]}{dt} &= \frac{E[S(t_k)S(t+dt)] - E[S(t_k)S(t)]}{dt} \\
&= \frac{E[S(t_k)(S(t) + dS)] - E[S(t_k)S(t)]}{dt} \\
&= \frac{E[S(t_k)dS]}{dt}
\end{aligned} \tag{4.29}$$

$$= \frac{E[S(t_k)(a(S(t), t)dt + b(S(t), t)dW(t)]}{dt}$$

$$= \frac{E[S(t_k)(a(S(t), t)]dt}{dt} + \frac{\overbrace{E[b(S(t), t)dW(t)]}^{=0}}{dt} \qquad (4.29)$$

$$= E[S(t_k)a(S(t), t)]$$

Replacing Equations 4.28 and 4.29 in Equation 4.27, we get

$$\frac{d\text{cov}(S(t_k), S(t))}{dt} = E[S(t_k)a(S(t), t)] - E[S(t_k)]E[a(S(t), t)] \qquad (4.30)$$

Notice that if the drift is independent of $S(t)$, the two terms on the left cancel and the covariance does not change as a function of the t. This means that in this case the covariance between $S(t_k)$ and $S(t_l)$, where $t_l > t_k$, is equal to the variance of $S(t_k)$. This is consistent with the log-normal case and the Wiener process we did in the previous section.

To get the variance (we need this for the initial conditions), we can solve an ordinary differential equation for the variance. Deriving an ordinary differential equation for the variance is very simple. From the definition of variance,

$$\text{var}(S(t)) = E[S^2(t)] - E^2[S(t)] \qquad (4.31)$$

we get

$$\frac{d\text{var}(S(t))}{dt} = \frac{dE[S^2(t)]}{dt} - 2E[S(t)]\frac{dE[S(t)]}{dt} \qquad (4.32)$$

To get $\frac{dE[S^2(t)]}{dt}$, we apply Ito's lemma to $S(t)^2$:

$$dS^2(t) = 2S(t)[a(S(t), t)dt + b(S(t), t)dW(t)] + b^2(S(t), t)dt \qquad (4.33)$$

This gives

$$\frac{dE[S^2(t)]}{dt} = 2E[S(t)a(S(t), t)] + E[b^2(S(t), t)] \qquad (4.34)$$

Replacing Equations 4.28 and 4.34 in Equation 4.32, we get

$$\frac{d\text{var}(S(t))}{dt} = 2E[S(t)a(S(t), t)] + E[b^2(S(t), t)] - 2E[S(t)]E[a(S(t), t)]$$

$$(4.35)$$

This equation must be solved to provide the initial conditions for the equation for the covariance. As mentioned in Chapter 2, these equations may not be closed. This means that it is possible that we don't get a finite number of equations to solve for the covariance. In such a case, it may be possible to use advanced mathematical software to generate equations for a sufficiently large number of moments.

Generating Scenarios by Numerical Integration of the Stochastic Differential Equations

The numerical integration of the stochastic differential equation

$$dS(t) = a(S, t)dt + b(S, t)dW \tag{4.36}$$

by finite differences is the most robust way of generating scenarios for pricing.

In the case of the numerical integration of ordinary (deterministic) differential equations by finite differences, the numerical scheme introduces a discretization error that translates into the numerical solution differing from the exact solution by an amount proportional to a power of the time step. This amount is the *truncation error* of the numerical scheme. We will deal with this issue extensively in Chapter 7.

In the case of the numerical integration of stochastic differential equations by finite differences, on the other hand, the interpretation of the numerical error introduced by the discretization scheme is more complicated. The reason for this is that unlike the case of ordinary differential equations, where the only thing we are interested in computing is the solution itself, when dealing with stochastic differential equations, there are two aspects that interest us. One aspect is the accuracy with which we compute the trajectories or paths of a realization of the solution. The other aspect is the accuracy with which we compute functions of the process such as expectations and moments. In the case of a plain European option, whose value is computed by calculating an expectation at known payoff time, it is clear that the accuracy we are interested in is the accuracy with which we can compute that expectation.

The order of accuracy with which a given scheme can approximate trajectories of the solution is not the same as the accuracy with which the same scheme can approximate expectations and moments of functions of the trajectories.

The convergence of the numerically computed trajectories to the exact trajectories is called *strong convergence*. The order of the numerical scheme that characterizes this convergence is called *order of strong convergence*. The convergence of the numerically computed moments of functions of the stochastic process to the exact values of those moments is called *weak con-*

vergence. The order of the numerical scheme that characterizes this convergence is called *order of weak convergence*.

Just as there is a comprehensive theory of convergence and stability for finite differences applied to deterministic ordinary differential equations, there is a similar theory for stochastic differential equations. The work by Kloeden and Platen (1995) is a comprehensive reference on this subject. We will discuss finite difference theory for partial differential equations in Chapter 7 in great detail. Although we will not cover the theory of finite difference for stochastic differential equations in this book, the information given in this chapter is sufficient for the purpose of judiciously building quality scenarios for pricing. For an exhaustive treatment of numerical schemes for stochastic differential equations, the reader is referred to Kloeden and Platen (1995).

The two most popular schemes for integrating stochastic differential equations in finance are the *explicit Euler scheme* and the *Milshtein scheme* (Milshtein, 1978).

Given a stochastic differential equation

$$dS(t) = a(S(t), t)dt + b(S(t), t)dW(t) \tag{4.37}$$

the Euler scheme advances the solution from time point t_i to $t_{i+1} = t_i + \Delta t$ as follows (the properties of this scheme when applied to ordinary differential equations will be discussed in detail in Chapter 7):

$$\hat{S}(t_{i+1}) = \hat{S}(t_i) + a(\hat{S}(t_i), t_i)\Delta t + b(\hat{S}(t_i), t_i)(W(t_{i+1}) - W(t_i)) \tag{4.38}$$

The corresponding formula for the Milshtein scheme is

$$\begin{aligned} \hat{S}(t_{i+1}) = \hat{S}(t_i) + a(\hat{S}(t_i), t_i)\Delta t + b(\hat{S}(t_i), t_i)(W(t_{i+1}) - W(t_i)) \\ + \tfrac{1}{2}b(\hat{S}(t_i), t_i)\frac{\partial b}{\partial S}(\hat{S}(t_i), t_i)\left[(W(t_{i+1}) - W(t_i))^2 - \Delta t \right] \end{aligned} \tag{4.39}$$

The Milshtein scheme only differs from the Euler scheme in the second line. Notice that the drift and volatility in the right-hand side of both schemes are evaluated at time t_i. As we will discuss in Chapter 7, this means that these are explicit schemes.

If the process $S(t)$ is multidimensional, the drift is a vector and the volatility is either a vector or a matrix, depending on the representation of $W(t)$ (see Chapter 2). For the multidimensional extension, see Kloeden and Platen (1995).

Using the standard log-normal process, we give a heuristic argument that shows why the order of strong convergence and the order of weak convergence differ. As a simple case study, we discuss exhaustively the distortions introduced by the Euler scheme in the log-normal process. This study illustrates the high level of caution that is warranted in using the Euler scheme.

Order of Strong Convergence   Given a stochastic differential equation,

$$dS(t) = a(S(t), t)dt + b(S(t), t)dW(t) \tag{4.40}$$

a finite difference scheme produces a numerical solution $\hat{S}(t_i), 0 \leq t_{i-1} < t_i \leq T$, $i = 1, \ldots, I$, of Equation 4.40. For simplicity, assume that the t_i are equally spaced, $\Delta = t_i - t_{i-1}$. The scheme has q order of strong convergence if

$$\lim_{\Delta \to 0} E_0 \left[\left| \hat{S} - S(T) \right| \right] \leq \alpha \Delta^q \tag{4.41}$$

where α is a constant that does not depend on Δ. In this definition, |.| denotes the Euclidian norm (the square root of the sum of the squares). This would be relevant if $S(t)$ were a multidimensional trajectory. In the one-dimensional case, which we are dealing with here, this norm is the same as the absolute value. The norm in the expectation operator enforces the pathwise interpretation of the scheme accuracy. The use of a norm is necessary because otherwise positive and negative deviations by the numerically computed trajectory from the exact trajectory may tend to cancel out, and the proximity of the two trajectories would not be captured.

In general, the explicit Euler scheme has an order of strong convergence of 0.5, which means that the error is proportional to $\sqrt{\Delta t}$. However, when the volatility of the process change is deterministic, the Euler scheme has an order of strong convergence of 1. The Milshtein scheme always has an order of strong convergence of 1, which means the error is proportional to Δt, regardless of whether the volatility is deterministic or not. As we just saw, the additional work required to implement the Milshtein scheme, as opposed to the Euler scheme, is insignificant. If capturing the details of the trajectories is important and the volatility is not deterministic, the Milshtein scheme should be preferred to the Euler scheme.

Order of Weak Convergence   Referring to the stochastic differential equation of the last subsection, let $f(S(T))$ denote a function of the trajectory of the solution. A finite difference scheme has q order of weak convergence if

$$\lim_{\Delta \to 0} \left| E_0[f(\hat{S}(T))] - E_0[f(S(T))] \right| \leq \beta \Delta^q \tag{4.42}$$

where β is a constant that does not depend on Δ.

Strong and Weak Convergence for the Euler Scheme   We motivate the difference between strong and weak convergence by a simplified and intuitive analysis of the Euler scheme applied to the standard log-normal stochastic differential equation. This analysis is not rigorous and is meant to show why the same scheme has different accuracy when it is used to compute trajectories than when it is used to compute expectations.

Consider the stochastic differential equation:

$$\frac{dS(t)}{S(t)} = \mu dt + \sigma d W(t) \tag{4.43}$$

If we assume that μ and σ are constant, we know the solution is

$$S(t) = S(0) \exp\left(\left(\mu - \frac{1}{2}\sigma^2\right)t + \sigma W(t)\right) \tag{4.44}$$

The Euler scheme applied to Equation 4.43 is

$$\hat{S}(t_{i+1}) = \hat{S}(t_i)(1 + \mu \Delta t + \sigma \Delta W(t_i)) \tag{4.45}$$

where $\Delta W(t_i) = W(t_{i+1}) - W(t_i)$. The numerical solution at time t_k is given by

$$\hat{S}(t_k) = S(0) \prod_{i=0}^{i=k-1} (1 + \mu \Delta t + \sigma \Delta W(t_i)) \tag{4.46}$$

Assuming that there are I time steps in the interval $0 \leq t \leq T$, the error for strong convergence is

$$E\left[|\hat{S}(T) - S(T)|\right] \tag{4.47}$$

$$= E\left[\left|\prod_{i=0}^{i=I-1} (1 + \mu \Delta t + \sigma \Delta W(t_i)) - \exp\left(\left(\mu - \frac{1}{2}\sigma^2\right)T + \sigma W(T)\right)\right|\right]$$

where we assume that $S(0) = 1$ for simplicity. To determine how well the product in the right approximates the exponential, we expand $\exp\left(\left(\mu - \frac{1}{2}\sigma^2\right)\Delta t + \sigma \Delta W(t_i)\right)$ in Taylor series, keeping terms just past order Δt:

$$\exp\left(\left(\mu - \frac{1}{2}\sigma^2\right)\Delta t + \sigma W(t_i)\right) = 1 + \left(\mu - \frac{1}{2}\sigma^2\right)\Delta t + \sigma \Delta W(t_i)$$

$$+ \frac{1}{2}\left(\left(\mu - \frac{1}{2}\sigma^2\right)\Delta t + \sigma \Delta W(t_i)\right)^2 \tag{4.48}$$

$$+ \frac{1}{6}\left(\left(\mu - \frac{1}{2}\sigma^2\right)\Delta t + \sigma \Delta W(t_i)\right)^3 + \cdots$$

$$= 1 + \left(\mu - \frac{1}{2}\sigma^2\right)\Delta t + \sigma \Delta W(t_i)$$

$$+ \frac{1}{2}\sigma^2 \overbrace{\Delta W(t_i)^2}^{=\Delta t}$$

$$+ \left(\mu - \frac{1}{2}\sigma^2\right)\sigma \Delta t \Delta W(t_i)$$

$$+ \frac{1}{6}\sigma^3 \Delta W(t_i)^3 + \mathcal{O}(\Delta t^2) \tag{4.48}$$

$$= 1 + \mu \Delta t + \sigma \Delta W(t_i)$$

$$+ \left(\mu - \frac{1}{2}\sigma^2\right)\sigma \Delta t \Delta W(t_i)$$

$$+ \frac{1}{6}\sigma^3 \Delta W(t_i)^3 + \mathcal{O}(\Delta t^2)$$

Defining $c = (\mu - \frac{1}{2}\sigma^2)\sigma$, we have

$$1 + \mu \Delta t + \sigma \Delta W(t_i) = \exp\left(\left(\mu - \frac{1}{2}\sigma^2\right)\Delta t + \sigma \Delta W(t_i)\right) - c\Delta t \Delta W(t_i)$$

$$- \frac{1}{6}\sigma^3 \Delta W(t_i)^3 - \mathcal{O}(\Delta t^2) \tag{4.49}$$

The product in Equation 4.47 can be expanded approximately as follows:

$$\prod_{i=0}^{i=I-1} [1 + \mu \Delta t + \sigma \Delta W(t_i)] \tag{4.50}$$

$$= \prod_{i=0}^{i=I-1}\left[\exp\left(\left(\mu - \frac{1}{2}\sigma^2\right)\Delta t + \sigma \Delta W(t_i)\right) - c\Delta t \Delta W(t_i) - \frac{1}{6}\sigma^3 \Delta W(t_i)^3\right]$$

$$= \exp\left(\left(\mu - \frac{1}{2}\sigma^2\right)T + \sigma W T\right) + I\mathcal{O}(\Delta t \Delta W) + I\mathcal{O}(\Delta W^3) + I\mathcal{O}(\Delta t^2)$$

where ΔW is any $\Delta W(t_i)$. Replacing this in Equation 4.47 and leaving out the $\mathcal{O}(\Delta t^2)$ term, we have

$$E\left[|\hat{S}(T) - S(T)|\right] = E\left[|I\mathcal{O}(\Delta t \Delta W) + I\mathcal{O}(\Delta W^3)|\right]$$

$$= \left[\left|\frac{T}{\Delta t}\mathcal{O}(\Delta t \Delta W) + \frac{T}{\Delta t}\mathcal{O}(\Delta W^3)\right|\right]$$

$$= TE\left[\left|\underbrace{\frac{1}{\Delta t}\mathcal{O}(\Delta t \Delta W)}_{\mathcal{O}\sqrt{\Delta t}} + \underbrace{\frac{1}{\Delta t}\mathcal{O}(\Delta W^3)}_{\mathcal{O}\sqrt{\Delta t}}\right|\right] \tag{4.51}$$

$$= \mathcal{O}(\sqrt{\Delta t})$$

To analyze the weak convergence, we should be specific about the function $f(.)$ in the weak convergence statement

$$\lim_{\Delta \to 0} \left| E_0[f(\hat{S}(T))] - E_0[f(S(T))] \right| \le \beta \Delta^q \qquad (4.52)$$

For simplicity, we consider as example the expectation of the process itself.

$$\lim_{\Delta \to 0} \left| E_0[f(\hat{S}(T))] - E_0[f(S(T))] \right| \qquad (4.53)$$

As with the strong convergence case, we replace the Euler discretized process, Equation 4.45, in the last expression:

$$\left| E[\hat{S}(T)] - E[S(T)] \right|$$

$$= \left| E\left[\prod_{i=0}^{i=I-1} (1 + \mu \Delta t + \sigma \Delta W(t_i)) \right] - E\left[\exp\left(\left(\mu - \frac{1}{2}\sigma^2 \right)T + \sigma W(T) \right) \right] \right| \qquad (4.54)$$

When we replace the expansion of the product given by Equation 4.50 in the last equation, the terms with ΔW in the expansion will not contribute to the expectation in the Equation 4.54:

$$\left| E[\hat{S}(T)] - E[S(T)] \right| = \left| E\left[\exp\left(\left(\mu - \frac{1}{2}\sigma^2 \right)t + \sigma W(t) \right) + I\mathcal{O}\Delta t^2 \right] \right.$$

$$\left. - E\left[\exp\left(\left(\mu - \frac{1}{2}\sigma^2 \right)t + \sigma W(t) \right) \right] \right| \qquad (4.55)$$

$$= I\mathcal{O}(\Delta t^2)$$

$$= \frac{T}{\Delta t}\mathcal{O}(\Delta t^2)$$

$$= \mathcal{O}(\Delta t)$$

Now we can see clearly why the order of convergence is different when we look at paths and when we look at properties such as the expectation. When we look at properties such moments, the odd powers of ΔW don't contribute to the expectation that expresses the convergence. This is because in weak convergence we take the expectation first and then the norm. When we look at the individual paths, on the other hand, these terms are the main contributors to the difference between the exact and the numerical solutions. This is because we take the norm first and then the expectation.

We now illustrate that the order of strong convergence of the Euler scheme is 1 when the volatility is deterministic by considering the simple case:

$$dS = \mu dt + \sigma dW \qquad (4.56)$$

The Euler scheme applied to this equation is

$$\hat{S}(t_{i+1}) = \hat{S}(t_i) + \mu(t_i)\Delta t + \sigma(t_i)\Delta W(t_i) \qquad (4.57)$$

The approximate solution at time T is

$$\hat{S}(T) = \hat{S}(0) + \sum_{i=0}^{i=I-1} \mu(t_i)\Delta t + \sum_{i=0}^{i=I-1} \sigma(t_i)\Delta W(t_i) \qquad (4.58)$$

The exact solution at time T is

$$S(T) = S(0) + \int_0^T \mu(t)dt + \int_0^T \sigma(t)dW(t) \qquad (4.59)$$

We consider now the difference

$$\hat{S}(T) - S(T) = \underbrace{\sum_{i=0}^{i=I-1} \mu(t_i)\Delta t - \int_0^T \mu(t)dt}_{\mathcal{O}(\Delta t)}$$

$$+ \sum_{i=0}^{i=I-1} \sigma(t_i)\Delta W(t_i) - \int_0^T \sigma(t)dW(t) \qquad (4.60)$$

where the difference between the first two terms on the right is of order Δt because the first term on the right is a first-order approximation to the integral represented by the second term. To characterize the last two terms on the right, we notice that those terms are Gaussian. Therefore,

$$E\left[\sum_{i=0}^{i=I-1} \sigma(t_i)\Delta W(t_i)\right] = 0 \qquad (4.61)$$

$$\text{var}\left[\sum_{i=0}^{i=I-1} \sigma(t_i)\Delta W(t_i)\right] = \sum_{i=0}^{i=I-1} \sigma(t_i)^2 \Delta t \qquad (4.62)$$

We can now express the third term in Equation 4.60 as follows:

$$\sum_{i=0}^{i=I-1} \sigma(t_i)\Delta W(t_i) = \sqrt{\frac{\sum_{i=0}^{i=I-1} \sigma(t_i)^2 \Delta t}{T}}\, W(T) \qquad (4.63)$$

To characterize the last term in Equation 4.60, we also need its expectation and variance:

$$E\left[\int_0^T \sigma(t)dW(t)\right] = 0 \qquad (4.64)$$

$$\text{var}\left[\int_0^T \sigma(t)dW(t)\right] = \int_0^T \sigma(t)^2 dt \qquad (4.65)$$

Therefore,

$$\int_0^T \sigma(t)dW(t) = \sqrt{\frac{1}{T}\int_0^T \sigma(t)^2 dt}\, W(T) \qquad (4.66)$$

We can now express the difference of the last two terms in Equation 4.60 as follows:

$$\sum_{i=0}^{i=I-1} \sigma(t_i)\Delta W(t_i) - \int_0^T \sigma(t)dW(t) = \frac{W(T)}{\sqrt{T}}\left(\underbrace{\sqrt{\sum_{i=0}^{i=I-1}\sigma(t_i)^2 \Delta t}}_{A + \mathcal{O}(\Delta t)} - \underbrace{\sqrt{\int_0^T \sigma(t)^2 dt}}_{A}\right)$$

$$= \frac{W(T)}{\sqrt{T}}\left(\sqrt{A + \mathcal{O}(\Delta t)} - \sqrt{A}\right) \qquad (4.67)$$

$$= \frac{W(T)}{\sqrt{T}}\left(\sqrt{A + \mathcal{O}(\Delta t)} - \sqrt{A}\right)$$

$$= \frac{W(T)}{\sqrt{T}}\mathcal{O}(\Delta t)$$

where we exploited the fact that the sum in the first line of Equation 4.67 is a first-order approximation of the integral in the same line, and where we expanded the square root in the second line in Taylor series. To first order, Equation 4.60 is of first order in Δt:

$$\hat{S}(T) - S(T) = \mathcal{O}(\Delta t) + \frac{W(T)}{\sqrt{T}}\mathcal{O}(\Delta t) \qquad (4.68)$$

Taking the absolute value of this difference is also of first order in Δt. The expectation of the absolute value is also of first order in Δt. Therefore, the Euler method applied to the simple SDE in Equation 4.56 has order of strong convergence equal to 1. In this case, there is nothing to be gained by using the Milshtein scheme in place of the Euler scheme to construct scenario trajectories.

BROWNIAN BRIDGE

The *Brownian bridge* is a very useful device for constructing trajectories. The basic idea of the Brownian bridge is as follows. Assume you have a Wiener process defined by a set of time-indexed random variables

$\{W(t_1),\ W(t_2),\dots\}$. How do you insert a random variable $W(t_k)$, where $t_i \leq t_k \leq t_{i+1}$, into the set in such a manner that the resulting set still constitutes a Wiener process? You can view the Brownian bridge as a sort of interpolation that allows you to introduce intermediate points in the trajectory of a Wiener process when that trajectory is known at discrete time points. There are practical reasons why it is a good idea to be able to do this. For example, assume that you have a scenario set that gets reused by a number of pricing applications. Assume that some of the applications may require knowledge of the scenario set at a specific point in time not included in the original set. The Brownian bridge gives you a way of generating that missing part of the trajectories in the scenario sets without having to reconstruct the trajectories. A more profound reason, which we will explore in detail, has to do with the way the Brownian bridge is constructed. By adding one more element into the $\{W(t_1),$ $W(t_2),\dots\}$ set, we increase the dimensionality of this set. In order to add a new element into the set, the Brownian bridge uses a new random variable whose variance is lower than the variance of the new element that is added. It turns out that increasing the dimensionality of a set of random variables by using an additional random variable of smaller variance is very desirable when quasi-random sequences are used. This is of significant importance in scenario generation.

Brownian Bridge Construction

Given $W(t)$ and $W(t + \Delta t_1 + \Delta t_2)$, we want to find $W(t + \Delta t_1)$. We assume that we can get the middle point by a weighted average of the two end points plus an independent normal random variable:

$$W(t + \Delta t_1) = \alpha W(t) + \beta W(t + \Delta t_1 + \Delta t_2) + \gamma Z \tag{4.69}$$

where α, β, and γ are constants to be determined, and Z is a standard normal random variable.

$W(t + \Delta t_1)$ must satisfy the following conditions:

$$\text{cov}\,[W(t + \Delta t_1), W(t)] = t \tag{4.70}$$

$$\text{cov}[W(t + \Delta t_1), W(t + \Delta t_1 + \Delta t_2)] = t + \Delta t_1 \tag{4.71}$$

$$\text{var}\,[W(t + \Delta t_1)] = t + \Delta t_1 \tag{4.72}$$

These conditions give us the following equations for α, β, and γ:

$$\begin{aligned} \alpha + \beta &= 1 \\ \alpha t + \beta(t + \Delta t_1 + \Delta t_2) &= t + \Delta t_1 \\ \alpha^2 t + 2\alpha\beta t + \beta^2(t + \Delta t_1 + \Delta t_2) + \gamma^2 &= t + \Delta t_1 \end{aligned} \tag{4.73}$$

Solving these equations (this is very straightforward, despite the non-linearities in α and β), we get

$$\alpha = \frac{\Delta t_2}{\Delta t_1 + \Delta t_2} \qquad (4.74)$$

$$\beta = 1 - \alpha \qquad (4.75)$$

$$\gamma = \sqrt{\Delta t_1 \alpha} \qquad (4.76)$$

The variance of the normal random variable that was added in order to construct $W(t + \Delta t_1)$ is $\gamma^2 = \Delta t_1 \alpha$. If instead of using the Brownian bridge, we would have created $W(t + \Delta t_1)$ in the standard way,

$$W(t + \Delta t_1) = W(t)\sqrt{\Delta t_1}Z \qquad (4.77)$$

we would have used a normal random variable with variance Δt_1. In the case of $\Delta t_1 = \Delta t_2$, which corresponds to adding a component halfway between endpoints, the variance of the normal deviate used in the Brownian bridge is half the variance of the normal deviate used in Equation 4.77 (since in this case $\alpha = \frac{1}{2}$).

Generating Scenarios with Brownian Bridges

We can use the Brownian bridge to generate a Wiener path and then use the Wiener path to produce a trajectory of the process we are interested in. We can use points from the Wiener path to get $W(t_i)$ and $W(t_{i-1})$ and replace these values in the expression for analytical advancement, Equation 4.6, or in our numerical integration scheme, such as Equations 4.38 or 4.39.

The simplest strategy for generating a Wiener path using the Brownian bridge is to divide the time span of the trajectory into two equal parts and apply the Brownian bridge construction to the the middle point. We then repeat the procedure for the left and right sides of the time interval. To illustrate how this works, consider a case where you want to compute a Wiener trajectory from $t = 0$ to $t = T$, at four equidistant points.

We want to compute $W(t_i)$, $0 = 1,..., 4$ where $t_i = i\Delta t$, with $\Delta t = \frac{t}{4}$, and initial condition $W(t_0) = W(0) = 0$. In this case, $\alpha = \frac{1}{2}$ (see Equation 4.74). These are the steps:

$$
\begin{aligned}
W(t_0) &= 0 \\
W(t_4) &= W(t_0) + \sqrt{t_4}Z_4 \\
&= \sqrt{t_4}Z_4 \\
W(t_2) &= \frac{1}{2}(W(t_0) + W(t_4)) + \sqrt{(t_2 - t_0)\alpha}Z_2
\end{aligned}
\qquad (4.78)
$$

$$= \frac{1}{2}W(t_4) + \sqrt{\frac{t_2 - t_0}{2}} Z_2$$

$$W(t_1) = \frac{1}{2}(W(t_0) + W(t_2)) + \sqrt{(t_1 - t_0)\alpha} Z_1$$

$$= \frac{1}{2}W(t_2) + \sqrt{\frac{t_1 - t_0}{2}} Z_1 \qquad (4.78)$$

$$W(t_3) = \frac{1}{2}(W(t_2) + W(t_4)) + \sqrt{(t_3 - t_2)\alpha} Z_3$$

$$= \frac{1}{2}(W(t_2) + W(t_4)) \sqrt{\frac{t_3 - t_2}{2}} Z_3$$

This is very easy to generalize to any number of time points if the number of time points is a power of two. Each Z_i is the ith component of a multidimensional standard normal random variable where the dimensions are uncorrelated. Notice that as you "fill in" the Wiener path, the additional variance of the normal components you add to the average of the two immediate W's has decreasing value. Of course, the total variance of all the Wiener increments $(W(t_{i+1}) - W(t_i))$ does not depend on how you construct the path. However, the fact that in the Brownian bridge approach you are using random variables that are multiplied by a factor of decreasing magnitude means that the importance of those variables also decreases as you fill in the path. The dimensions of the random variables with larger variance need to be covered, or sampled, more efficiently than the dimensions with smaller variance. In *standard Monte Carlo* this is not an issue because standard Monte Carlo, where we sample from a joint normal distribution, is equally efficient at sampling from any dimension. But, as we will see in the next chapter, standard Monte Carlo is very slow. An alternative to standard Monte Carlo, called *quasi-random sequence Monte Carlo*, on the other hand, differs in its ability to cover lower dimensions, as compared with higher dimensions. This method for path construction, where the variance is concentrated in the first few dimensions (these are the ones you build first following the procedure above), reduces the burden on the simulation from having to sample efficiently from the higher dimensions. The effect of this way of constructing Wiener paths has been called *dimensionality reduction* in the literature. But it is important to understand that this approach does not reduce the number of dimensions. What it does is change the problem around such that some dimensions (these are called *higher dimensions* simply because of the order in which they occur in the algorithm described by Equation 4.78) face less activity by the random variables used to get the Z_i's than others. This reduces the need to carefully sample from such dimensions. This is precisely what we need in order to use quasi-random sequences effectively. These issues are discussed in detail by Caflisch, Morokoff, and Owen, 1997.

As we noted after Equation 4.7, the traditional forward construction of the Wiener path,

$$W(t_i) = W(t_{i-1}) + \sqrt{t_i - t_{i-1}} Z_i \qquad (4.79)$$

weighs each Z_i by the same factor (assuming the time intervals are the same), causing all the dimensions of Z to be equally important.

At this point we can ask two questions about the Brownian bridge approach to trajectory building.

■ Why not use an approach like this directly on the process of interest, rather than on the driving Wiener process? For example, if we are interested in constructing a path for process $S(t)$, why not use something like the Brownian bridge directly on $S(t)$?

■ If we are dealing with a multidimensional Wiener process, where each $\hat{W}(t_i)$ is a vector of correlated variables, and we apply the Brownian bridge approach to each of the components of $\hat{W}(t)$, will this spoil the correlation that must exist between the components of $\hat{W}(t)$?

The answer to these two questions touches on related issues. As far as the first question, the reason why the Brownian bridge is so straightforward is because we only need the variance to characterize the Wiener process (the expectation is satisfied automatically since we use standard normals to generate the Wiener process), and because the covariance between $W(t_k)$ and $W(t_l)$ only depends on the minimum of (t_k, t_l). This is not the case in general. A process may need multiple moments to be characterized, and we will not be able to construct it with the simple argument that worked so well for the Wiener process.

As far as the second question, the answer is no. If you have a multidimensional Wiener process, you can safely use the Brownian bridge construction in each component and your correlations will be what they are supposed to be. This point is deeper than it seems, so we will elaborate. When we have a multidimensional process (don't confuse this notion of multidimensional, which means a process driven by several, perhaps correlated Wiener processes, with the fact that each trajectory is characterized by time-indexed multidimensional random variables), the correlation between the values of the various components is determined by the correlation between the changes in values. To clarify this, consider a process with K dimensions:

$$\begin{aligned} dS_k(t) = & \, a_k(S_1((t), \dots, S_K(t), t))dt \\ & + \sigma_K(S_1((t), \dots, S_K(t), t))dW_K(t) \; k = 1, \dots, K \end{aligned} \qquad (4.80)$$

In this representation we assume that $\sigma_k(.)$ is a scalar and that $W_k(t)$, $k = 1, \dots, K$ are the components of a multidimensional Wiener process. Chapter 2 discusses other representations of multidimensional processes. The correlation of the process levels, that is correlation $(S_k(t), S_l(t))$, is determined by the correlation of the process changes, $(dS_k(t), dS_l(t))$, but these two correlations are not equal in general. In the case of Wiener processes, however, they are equal. This allows us to preserve the correlation across dimensions by properly correlating the standard normals used in the bridge construction.

To see that the correlation of two Wiener processes is the same as the correlation of their increments, we consider two Wiener processes, $W_1(t)$ and $W_2(t)$, such that $dW_1(t)dW_2(t) = \rho dt$, and we find the correlation between $W_1(t)$ and $W_2(t)$, which we denote by ρ_{W_1, W_2}. We do this in a more rigorous way than needed in this simple case because this illustrates a general way that will work with more complicated processes:

$$
\begin{aligned}
\rho_{W_1(t), W_2(t)} &= \frac{\mathrm{cov}\,[\,W_1(t), W_2(t)\,]}{\underbrace{\sqrt{\mathrm{var}\,[\,W_1(t)\,]}}_{=\sqrt{t}}\,\underbrace{\sqrt{\mathrm{var}\,[\,W_2(t)\,]}}_{=\sqrt{t}}} \\[2mm]
&= \frac{\mathrm{cov}\,[\,W_1(t), W_2(t)\,]}{t} \\[2mm]
&= \frac{1}{t}(\,\mathrm{E}[\,W_1(t)\,W_2(t)\,] - \underbrace{\mathrm{E}[\,W_1(t)\,]}_{=0}\,\underbrace{\mathrm{E}[\,W_2(t)\,]}_{=0}\,) \\[2mm]
&= \frac{1}{t}\mathrm{E}[\,W_1(t)\,W_2(t)\,]
\end{aligned}
\tag{4.81}
$$

To get $\mathrm{E}[\,W_1(t)\,W_2(t)\,]$, apply Ito's lemma to $g(W_1, W_2) = W_1(t)W_2(t)$:

$$
\begin{aligned}
dg(t) &= \underbrace{\frac{\partial g}{\partial W_1}}_{=W_2}\,dW_1 + \underbrace{\frac{\partial g}{\partial W_2}}_{=W_1}\,dW_2 + \underbrace{\frac{1}{2}\frac{\partial^2 g}{\partial W_1^2}\,dW_1^2}_{=0} \\[2mm]
&\quad + \underbrace{\frac{\partial^2 g}{\partial W_1 \partial W_2}}_{=1}\,\underbrace{dW_1 dW_2}_{=\rho dt} + \underbrace{\frac{1}{2}\frac{\partial^2 g}{\partial W_2^2}\,dW_2^2}_{=0} \\[2mm]
&= W_2(t)dW_1(t) + W_1(t)dW_2(t) + \rho dt
\end{aligned}
\tag{4.82}
$$

We now take expectation of both sides and integrate

$$
\begin{aligned}
\mathrm{E}[dg(t)] &= \underbrace{\mathrm{E}[\,W_2(t)dW_1(t)\,]}_{=0} + \underbrace{\mathrm{E}[\,W_1(t)dW_2(t)\,]}_{=0} + \rho dt \\[2mm]
d\mathrm{E}[g(t)] &= \rho dt \\
\mathrm{E}[g(t)] &= \rho t
\end{aligned}
\tag{4.83}
$$

Replacing for $g(W_1, W_2)$, we get

$$E[W_1(t)W_2(t)] = \rho t \tag{4.84}$$

Substituting this in Equation 4.81, we confirm that

$$\rho_{W_1, W_2} = \frac{1}{t}E[W_1(t)W_2(t)]$$
$$= \rho \tag{4.85}$$

When we do the Brownian bridge for a multidimensional Wiener process, we do the procedure in Equations 4.78 on each dimension. Equation 4.85 suggests that we can get the correct correlation between dimensions if we impose that correlation on the normal random variables that enter in the construction procedure in Equation 4.78. To verify that this is the case, consider a Brownian bridge applied to two Wiener processes, W_1 and W_2, such that $dW_1(t)dW_2(t) = \rho dt$:

$$W_1(t_1) = \alpha W_1(t_0) + (1 - \alpha)W_1(t_2) + \beta Z^{(1)} \tag{4.86}$$

$$W_2(t_1) = \alpha W_2(t_0) + (1 - \alpha)W_2(t_2) + \beta Z^{(2)} \tag{4.87}$$

where $Z^{(1)}$ and $Z^{(2)}$ are the standard normal random variables used with dimensions 1 and 2, respectively. It is straightforward to verify that $\rho_{W_1(t), W_2(t)} = \rho$ if cov $[Z^{(1)}, Z^{(2)}] = \rho$.

The fact that the correlation between the level and the changes is the same for Wiener processes can also be expressed as follows. The correlation between finite changes across dimensions are the same as the correlation between infinitesimal changes across dimensions.

This is not the case in general. To illustrate this, consider the case of two standard log-normal processes:

$$\frac{dS_1}{S_1} = \mu_1 dt + \sigma_1 dW_1(t) \tag{4.88}$$

$$\frac{dS_2}{S_2} = \mu_2 dt + \sigma_2 dW_2(t) \tag{4.89}$$

where $dW_1(t)dW_2(t) = \rho dt$. We want to get the correlation of $S_1(t)$ and $S_2(t)$ as a function of ρ:

$$\rho_{S_1, S_2} = \frac{1}{\sqrt{\text{var}[S_1]\text{var}[S_2]}}(E[S_1 S_2] + E[S_1]E[S_2]) \tag{4.90}$$

Using the same approach as before, define $g(S_1, S_2) = S_1(t)S_2(t)$ and apply Ito's lemma:

$$
\begin{aligned}
d(S_1(t)S_2(t)) &= S_2 dS_1 + S_1 dS_2 + S_1 S_2 \sigma_1 \sigma_2 \rho dt \\
&= S_1 S_2 (\mu_1 + \mu_2 + \sigma_1 \sigma_2 \rho) dt \\
&\quad + S_1 S_2 \sigma_1 dW_1(t) + S_1 S_2 \sigma_2 dW_2(t)
\end{aligned}
\tag{4.91}
$$

Taking expectation on both sides and considering that μ_1, μ_2, σ_1, and σ_2 are constant, we get

$$
\frac{dE[S_1 S_2]}{E[S_1 S_2]} = (\mu_1 + \mu_2 + \rho \sigma_1 \sigma_2) dt
\tag{4.92}
$$

This can be integrated to give

$$
E[S_1 S_2] = S_1(0)S_2(0) \exp(\mu_1 + \mu_2 + \rho \sigma_1 \sigma_2)t
\tag{4.93}
$$

since

$$
\begin{aligned}
E(S_1(t)) &= S_1(0)\exp(\mu_1 t) \\
E(S_2(t)) &= S_2(0)\exp(\mu_2 t) \\
\text{var}(S_1(t)) &= S_1^2(0)\exp(2\mu_1 t)(\exp(\sigma_1^2 t) - 1) \\
\text{var}(S_2(t)) &= S_2^2(0)\exp(2\mu_2 t)(\exp(\sigma_2^2 t) - 1)
\end{aligned}
\tag{4.94}
$$

Replacing in Equation 4.91, we get

$$
\rho_{S_1 S_2} = \frac{\exp(\sigma_1 \sigma_2 \rho t) - 1}{\sqrt{(\exp(\sigma_1^2 t) - 1)(\exp(\sigma_2^2 t) - 1)}}
\tag{4.95}
$$

As $t \to 0$, $\rho_{S_1 S_2} = \rho$, but as time increases, $\rho_{S_1 S_2}$ decreases.

In conclusion, if we have a general multidimensional stochastic process, approximations of finite increments of the process will influence the correlation of process values across dimensions.

JOINT NORMALS BY THE CHOLESKI DECOMPOSITION APPROACH

The standard procedure for generating a set of correlated normal random variables is through a linear combination of uncorrelated normal random variables. Assume we have a set of n independent standard normal random variables Z_i, $i = 1,\ldots, n$, and we want to build a set of n correlated standard normals $\tilde{Z}_i$, $i = 1,\ldots, n$, with correlation matrix R.

We express these variables as column vectors $Z = \{Z_1, \ldots, Z_n\}^T$ and $\tilde{Z} = \{\tilde{Z}_1, \ldots, \tilde{Z}_n\}^T$ and assume that we can accomplish this by the following linear combination:

$$\tilde{Z} = AZ \tag{4.96}$$

where A is a square matrix to be determined. Multiplying both sides of Equation 4.96 by their transpose, we get

$$\tilde{Z}\tilde{Z}^T = (AZ)(AZ)^T \tag{4.97}$$

Since $(AZ)^T = Z^T A^T$, we have

$$\tilde{Z}\tilde{Z}^T = A(ZZ^T)A^T \tag{4.98}$$

We also have that the correlation matrix of the $\tilde{Z}_i$ is given by the expectation of $\tilde{Z}\tilde{Z}^T$. The expectation of ZZ^T is the identity matrix, because the Z_i are independent. Since the matrix A is assumed to be deterministic, taking expectation of both sides of Equation 4.98 gives

$$\begin{aligned}
E[\tilde{Z}\tilde{Z}^T] &= E[A(ZZ^T)A^T] \\
R &= AE[ZZ^T]A^T \\
&= AIA^T \\
&= AA^T
\end{aligned} \tag{4.99}$$

An expression of the form

$$R = AA^T \tag{4.100}$$

where A is a lower triangular matrix, is called the *Choleski decomposition* of matrix R, and the A, A^T are called the *Choleski factors*. Press et al., 1992, give a numerical implementation of this algorithm. A procedure called *singular value decomposition* (Press et al., 1992) also accomplishes the same result and is sometimes used instead of the Choleski decomposition. The Choleski decomposition is a simpler and safer alternative for the following reasons.

■ The Choleski decomposition will only work with a valid correlation or covariance matrix. For a covariance matrix to be valid, the series of observations from which the matrix was generated must be sufficiently long. If the number of observations is insufficient, the Choleski decomposition will fail (the Choleski decomposition only works with positive definite matrices).

■ The covariance matrix entries must be stated with enough numerical precision. Even if the number of observations are enough to generate a valid covariance matrix, an insufficient number of valid digits in the numerical representation of the matrix may be sufficient to ruin it. This is particularly true of large covariance matrices. A large covariance matrix is an extremely rigid mathematical entity. Any attempt to tinker with the entries of a large covariance matrix will almost certainly invalidate it. If the matrix is invalid because of insufficient accuracy or because it was improperly manipulated, this will also be revealed by the failure of the Choleski decomposition.

Notice that the second observation also implies that we cannot investigate the effect of correlation on the price of a derivative by simply perturbing an entry in the correlation matrix of the underlying assets.

QUASI-RANDOM SEQUENCES

Quasi-random sequences allow us to conduct simulations that under some conditions may be far more efficient than standard Monte Carlo. The basic problem with standard Monte Carlo is that, unless special techniques are used (which we will discuss in the next chapter), it is intrinsically slow.

Despite this problem with speed, which in many cases can be addressed with the techniques we will discuss in Chapter 5, standard Monte Carlo has two two highly desirable properties when applied to financial pricing.

■ In most cases, simulation with standard Monte Carlo has a clearly defined convergence law. This allows us to stop simulating when we have reached the desired level of accuracy. This means that we have a clearly defined termination criterion to stop simulating at the right time.
■ The efficiency of a simulation with standard Monte Carlo is not sensitive to the dimensionality of the problem.

Although these two properties are highly valuable, the fact that standard Monte Carlo can be very slow in financial pricing has motivated the search for alternatives. The outcome of this search are so-called "quasi-random sequences." These are sequences of numbers that fill in a multidimensional unit hypercube in a way that they can be used in replacement of a multidimensional uniform distribution. As we will see, quasi-random sequences can lead to dramatic increases in speed, but this comes at the cost of negating, to some extent, the good properties of standard Monte Carlo mentioned above.

- Although simulating with quasi-random sequences has a convergence law, it is preferable to determine a termination criterion by calibrating the quasi-random sequence computation with standard Monte Carlo results. In other words, we have a less clearly defined termination criterion.
- The efficiency of a simulation with a quasi-random sequence becomes increasingly penalized as the dimensionality of the problem grows.

The second point, which at first sight might appear to be a disadvantage, can be significantly ameliorated if the problem can be reformulated in a way that most of the variability of the underlying stochastic factors becomes concentrated in a few dimensions. In this case, the speed potential of quasi-random sequences can be more fully realized. This is precisely what happens when we build scenarios using the Brownian bridge approach.

The reason why regular Monte Carlo is slow is because randomly sampling from a multidimensional distribution does not fill in the space with the regularity that would be desirable. Random points tend to cluster, and this clustering limits the efficiency with which regular Monte Carlo can capture payoff features. This clustering is best observed in low dimensions. Figure 4.1 shows what happens when we plot in the unit square points drawn from a two-dimensional uniform distribution.

Clearly, the points don't fill in the square uniformly, but have the tendency to cluster. When the two-dimensional uniform deviates are mapped to two-dimensional standard normals, the clustering remains. When applied to option pricing, this clustering causes a simulation with few random samples to miss features that determine the option value. As we will see in the next chapter, the number of samples needed for accurate pricing using straight Monte Carlo is surprisingly large.

Since the purpose of simulation in pricing is to compute an expectation, another alternative we may consider is to make a uniform grid in the $[0, 1]^d$ cube and then use those grid points to evaluate the payoff and distribution functions that are involved in the expectation. In this approach, we would use a standard multidimensional integration technique to evaluate the expectation numerically. To illustrate how this would work, consider a call option on a log-normal stock with maturity $t = T$.

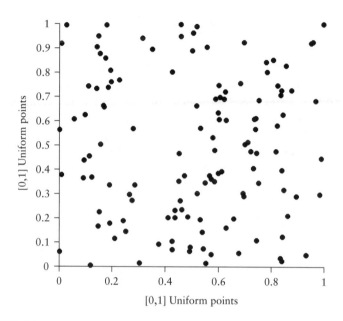

FIGURE 4.1 Illustrating clustering. 128 uniform deviates in the unit square.

The price is given by

$$
V(0) = E_0^\beta[\exp^{-rT}\max[0, S(T) - K]]
$$

$$
= E_0^\beta\left[\exp^{-rT}\max\left[0, S(0)\exp\left(\left(r - \frac{1}{2}\sigma^2\right)T + W(T)\right) - K\right]\right] \quad (4.101)
$$

$$
= E_0^\beta\left[\exp^{-rT}\max\left[0, S(0)\exp\left(\left(r - \frac{1}{2}\sigma^2\right)T + \sqrt{T}Z\right) - K\right]\right]
$$

Since Z is a standard normal and the standard normal density function is given by

$$
\Phi(\xi) = \frac{1}{\sqrt{2\pi}}\exp\left(-\frac{\xi^2}{2}\right) \quad (4.102)
$$

the value is

$$
V(0) = \exp^{-rT}\int_{-\infty}^{\infty}\max\left[0, S(0)\exp\left(\left(r - \frac{1}{2}\sigma^2\right)T + \sqrt{T}\xi\right) - K\right]
$$

$$
\times \frac{1}{\sqrt{2\pi}}\exp\left(-\frac{\xi^2}{2}\right)d\xi \quad (4.103)
$$

We can write this integral in terms of the inverse of the standard density function:

$$V(0) = \exp^{-rT} \int_0^1 \max\left[0, S(0)\exp\left(\left(r - \frac{1}{2}\sigma^2\right)T + \sqrt{T}\Phi^{-1}(u)\right) - K\right]du$$

(4.104)

The integrand in this equation is well behaved, and we would expect that a few equally spaced points in the [0, 1] interval should be enough to compute the integral with good accuracy. It is easy to verify that for $T = 1$, $r = 0.1$, $S(0) = 100$, $K = 100$, and $\sigma = 0.3$, just four equally spaced points in the unit interval, we can compute the price with three digits of accuracy!

Notice that the integral in Equation 4.104 can also be interpreted as an expectation over uniform random samples:

$$V(0) = \exp^{-rT} E\left[\max\left[0, S(0)\exp\left(\left(r - \frac{1}{2}\sigma^2\right)T + \sqrt{T}\Phi^{-1}(u)\right) - K\right]\right]$$

(4.105)

If we compute this expectation by sampling, without repeats, from equally spaced points u_i in the unit interval, the expression

$$V(0) \approx \exp^{-rT}\frac{1}{N}\sum_{i=1}^{i=N} \max\left[0, S(0)\exp\left(\left(r - \frac{1}{2}\sigma^2\right)T + \sqrt{T}\Phi^{-1}(u_i)\right) - K\right]$$

(4.106)

is equivalent to a first-order integration of Equation 4.104, since $\Delta u = \frac{1}{N}$:

$$V(0) \approx \exp^{-rT}\sum_{i=1}^{i=N} \max\left[0, S(0)\exp\left(\left(r - \frac{1}{2}\sigma^2\right)T + \sqrt{T}\Phi^{-1}(u_i)\right) - K\right]\Delta u$$

(4.107)

Clearly, since the numerical integration of Equation 4.104 can be done efficiently with a few equally spaced points in the unit interval, this also means that computing the expectation in Equation 4.105 by sampling from equally spaced points in the unit interval is very effective, since both approaches are equivalent.

Unfortunately, there are two fatal flaws with this approach.

■ The number of data points needed to sample from grids explodes like N^d, where N is the number of points per dimension and d is the number of dimensions. This constitutes an insurmountable computational barrier. This is the same type of difficulty faced by the finite difference approach, which limits the number of dimensions that can be practically handled to three or less.

■ It is not possible to incrementally enlarge the size of the grid and at the same time keep the grid uniform. This means that with a uniform grid approach it is not possible to have a termination criterion that can be invoked incrementally. This is a very serious limitation.

Quasi-random sequences are a deterministic way of filling in multidimensional unit intervals with the following characteristics.

■ The intervals are filled in more evenly than with Monte Carlo. The evenness is captured by the concept of *discrepancy*. The discrepancy increases as the number of dimensions increases.

■ As the number of dimensions increases, quasi-random sequences become increasingly less capable of evenly filling in the space. In high dimensions (typically over 30) they leave holes in the sampling space, leading to a steadily decreasing ability to capture the variability of random variables associated with those dimensions.

■ It is possible to define a theoretical error bound in an incremental way. However, unlike the case of regular Monte Carlo, with quasi-random sequences the actual numerical error can be drastically different from the theoretical error bound. For this reason there is a need to use standard Monte Carlo to calibrate simulations with these sequences

Figure 4.2 shows a plot of 256 points of a two-dimensional Sobol sequence. When compared with Figure 4.1, it is clear that the Sobol points cover the unit square more uniformly.

Figure 4.3 shows a plot of dimensions one and six of a six-dimensional Sobol sequence. Comparing this figure with the previous one, we see that Figure 4.3 shows a more visible pattern of points and has a less "random" look. As the number of dimensions increases, the points of quasi-random sequences tend to leave open spaces that eventually may make the use of standard Monte Carlo more advantageous.

There is one fundamental distinction between random or pseudorandom numbers and quasi-random sequences that we will remark here and elaborate more on later in the chapter. Notice that when dealing with truly random numbers, we can construct random points in $[0,1]^d$ by making multiple calls from the same uniform random number generator and assigning each outcome to a different dimension. This is how Figure 4.1 was produced. This is not the

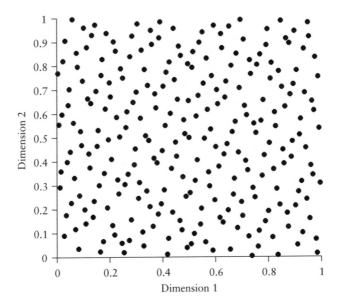

FIGURE 4.2 Two-dimensional Sobol sequence. 256 Sobol points in the unit square.

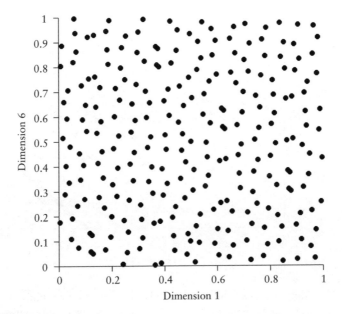

FIGURE 4.3 Dimensions one and six of a six-dimensional Sobol sequence. 256 Sobol points in one unit square.

way quasi-random sequences work. A two dimensional quasi-random sequence, for example, cannot be built by assigning the outcomes of one-dimensional sequences to two dimensions. This is a fundamental difference in practical applications. It is commonly stated that software applications can be made to work with pseudorandom numbers or with quasi-random numbers by simply replacing the algorithm that produces the input to the Choleski construction of correlated normals. This is a simplistic view that can lead to serious trouble if the implementation is not done properly. With pseudorandom numbers, the algorithm that produces the input needed to get correlated normals does not need to know the dimensionality of the problem. With quasi-random sequences this is not the case. This fact has implications in the object design of financial software.

To visualize what may happen if you use one-dimensional quasi-random sequences to build multidimensional random variables, consider Figure 4.4.

The points not only don't fill the unit square uniformly; they are restricted to a subspace. If we use this as the source of uniforms for our simulation, we simply get the wrong answer.

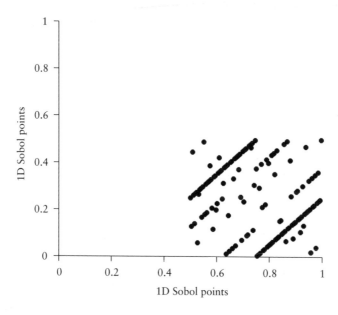

FIGURE 4.4 Making a "two"-dimensional distribution with one-dimensional Sobol points. 128 Sobol points from a one-dimensional sequence alternatively assigned to dimensions one and two.

The Concept of Discrepancy

The *local discrepancy*, $D(C_j; N)$, of a quasi-random sequence is defined as

$$D(C_j; N) = \frac{\text{Number of points in } C_j}{\text{Total number of points}} - \text{Volume of } C_j \qquad (4.108)$$

where C_j is a subcube of the hypercube.

The *discrepancy*, $D^*(N)$, is defined as

$$D^*(N) = \sup_{C_j}[D(C_j; N)] \qquad (4.109)$$

The most popular quasi-random sequences, such as the Halton, Sobol, Faure, and Niederreiter sequences, have discrepancies that satisfy

$$D^*(N) \le c(d)\frac{(\log N)^d}{N} + \mathcal{O}\left(\frac{(\log N)^{d-1}}{N}\right) \qquad (4.110)$$

where $c(d)$ depends only on d and is independent of the total number of points, N.

Discrepancy and Convergence: The Koksma-Hlawka Inequality

The convergence of an integral approximated by quasi–Monte Carlo simulation is characterized by the *Koksma-Hlawka inequality*. The purpose of this section is to show that although we can make a theoretical statement about convergence in quasi–Monte Carlo, this statement is presented in a manner that has limited practical value. For detailed derivations and proofs, the reader is referred to the book by Niederreiter, 1992.

Assume we are interested in approximating the integral

$$\int_{C^s} f(u)\,du \qquad (4.111)$$

where C^s is an s-dimensional unit hypercube. We define the *variation in the sense of Vitali* by

$$G^{(s)}(f; 1, \ldots, s) = \int_0^1 \cdots \int_0^1 \left|\frac{\partial^s f}{\partial u_1, \ldots, \partial u_s}\right| du_1, \ldots, du_s \qquad (4.112)$$

With this, we define the *variation of f in the sense of Krause* as

$$G(f) = \sum_{k=1}^{k=s} \sum_{1 \le i_1 \cdots \le i_k \le s} G^{(k)}(f; i_1, \ldots, i_k) \qquad (4.113)$$

The Kokma-Hlawka inequality is

$$\left| \frac{1}{N} \sum_{n=1}^{n=N} f(x_n) - \int_{C^s} f(u)\,du \right| \le G(f)D^*(N) \qquad (4.114)$$

where x_n are multidimensional samples from C^s.

We can now appreciate that this criterion for convergence is extremely difficult to change into a numerical statement. The reason for this is that these variations involve higher derivatives of the function we are trying to integrate. Obviously, in most interesting cases when we resort to numerical integration with simulation, we don't know the analytical form of function $f(.)$.

Proper Use of Quasi-Random Sequences

In constructing scenario trajectories, we need to advance the stochastic process, $S(t)$, from one point in time to the next. To get a particular trajectory we can work with $S(t)$ directly or we can first construct a Wiener path and then use the path or the Wiener process, $W(t_i)$, or the Wiener increments, $W(t_{i+1}) - W(t_i)$, to get $S(t_i)$. The sequence of time points depends on whether we are using the Brownian bridge approach or not. If we are not using the Brownian bridge, we proceed sequentially from t_1 to t_I. In this case, it does not really matter whether we work with $S(t)$ directly or build $W(t)$ first.

One-Dimensional Scenarios   Figure 4.5 shows the building of a one-dimensional scenario set with pseudorandom numbers.

Figure 4.6 indicates the building of a one-dimensional scenario set with pseudorandom numbers.

The main difference in these two approaches is the call of the quasi-random sequence generator. This happens before a particular trajectory is built.

If we are using the Brownian bridge concept, the inner loop in Figure 4.6 must be changed to reflect the order in which the new $W(t_i)$ are created with the Brownian bridge. In the case of a four-point trajectory, this order is $i = 4, 2, 3$.

Multidimensional Scenarios   If we are building multidimensional scenario sets, the pseudocode for standard pseudo–Monte Carlo is shown in Figure 4.7. Here we assume that the correlation matrix of the $d\vec{S}(t)$ does not depend on time. If the correlation matrix is time dependent, there are two alternatives. The Choleski factorization can be done k times before the j-loop is started and the matrix array of Choleski factors can be kept in memory, or the Choleski decomposition is done at every time step. In the latter case there is significantly more numerical work.

---

for (j=1;j ≤ J; j++)
{

   for (i=1;i ≤ I; i++)
   {

      Sample uniform random variable, U_j.
      Using U_i, compute standard normal.
      Get $W(t_{i+1}) - W(t_i)$.
      Get $S(t_{i+1})$ by replacing $W(t_{i+1}) - W(t_i)$ in exact solution
      advancement or in numerical scheme.

   }

}

FIGURE 4.5 Pseudocode for one-dimensional scenario set with pseudorandom numbers. The set has *J* trajectories, each trajectory has *I* time points.

---

for (j=1;j ≤ J; i++)
{

   Sample an I-dimensional quasi-random sequence.
   for (i=1;i ≤ I; i++)
   {

      Select the ith dimension from the quasi-random sequence; this is the
      uniform "random" sample U_i.
      Using U_i, compute standard normal.
      Get $W(t_{i+1}) - W(t_i)$.
      Get $S(t_{i+1})$ by replacing $W(t_{i+1}) - W(t_i)$ in exact solution
      advancement or in numerical scheme.

   }

}

FIGURE 4.6 Pseudocode for one-dimensional scenario trajectory with quasi-random sequences (no Brownian bridge). The set has *J* trajectories, each trajectory has *I* time points.

The use of quasi-random sequences for building multidimensional trajectories is more involved. If we are not using the Brownian bridge idea, the pseudocode is as shown in Figure 4.8.

In this case, at each Monte Carlo cycle we need to produce an *Id*-dimensional quasi-random sequence. At each time step, we use *d* points from the quasi-random sequence to produce the correlated Wiener process across the dimensions of the processes $\vec{S}(t)$.

Get Choleski factors for correlation matrix of $d\vec{S}$.
for $(j=1; j \le J; j++)$
{

   for $(i=1; i \le I; i++)$
   {

      for $(k=1; k \le d; k++)$
      {

         Sample uniform random variable, U_j.
         Using U_j, compute standard normal.
         Get $W_k(t_{i+1}) - W_k(t_i)$.
         Get $S_k(t_{i+1})$ by replacing $W_k(t_{i+1}) - W(t_i)$ in exact solution
         advancement or in numerical scheme.

      }

   }

}

FIGURE 4.7 Pseudocode for d-dimensional scenario set with pseudorandom numbers. The set has J trajectories, each trajectory has I time points, the number of process dimension is d.

Get Choleski factors for correlation matrix of $d\vec{S}$.
for $(j=1; j \le J; j++)$
{

   Sample an Id-dimensional quasi-random sequence
   for $(i=1; i \le I; i++)$
   {

      Select set of d samples from the quasi-random sequence, $U_k, k=1 \ldots d$.
      Using the U_k and the Choleski factors, get correlated standard normals.
      for $(k=1; k \le d; k++)$
      {

         Get $W_k(t_{i+1}) - W_k(t_i)$.
         Get $S_k(t_{i+1})$ by replacing $W_k(t_{i+1}) - W(t_i)$ in exact solution
         advancement or in numerical scheme.

      }

   }

}

FIGURE 4.8 Pseudocode for multidimensional scenario trajectory with quasi-random sequences (no Brownian bridge). The set has J trajectories, each trajectory has I time points, the number of process dimensions is d.

If we want to use the Brownian bridge approach with multidimensional trajectories, we would sweep the i-loop in Figure 4.8 in the sequence required by the Brownian bridge. The issue arises, however, as to how to select the order of trajectories in the k-loop. It might be advantageous to order the trajectories from larger volatility to smaller volatility, thereby ensuring that the higher volatility processes get affected by the lower dimensions of the quasi-random sequence.

INTEREST RATE SCENARIOS

In the "Scenario Nomenclature" section earlier this chapter, we defined a spot trajectory as a set of values $\hat{S}^j(t_i)$, $i = 1, \dots, I$ that are an approximation to the exact realizations of the solution to the stochastic differential equation describing $S(t)$. If we have a vector of processes, $\hat{S}(t)$, we speak of a multidimensional trajectory. These trajectories are lines in the $S - t$ domain, and in the case of multidimensional processes, the trajectories are sets of lines. In the case of interest rates in general, a trajectory does not consist of a single line but of a family of forward curves. Here we discuss how to generate arbitrage-free interest rate scenarios. These scenarios are useful for pricing, but they can also be used for risk management calculations if the time horizon is short.

We will discuss the dynamics of forward-rated and LIBOR rates.

HJM for Instantaneous Forwards

To gain insight into the dynamics of interest rates, we first derive the equation that governs the *instantaneous forward rate*. The basic framework for the dynamics of forward rates is the *Heath-Jarrow-Morton model* of interest rates (Heath, Jarrow, and Morton, 1992). The discussion presented here is a summary. For more detail, the reader is referred to the specialized literature.

The instantaneous forward rate observed at time t and maturity at time T is denoted by $f(t, T)$. We postulate the following SDE for $f(t, T)$ (the reason for this is the practicalities of implementation):

$$df_t(t, T) = \mu(t, T, T - t)dt + f(t, T)^{\gamma}\sigma(T - t)dW \qquad (4.115)$$

where γ is a constant, and the argument in σ indicates that we assume stationary volatility. The subscript in df_t indicates that the differential results from a change in t. We need to determine μ. To do this, we require that the drift at time t of a zero coupon bond, $B(t, T)$, maturing at T should be $f(t, t)$. The price of such a bond is

$$B(t, T) = \exp\left(-\int_t^T f(t, s)ds\right) \qquad (4.116)$$

To construct the process for $B(t, T)$, we define

$$G(t, T) = \int_t^T f(t, s) ds \tag{4.117}$$

Hence,

$$dG_t(t, T) = -f(t, t) dt + \int_t^T df_t(t, s) ds \tag{4.118}$$

Replacing df from Equation 4.115, this becomes

$$dG = (-f(t, t) + a) dt + b \, dW \tag{4.119}$$

where

$$a = \int_t^T \mu(t, s, s - t) ds \tag{4.120}$$

$$b = \int_t^T f(t, s)^\gamma \sigma(s - t) ds \tag{4.121}$$

Using Ito's lemma, the process for the bond price is

$$dB(t, T) = -B(t, T) dG + \frac{1}{2} B(dG)^2 \tag{4.122}$$

Replacing from dG from Equation 4.119, we get

$$\frac{dB}{B} = f(t, t) dt + \left(-a + \frac{1}{2} b^2\right) dt + b \, dW \tag{4.123}$$

Since in the risk neutral measure the drift of $dP(t, T)$ must be equal to $f(t, t)$, the following relationship must be satisfied:

$$-a + \frac{1}{2} b^2 = 0 \tag{4.124}$$

Replacing for a and b, we get

$$\int_t^T \mu(t, s, s - t) ds = \frac{1}{2} \left(\int_t^T f(t, s)^\gamma \sigma(s - t) ds\right)^2 \tag{4.125}$$

Differentiating both sides with respect to T, we get the familiar HJM drift:

$$\mu(t, T, T - t) = f(t, T)^\gamma \sigma(T - t) \int_t^T f(t, s)^\gamma \sigma(s - t) ds \tag{4.126}$$

The HJM approach can also be formulated for noninstantaneous forward rates. However, in practice many products are priced from LIBOR rates, rather than forward rates. The next section describes the analytics needed to construct LIBOR rate scenarios.

LIBOR Rate Scenarios

The *LIBOR rate* observed at time t, applicable to the time interval t_i, t_{i+1}, is defined by

$$L(t, t_i, t_{i+1}) = \frac{1}{t_{i+1} - t_i}\left(\frac{B(t, t_i)}{B(t, t_{i+1})} - 1\right) \tag{4.127}$$

Our objective is to advance a sequence of LIBOR rates $\{L(t, t_1, t_2),$ $L(t, t_2, t_3), \ldots, L(t, t_{n-1}, t_n)\}$ from observation time t to observation time $t + \Delta t$. To do this we will derive stochastic differential equations for each of the LIBOR rates and we will solve these equations numerically. Notice that as we advance the rates, the observation time eventually reaches the period over which the LIBOR rate is defined. When this happens, that particular rate is fixed and no longer changes. To simplify the algebra, we will use the following notation:

$$L_i = L(t, t_i, t_{i+1})$$
$$\tau = t_{i+1} - t_i = \text{constant} \tag{4.128}$$

To derive the SDE governing L_i, we apply Ito's lemma to get $\frac{dL_i}{L_i}$:

$$\frac{dL_i}{L_i} = \frac{d\left(\dfrac{B_i}{B_{i+1}} - 1\right)}{\dfrac{B_i}{B_{i+1}} - 1}$$

$$= \frac{\dfrac{B_i}{B_{i+1}}}{\dfrac{B_i}{B_{i+1}} - 1}\left(\frac{dB_i}{B_i} - \frac{dB_{i+1}}{B_{i+1}} - \frac{dB_i}{B_i}\frac{dB_{i+1}}{B_{i+1}} + \left(\frac{dB_{i+1}}{B_{i+1}}\right)^2\right) \tag{4.129}$$

From Equation 4.127 we get

$$\frac{\dfrac{B_i}{B_{i+1}}}{\dfrac{B_i}{B_{i+1}} - 1} = \frac{1 + \tau L_i}{\tau L_i} \tag{4.130}$$

We now express the dynamics of $\frac{dB}{B}$ in the risk neutral world (where bond prices have an instantaneous rate of return equal to the instantaneous risk free rate, $r(t)$):

$$\frac{dB_i}{B_i} = r(t)dt + \sigma_i dW(t) \tag{4.131}$$

The important thing to remark here is that the Wiener process W is the same for all the bonds. If the bond returns are not perfectly correlated, then

W is a vector or a multidimensional Wiener process, and σ_i is also a vector (we discussed this extensively in Chapter 2). Here we assume that the proper interpretation of W as a scalar or vector is understood. Replacing Equations 4.130 and 4.131 into Equation 4.129, we get

$$\frac{dL_i}{L_i} = \frac{1 + \tau L_i}{\tau L_i}[\sigma_i dW - \sigma_{i+1} dW - \sigma_i \sigma_{i+1} + \sigma_{i+1}\sigma_{i+1}] \qquad (4.132)$$

This can be rewritten as

$$\frac{dL_i}{L_i} = \frac{1 + \tau L_i}{\tau L_i}(\sigma_i - \sigma_{i+1})d\underbrace{(W - \sigma_{i+1}t)}_{W_{i+1}} \qquad (4.133)$$

where the quantity W_{i+1} on the right is a Wiener process in a particular measure. This measure is the one induced by B_{i+1} (this is the case because this expression was derived by considering the process for $\frac{B_i}{B_{i+1}}$).

Introducing the definition,

$$\gamma_i = \frac{1 + \tau L_i}{\tau L_i}(\sigma_i - \sigma_{i+1}) \qquad (4.134)$$

the SDEs for the LIBOR rates are

$$\frac{dL_i}{L_i} = \gamma_1 dW_2$$

$$\vdots$$

$$\frac{dL_{i-1}}{L_{i-1}} = \gamma_{i-1} dW_i \qquad (4.135)$$

$$\frac{dL_i}{L_i} = \gamma_i dW_{i+1}$$

$$\vdots$$

$$\frac{dL_{n-1}}{L_{n-1}} = \gamma_{n-1} dW_n \qquad (4.136)$$

where each W_i is a Wiener process in a *different* measure. We cannot generate scenarios if the Wiener processes are in different measures. For the construction of the Wiener processes to make sense, all of them must be expressed in the same measure. In this case this issue is very easy to deal with, because successive W_i processes can be generated recursively in terms of a *single* Wiener process.

Two successive W_i processes are related as follows:

$$W_i = W - \sigma_i t$$
$$W_{i+1} = W - \sigma_{i+1} t \qquad (4.137)$$

This gives

$$W_{i+1} = W_i + (\sigma_i - \sigma_{i+1})t \qquad (4.138)$$

Using Equation 4.134, we get

$$W_{i+1} = W_i + \frac{\tau L_i}{1 + \tau L_i} \gamma_i t \qquad (4.139)$$

This shows that we can write the process W_{i+1} (which is a Wiener process in the measure induced by B_{i+1}) as W_i (which is a Wiener process in the measure induced by B_i), plus a drift. This means that we can construct scenarios by generating one of the W_i processes and then expressing the rest of the Ws recursively in terms of the first one. In this way, the scenarios would be constructed by drawing random numbers in the same measure. Notice that the drifts in Equation 4.139 are path dependent. This is not a problem if we proceed as follows. Given the initial term structure of LIBOR rates, we obtain initial values for L_i. We next select a starting Wiener process index and generate $\Delta W_i = \sqrt{\Delta t}\, Z$, where Z is a standard normal random variable and Δt is the integration step. We then compute the remaining Wiener increments recursively as follows:

$$\Delta W_{i+1}(t) = \Delta W_i(t) + \frac{\tau L_i(t)}{1 + \tau L_i(t)} \gamma_i(t)\Delta t, \quad i = 1,\ldots, n-1 \qquad (4.140)$$

We next need to update the LIBOR rates. To do this, we observe that Equation 4.136 has a local log-normal structure if we assume that γ_i is constant. We then get

$$L_i(t + \Delta t) = L_i(t) \exp\left(-\frac{1}{2}\gamma_i^2 + \gamma_i \Delta W_{i+1}\right), \quad i = 1,\ldots, n-1 \qquad (4.141)$$

We can now increment time by Δt and use Equation 4.140 to get the next set of Wiener increments, which we then insert in Equation 4.141 to get the next LIBOR increments. This procedure captures the complicated path dependency of the drifts in an explicit manner (details about the concept of explicit computations will be given in Chapter 7). It is possible to improve on this simple approach to the integration of Equation 4.136 by making a predictor-corrector update of the drift in Equation 4.140. To do this, we first compute a preliminary update $\tilde{L}_i(t + \Delta t)$. We then use the average $\frac{1}{2}(\tilde{L}_i(t + \Delta t) + L_i(t))$ in place of $L_i(t)$ in Equation 4.140 to generate a new set of ΔW_{i+1}, which we finally use in Equation 4.141 to get a final update for $L_i(t + \Delta t)$. This allows us to take very large integration steps (of the order of 0.5 years for realistic market data) and still properly capture the path dependency. The concept of predictor corrector will be fully explored in Chapter 7.

To carry out the recursive update of the Wiener processes, we can start with any W_i. It is convenient, however, to use the W_i of the LIBOR rate that will still be alive and as close as possible to the horizon of the scenarios we are building (the smallest t_i, such that $t_i \geq t_{max}$, where t_{max} is the maximum integration time of Equation 4.136). This means that typically we start with a Wiener process corresponding to a high maturity and work backward to lower maturities.

PRINCIPAL COMPONENT ANALYSIS TO APPROXIMATE CORRELATION MATRICES

In the generation of trajectories for multidimensional processes, such as the LIBOR trajectories we described in the last section, it is often desirable to reduce the stochastic dimensionality of the scenarios, while at the same time capturing features considered important. Among the considerations for doing this are the following.

- Market practice in some cases relies on models that assume a low dimensionality. Calibrating against such models may motivate reducing the number of dimensions.
- By doing our simulations with reduced stochastic dimensions it may become possible to perform a quality check on the simulated results by comparing with results from techniques that are reliable but that only work in very low dimensions, such as finite differences and trees.
- Reducing the number of dimensions may enable us to gain a better understanding of the processes involved. Historical data shows that correlation contains relatively stable information as well as noise. Dimensionality reduction can help separate the two and facilitate modeling of the stable information.

A standard procedure for reducing the dimensionality of a process is as follows. Given a vector process, L, of length n, defined by

$$dL = adt + \sigma b dW \qquad (4.142)$$

where L and a are n-vectors, σ is an n-vector, b is an $n \times m$ matrix, and dW is an n-vector of independent Wiener processes, our objective is to get the matrix b such that

$$E[(\sigma b d W)(\sigma b d W)^T] = E[(\sigma b d W)(d W^T b^T \sigma^T)] = \sigma \hat{C} \sigma^T dt \quad (4.143)$$

where $\hat{C} = bb^T$ is an approximation to the measured correlation matrix of dL, C. The measured correlation matrix can be factored as

$$C = ADA^T \quad (4.144)$$

where A is the matrix of eigenvectors of C, and D is the diagonal matrix of ordered eigenvalues of C. The procedure consists of eliminating the $n - m$ smallest elements of D. We call this resulting matrix D^*. We construct the matrix,

$$\tilde{b} = A\sqrt{D^*} \quad (4.145)$$

where $\sqrt{D^*}$ is a diagonal matrix with the square root of the elements of D^*. This b matrix is $n \times m$.

Now consider the matrix $C^* = \tilde{b}\tilde{b}^T$. This matrix will look very much like a correlation matrix, except that its diagonal entries are not equal to one. We can define

$$b_{ij} = \frac{\tilde{b}_{ij}}{\sqrt{C^*_{ii}}}, \quad i = 1, \ldots, n; \, j = 1, \ldots, m \quad (4.146)$$

It is easy to verify that with this rescaling, the quantity bb^T is a matrix with ones on the diagonal. This definition of b allows us to reduce the number of independent Wiener processes from n down to m, while at the same time preserving the individual volatilities of each element in the vector L.

CHAPTER 5

European Pricing with Simulation

As we saw in Chapter 3, the price of a derivative security can be expressed as an expectation of discounted payoffs. In the case of European derivatives, where the times when future cash flows occur are known, Monte Carlo simulation is a robust and well-established way to get an estimate of this expectation. In the case of derivatives with early exercise features, such as American or Bermudan options, pricing with simulation is a much more challenging problem. It is only due to very recent advances that simulation can be viewed as a practical approach for pricing early exercise derivatives.

In this chapter we will discuss some of the standard methods and issues associated with pricing European derivatives. The discussion on methods and issues is by no means exhaustive, but it consists of a selection made on the basis of practicality and usefulness.

ROLES OF SIMULATION IN FINANCE

When we refer to *simulation*, what we have in mind is known as the *Monte Carlo method* (*pseudo–Monte Carlo* and *quasi–Monte Carlo* are variations). The book by Hammersley and Handscomb (1964) is an excellent general source on the Monte Carlo method. The texts by Bratley, Fox, and Schrage (1987) and by Law and Kelton (2000) are good general references on simulation.

There are two primary areas in the application of the Monte Carlo method in finance, with distinct requirements and issues: pricing and risk management. In the next two subsections we briefly describe some of the main differences between these two applications of simulation.

Monte Carlo in Pricing

In this case we are interested in computing (or estimating) an expectation. In the case of a European derivative, we are interested in the expectation

$$V(0) = B(0)E_0^B\left[\frac{V(T)}{B(T)}\right] \tag{5.1}$$

where $B(.)$ is the normalizing asset and $V(T)$ is the known payoff at maturity.

In the case of an option with early exercise, we are interested in

$$V(0) = B(0) \sup_{\tau \in \{0, T\}} E_0^B\left[\frac{F(\tau)}{B(\tau)}\right] \tag{5.2}$$

where τ is a stopping time and $F(\tau)$ is the payoff at $t = \tau$. What is important about these two problems is that we are trying to compute expectations and we assume that the distribution properties of the function whose expectation we want are determined by underlying processes (Ito or Poisson processes, for example). These processes are given to us as part of the problem formulation, and we accept the distributions that result for $\frac{V(T)}{B(T)}$. Typically, we are not looking for properties other than the expectation. In applying Monte Carlo to pricing a European derivative, we face two challenges.

- How do we construct the function $\frac{V(T)}{B(T)}$ from the underlying processes?
- How do we estimate the expectation efficiently and accurately?

The first item is important, because we may not have an analytical formula for $\frac{V(T)}{B(T)}$ as a function of the underlying processes. In fact, in many cases of practical interest, we don't. The second item is important because we must get the answer with known error bounds (if at all possible) and within time constraints.

In computing the distribution of the discounted payoffs, we must work with processes that are specified in an appropriate measure. In its simplest form, Monte Carlo pricing is carried out in the pricing measure used to derive the derivative price. However, since we are only interested in an expectation, we do not necessarily have to carry out our simulation in the pricing measure. We may be able to carry out our simulation in a measure other than the pricing measure, but one that is more suitable for speed and accuracy. Or, we may be able to work with a function that is not the discounted payoff, but one with the same expectation as the discounted payoff. These aspects are quite different in risk management applications of simulation.

In summary, here are the main challenges in simulation applied to pricing.

- **Speed:** The computation of the expectation should be fast enough to be satisfactory for trading. At the time of this writing, this amounts to the order of a second or less on high-end desk computers.
- **Accuracy:** Accuracy should be good enough for trading and hedging.
- **Early exercise:** Although significant advances have occurred in this area, at the time of this writing the use of simulation in early exercise still has room for significant improvements. We will discuss this topic extensively in the next chapter.

Monte Carlo in Risk Management

The applications of Monte Carlo simulations to risk management have to do with estimating losses that can occur with a given probability over a given time horizon. The area where this is relevant is known as *value-at-risk computations* (Jorion (2000) is a comprehensive source on this subject). In value-at-risk-computations we want to arrive at statements such as, "We are 90 percent confident that over the next 24 hours there is less than a 1 percent chance that losses will exceed 20 million dollars." This statement tells us that in risk management we are typically interested in resolving the tails of distributions. This poses different challenges than estimating the expectation, which is what matters in pricing.

The appropriate measure for risk management applications of simulation is the market or real world measure. This may or may not be critical, depending on the time horizon and the nature of the portfolio. Furthermore, the fact that we are interested in events that occur in the tails of distributions also means that we are interested in the dependency structure of extreme events. This dependency is not properly described by correlations and brings in considerations quite different from what is relevant to pricing. A good reference in this area is in Embrechts, Resnik, and Samorodnitsky (1999).

Furthermore, unlike pricing applications, the demand on accuracy in risk management applications refers to the aggregation of a large number of financial contracts, not to the individual contracts. The same can be said of computational speed. We will not elaborate on risk management applications of simulation in this book.

To summarize, the main challenges of simulation in risk management are presented below.

- **Speed:** The entire portfolio of the institution must be completed over a period of a few hours. This may mean that the methodology of pricing used for the purpose of risk management could be different than the one used for trading.

■ **Reliability:** The results obtained must pass backtesting standards. This is a modeling issue, highly influenced by statistical considerations.

■ **Relevance:** This refers to the question of whether the results of simulation can be used for decision making or purely for compliance with regulatory requirements.

THE WORKFLOW OF PRICING WITH MONTE CARLO

The following items describe the principal ideas in Monte Carlo pricing. We will discuss these items in much greater detail in the rest of the chapter.

■ In its simplest form, pricing with Monte Carlo works by evaluating the payoff function repeatedly and taking the average of these evaluations. Each evaluation is called a *Monte Carlo cycle*. In more refined implementations, the evaluation that is conducted at each Monte Carlo cycle is not of the payoff function but of a different function with the same expectation but more desirable statistical properties.

■ Each evaluation is preceeded by the computation of underlying assets or processes. In the case of a simple European equity option, for example, the evaluation of the payoff function requires knowledge of the underlying price at maturity. The underlying price needed to evaluate the payoff function is captured in the concept of *scenario*. The computation of scenarios may require sampling from a known distribution function or may require the solution of stochastic differential equations. Each Monte Carlo cycle requires the computation of a *scenario*. We discussed the generation of scenarios in detail in Chapter 4.

■ Each Monte Carlo cycle gives us a number (the evaluation of the payoff function or of some other, more statistically suitable function), which is the realization of a random variable. In simple Monte Carlo, the random variables whose values are realized in each cycle all have the same properties and are independent. These properties are called *properties of the population* or *properties of the parent distribution*. Monte Carlo simulation consists of producing a finite sample from an infinite population. In some implementations of Monte Carlo, the random variables that get realized at each cycle may not be independent.

■ The objective of Monte Carlo simulation in pricing is to infer primarily the mean, but perhaps also other moments of the parent distribution, namely, the distribution of the properly normalized payoffs (which is unknown to us, of course), from the properties of the sample generated by the Monte Carlo cycles.

■ In order to infer the statistical properties of the parent distribution, we need to work with estimators of those properties. A good Monte Carlo simulation hinges on the design of efficient estimators.

ESTIMATORS

An *estimator* is a random variable that we can use to infer the statistical properties of the parent distribution. For example, the mean of the sample is an estimator of the mean of the population. Since estimators are random variables, they have their own distributions. The estimator computed from a sample is a realization of a random variable. An *efficient estimator* is one whose distribution is highly concentrated around the true value of the statistical parameter we are trying to measure. An *unbiased estimator* is one whose expectation is the statistical quantity we are estimating.

Estimation of the Mean

Assume n independent and identically distributed (IID) random variables $\{X_1, \ldots, X_n\}$. Each X_i is a normalized (discounted) evaluation of the payoff function as a result of the ith Monte Carlo cycle. Consider the sample mean:

$$\overline{X} = \frac{1}{n} \sum_{i=1}^{i=n} X_i \tag{5.3}$$

The mean of the sample is an estimator of the mean of the population. Is it an unbiased estimator of the population mean? To answer this question, we simply take the expectation of $\overline{X}$:

$$\mathrm{E}[\overline{X}] = \frac{1}{n} \mathrm{E}\left[\sum_{i=1}^{i=n} X_i\right]$$

$$= \frac{1}{n} \sum_{i=1}^{i=n} \mathrm{E}[X_i] \tag{5.4}$$

Since the expectation of each X_i is the same as the expectation of the population,

$$\frac{1}{n} \sum_{i=1}^{i=n} \mathrm{E}[X_i] = \frac{1}{n} n \mathrm{E}[X] \tag{5.5}$$

This gives

$$E[\overline{X}] = E[X] \tag{5.6}$$

which shows that the expectation of the sample is an unbiased estimator of the expectation of the population.

How good is this estimator? To answer this, we look at the variance of $\overline{X}$:

$$
\begin{aligned}
\sigma_{\overline{X}}^2 &= \mathrm{var}(\overline{X}) \\
&= \mathrm{var}\left[\frac{1}{n}\sum_{i=1}^{i=n} X_i\right] \\
&= \frac{1}{n^2}\sum_{i=1}^{i=n} \mathrm{var}(X_i) \\
&= \frac{1}{n^2}\sum_{i=1}^{i=n} \sigma_X^2 \\
&= \frac{1}{n^2} n \sigma_X^2
\end{aligned}
\tag{5.7}
$$

Here we made use of the fact that the X_i are independent random variables from a parent distribution with variance σ_X^2. This gives us:

$$\sigma_{\overline{X}}^2 = \frac{\sigma_X^2}{n} \tag{5.8}$$

This tells us that the standard error of the mean estimator is inversely proportional to the square root of the number of samples. Notice that the estimator of the mean is the sum of independent random variables. The *central limit theorem* tells us that the mean estimator is normally distributed.

If we assume that the computational work involved in estimating the mean is linearly proportional to the number of cycles, then

$$\text{Computational work} \propto n \propto \frac{\sigma_X^2}{(\text{Error})^2} \tag{5.9}$$

This tells us that if the computational time needed to get a sample X_i is independent of the total number of samples, then in order to double the accuracy we must quadruple the computational work.

However, it is perfectly possible to have a situation where in order to increase the accuracy of the *estimation* the computational work needed to compute X_i *increases*. In such a case this scaling law breaks down and the relationship between computational work and accuracy may become far worse. To visualize how this link between the number of Monte Carlo cycles and the effort within each cycle may arise, consider a case where the X_i are computed through some numerical approximation. Clearly, if we are conducting a relatively crude Monte Carlo with a small number of samples, it may not make sense to excessively refine the computation of each X_i. As we increase the number of cycles, and as a result we expect to get a better estimation of the mean, then it would make sense to refine the computation of each X_i. This means that in such a case, the more Monte Carlo cycles we run to estimate the mean, the more work we do in each cycle. This happens when the computation of the payoff function involves the numerical solution of stochastic differential equations. This link between the computational work of each cycle and the total number of cycles may lead to a computational barrier, where the amount of work needed to further increase the accuracy of the estimation becomes unmanageable. We will discuss this in greater detail later.

At this point we can make two significant observations.

- In numerical analysis there is an informal concept known as the *curse of dimensionality*. This refers to the fact that the computational load (CPU time, memory requirements, etc.) may increase exponentially with the number of dimensions in the problem. The computational work needed to estimate the expectation through Monte Carlo does not depend explicitly on the dimensionality of the problem. This means that there is no curse of dimensionality in Monte Carlo computations when we are only interested in a simple expectation. This is the case with European options. Unlike other methodologies, such as finite differences, where the computational burden increases with the number of dimensions, there is no such limitation with Monte Carlo. As we will see later, the situation is less rosy when we deal with early exercise.
- The standard error of the mean estimation depends on the standard deviation of the population. Since we don't know the variance of the population, we must estimate it. However, the estimator of the variance of the population is a random variable, and it has a variance. This implies that there will be an error in our assessment of the standard error of the mean estimator.

Estimation of the Variance

An obvious candidate for estimating the variance of the population is the variance of the sample:

$$\hat{\sigma}_X^2 = \frac{1}{n} \sum_{i=1}^{i=n} (X_i - \overline{X})^2 \tag{5.10}$$

We now determine whether this estimator is unbiased:

$$
E\bar{\sigma}_X^2 = E\left[\frac{1}{n}\sum_{i=1}^{i=n}(X_i - \bar{X})^2\right]
$$

$$
= E\left[\frac{1}{n}\sum_{i=1}^{i=n}X_i^2 - 2\frac{1}{n}\bar{X}\sum_{i=1}^{i=n}X_i + \frac{1}{n}\sum_{i=1}^{i=n}\bar{X}^2\right]
$$

$$
= E\left[\frac{1}{n}\sum_{i=1}^{i=n}X_i^2 - 2\bar{X}\bar{X} + \frac{1}{n}n\bar{X}^2\right]
$$

$$
= E\left[\frac{1}{n}\sum_{i=1}^{i=n}X_i^2 - \bar{X}^2\right]
$$

$$
= \frac{1}{n}\sum_{i=1}^{i=n}E[X_i^2] - E[\bar{X}^2]
$$

$$
= \frac{1}{n}nE[X_i^2] - E[\bar{X}^2]
$$

$$
= E[X_i^2] - E[\bar{X}^2]
$$

$$
= (\sigma_X^2 + E^2[X]) - (\sigma_{\bar{X}}^2 + E^2[\bar{X}])
$$

$$
= (\sigma_X^2 + E^2[X]) - \left(\frac{\sigma_X^2}{n} + E^2[X]\right)
$$

$$
= \frac{n-1}{n}\sigma_X^2
$$

(5.11)

The expression

$$
\sigma_{\bar{X}}^2 = \frac{n-1}{n}\sigma_X^2 \tag{5.12}
$$

says that the variance of the sample is not an unbiased estimator of the variance of the population. This also tells us that the quantity

$$
s_{\bar{X}}^2 = \frac{n}{n-1}\sigma_{\bar{X}}^2 \tag{5.13}
$$

is an unbiased estimator of the variance of the population because the $\frac{n-1}{n}$ factor cancels:

$$
\begin{aligned}
E[s_X^2] &= \left[\frac{n}{n-1}\sigma_X^2\right] \\
&= E\left[\frac{n}{n-1}\frac{n-1}{n}\sigma_X^2\right] \\
&= \frac{n}{n-1}\frac{n-1}{n}E[\sigma_X^2] \\
&= \frac{n}{n-1}\frac{n-1}{n}\sigma_X^2 \\
&= \sigma_X^2
\end{aligned}
\tag{5.14}
$$

Since the estimator s^2 is a random variable, it has a variance (this is the variance of the variance estimator).

After some algebra, we can show that the variance of s^2 is given by

$$
\sigma_{s^2}^2 = \frac{1}{n}\left(E[X^4] - \frac{n-3}{n-1}E^2[X^2]\right)
\tag{5.15}
$$

If the parent distribution is Gaussian, then the variance of the variance estimator is

$$
\sigma_{s^2}^2 = \frac{2}{n-1}(\sigma_X^2)^2
\tag{5.16}
$$

For n large, this is approximately

$$
\sigma_{s^2}^2 = \frac{2}{n}(\sigma_X^2)^2
\tag{5.17}
$$

Let's now compare the standard deviation of the mean estimator and the standard deviation of the variance estimator:

$$
\text{Stand. dev. of mean est.} = \frac{\sigma_X}{\sqrt{n}}
$$

$$
\text{Stand. dev. of var. est.} = \sqrt{2}\frac{\sigma_X^2}{\sqrt{n}}
$$

where we should keep in mind that the second expression is only valid for Gaussian parents.

How about estimating the standard deviation, as opposed to the variance? We can use s as an estimator of the standard deviation. We can derive an expression for the standard deviation of the standard deviation estimator. For the case of a Gaussian parent distribution, it can be shown that the standard error in the estimation of the standard deviation is (Lupton, 1993)

$$\text{Stand. dev. of stand. dev. est.} = \frac{1}{\sqrt{2}} \frac{\sigma_X}{\sqrt{n}} \tag{5.18}$$

Assessment of this error may become important in value-at-risk computations.

SIMULATION EFFICIENCY

The *efficiency of an estimator* refers to the computational cost of achieving a given level of confidence in the quantity we are trying to estimate. Our primary concern in pricing is estimating the expected value of discounted cash flows. As we saw in the last section, both the uncertainty in estimating the expectation as well as the uncertainty in the error of our estimation depend on the variance of the population from which we sample. Clearly, if the variance of the population is smaller, we will need fewer samples to attain a given level of accuracy.

The simplest approach to computing the expectation of a payoff is to sample the discounted payoff function. However, we have other choices. For example, we could sample something that is not the discounted value of the payoff but which has the same expectation as the discounted payoff. This will work if in this way we manage to reduce the variance of the population. Another alternative is to distort the probability density of the discounted payoff such that the variance is reduced but the expectation remains the same.

If we do this, we may end up having an estimator of the expectation that has significantly smaller variance and allows us to get an accurate computation of the value with relatively few samples. However, whatever we do to reduce the variance of the population will most likely tend to increase the computational time per Monte Carlo cycle. As a result, in order to make a fair comparison between estimators, we must take into account not only their variance but also the computational work for each Monte Carlo cycle.

The total computational work required by an estimator with variance σ^2 scales as

$$\text{Work} = \tau n \tag{5.19}$$

where n is the number of cycles needed to achieve the accuracy we want, and τ is the computational work per cycle. Replacing for n,

$$\text{Work} \propto \tau \frac{\sigma^2}{\text{Error}} \qquad (5.20)$$

Assume now that two estimators with variance σ_1^2 and σ_2^2 and work per Monte Carlo cycle τ_1 and τ_2, respectively. Define $\eta = \frac{\tau_1}{\tau_2}$, the ratio of computational work per replication. We can now define an acceleration factor that results by using estimator 2 instead of estimator 1:

$$y = \eta \frac{\sigma_1^2}{\sigma_2^2} \qquad (5.21)$$

We would like y to be as large as possible. The next section discusses the main strategies available to accomplish this. We will then go into some of those strategies in greater detail.

Increasing Simulation Efficiency

If we do nothing about efficiency, the number of Monte Carlo replications we need to achieve acceptable pricing accuracy may be surprisingly large. It may in fact be so large that it renders a naive implementation of the Monte Carlo method all but useless given the practical requirements of trading and risk management. For example, to price a typical European call down to one cent per \$10 we may need over 1 million replications. In other instruments, such as index amortizing swaps, the computational time with naive Monte Carlo may be impractically long. As a result, in many cases variance reduction is not just a mathematical nicety, but a practical requirement.

The most commonly used strategies for variance reduction are the following.

- **Antithetic variates:** We construct the estimator by using two Brownian motion trajectories that are mirror images of each other. This causes cancellation of dispersion. This method tends to reduce the variance modestly, but it is extremely easy to implement and as a result, very commonly used.
- **Control variates:** The estimator includes a problem highly correlated with the one we want to solve. We must know the expectation of the correlated problem either analytically or numerically. The combined problem has less variance. The correlated problem is called the *control variate*. In either case, we must know the expectation of the control

variate very well, because any uncertainty in the control variate will contaminate our desired results. This is the methodology of choice in many pricing problems. If carried out properly, we can accomplish extremely high improvements in efficiency. Significant insight and understanding of the problem is required, however.

- **Importance sampling:** We take expectations using a different probability density than that of the problem we are solving. This is effectively an application of the Girsanov theorem, where the measure is distorted in a manner that the variance is reduced. It can be very effective in problems involving jumps.

- **Stratification:** We arrange the Monte Carlo replications within predetermined regions of the distribution, thus covering the space spanned by the random variables more evenly. Stratification can be particularly effective when important events that need to be captured occur in the tails of distributions.

- **Moment matching:** This consists in ensuring that the moments of the sample of the underlying processes are matched to the moments of the population. It follows the intuitive but rather vague notion that if we want to get the correct expectation, we should have the correct underlying process. It is straightforward to implement, but it is not guaranteed to work.

- **Low-discrepancy sequences:** We discussed this topic to some extent in the previous chapter. Also known as *quasi–Monte Carlo methods,* these approaches use sequences that cover the space of underlying random variables more evenly than regular Monte Carlo. Essentially, low-discrepancy sequences get around the problem known as *clustering,* which happens with regular Monte Carlo. Clustering means that random points generated by Monte Carlo in a multidimensional space will not be spread out in a manner that could be considered necessarily optimal for a given number of dimensions. Low-discrepancy sequences get around this problem by controlling the way sampling points are arranged in a multidimensional space. When the number of dimensions is small, the idea of evening out the arrangement of sampling points may appear intuitive and attractive. As the number of dimensions increases, however, attempts to even out the distribution of sampling points ends up translating into regions of space (you can visualize these as holes) that don't get sampled. Quasi–Monte Carlo methods were popularized in the early 1990s, but the fact that many of the interesting and useful properties of simulation depend on the use of (pseudo-) random numbers has affected the growth of the popularity of low-discrepancy methods.

Next, we will concentrate on the four of these strategies that have proven to be the most fruitful in pricing applications.

ANTITHETIC VARIATES

The easiest way to describe the method of antithetic variates is through a simple example. Assume we want to price a European call on a price process:

$$\frac{dS}{S} = r dt + \sigma dW \tag{5.22}$$

The solution of this SDE at maturity, $t = T$, is

$$S(T) = S(0)\exp\left(\left(r - \frac{1}{2}\sigma^2\right)T + \sigma\sqrt{T}Z\right) \tag{5.23}$$

where Z is a standard normal random variable. The payoff function is

$$V(T) = \max[S(T) - K, 0] \tag{5.24}$$

where K is the strike.

To apply the antithetic variate technique, we generate standard normal random numbers $Z_j, j = 1, \ldots, n$ and define two set of samples of the underlying price:

$$
\begin{aligned}
S_j^+(T) &= S(0)\exp\left(\left(r - \frac{1}{2}\sigma^2\right)T + \sigma\sqrt{T}Z_j\right) \\
S_j^-(T) &= S(0)\exp\left(\left(r - \frac{1}{2}\sigma^2\right)T + \sigma\sqrt{T}(-Z_j)\right)
\end{aligned}
\tag{5.25}
$$

Similarly, we define two sets of discounted payoff samples:

$$
\begin{aligned}
V_j^+(T) &= \max[S_j^+(T) - K, 0] \\
V_j^-(T) &= \max[S_j^-(T) - K, 0]
\end{aligned}
\tag{5.26}
$$

Now we construct our mean estimator by averaging these samples:

$$\overline{V}(0) = \frac{1}{n}\sum_{j=1}^{j=n} \frac{1}{2}(V_j^+ + V_j^-) \tag{5.27}$$

Notice that in constructing the estimator, it is important that we take each element in the sample to be the sum of V_j^+ and V_j^-. If we took the V_j^+ and V_j^- in succession, we would not have independent random variables in the sample and we would not be able to invoke the variance properties of the estimator, which assume the sample is made up of independent random variables.

Efficiency of Antithetic Variates

Each sampling in the simulation using the antithetic method involves roughly twice the work of straight Monte Carlo. It is not exactly twice because some efficiencies can be incorporated into the simulation architecture. However, it is reasonable to assume that the replication time will approximately double. Hence, the replication work ration is

$$\eta_{\text{antithetic}} \approx \frac{1}{2} \tag{5.28}$$

The acceleration factor (Equation 5.21) of the antithetic method is

$$y = \eta \frac{\sigma_1^2}{\sigma_2^2}$$

$$= \frac{1}{2} \frac{\text{var}[V^+]}{\text{var}\left[\frac{V^+ + V^-}{2}\right]} \tag{5.29}$$

$$= 2 \frac{\text{var}[V^+]}{\text{var}[V^+] + 2\text{cov}[V^+, V^-] + \text{var}[V^-]}$$

Since $\text{var}[V^+] = \text{var}[V^-]$, we have

$$y = \frac{1}{1 + \dfrac{\text{cov}[V, V^-]}{\text{var}[V^+]}}$$

$$= \frac{1}{1 + \rho_{V^+, V^-}} \tag{5.30}$$

For any variance reduction approach to be worthwhile, its acceleration factor must be greater than 1. This implies that for the antithetic method to work, we need V^+ and V^- to be negatively correlated:

$$\rho_{V^+, V^-} < 0 \tag{5.31}$$

This will happen if the payoff function is a monotonic function of Z. Notice that if the V^+ and V^- are perfectly negatively correlated, the efficiency factor becomes infinitely large. This means that in such a case we would know the answer with only one Monte Carlo cycle. This would happen if the payoff were a linear function of the random variable Z.

If the payoff is symmetric with respect to Z, then the efficiency factor will drop below 1, and the application of this method will result in greater computational effort, rather than less.

In summary, we can say the following about the antithetic method.

- Significant efficiency requires an almost linear payoff function. The function must be linear in the random variable where the antithetic variable is defined. In the case described here, this is the standard normal random variable. This situation almost never happens in practice, and the gains, if any, tend to be modest.
- There is typically insignificant additional coding effort needed to implement the antithetic method, and for this reason it is quite commonly used. However, care must be taken not to use this method blindly, since we may end up using more computer time, rather than less. Attempts to combine this method with other methods typically don't work well.

CONTROL VARIATES

This is typically a far more powerful way of reducing the variance in pricing than using antithetic variates. When properly designed, computations can be accelerated by one or even two orders of magnitude.

In financial applications of the control variate method, the emphasis has traditionally been on using a closely related financial instrument whose value is known analytically to compute the value of another instrument by simulation. The combination of the two instruments allows us to construct an estimator with much less variance if both instruments are closely related. The best-known example in finance is the *arithmetic average Asian option*, priced by simulation using the *geometric average Asian option* as control variate. While there is a closed form solution of the geometric average option, there is no analytical solution in the arithmetic average case.

The fact that we are pricing a financial instrument does not mean that we have to use another financial instrument as control variate. In fact, any other function of the same underlying processes whose expectation is known, and which is highly correlated with the instrument we are interested in will work. Also, we don't have to know the control variate's expectation analytically. Even if we know the control variate expectation numerically, the technique will work as long as we have a reasonably good assessment of the control variate expectation.

We need some nomenclature and definitions.

- $\overline{V}$ is the uncontrolled estimator of the value of the instrument we are interested in.
- $\overline{V}^c$ is the controlled estimator. This estimator has an expectation equal to or very close to the expectation we are seeking, but its variance is much smaller than that of $\overline{V}$.

■ $\overline{V}^a$ is the estimator of the value of another instrument closely related to the one we are interested in. We call this instrument the *control variate instrument*. In general, the control variate does not have to be a valid financial instrument at all, although in most cases it is. For simplicity, we will refer to the control variate as an instrument, or simply as the control variate.

■ V^a is the value of the control variate instrument. It is important that we should know this value very accurately.

■ β is a constant to be chosen optimally.

■ $\sigma_{V^a}^2$ is the variance of the control variate.

■ σ_V^2 is the variance of the instrument we are interested in.

The controlled estimator is constructed as follows:

$$\overline{V}^c = \overline{V} + \beta(V^a - \overline{V}^a) \tag{5.32}$$

In terms of samples, this can be written as

$$\overline{V}^c = \frac{1}{n}\sum_{j=1}^{j=n} V_j + \beta\left(V^a - \frac{1}{n}\sum_{j=1}^{j=n} V_j^a\right) \tag{5.33}$$

We can select an optimal β by minimizing the variance of the controlled estimator:

$$\text{var}[\overline{V}^c] = \sigma_V^2 - 2\beta\rho_{V,V^a}\sigma_V\sigma_{V^a} + \beta^2\sigma_{V^a}^2 \tag{5.34}$$

The minimum variance corresponds to

$$\frac{\partial\text{var}[\overline{V}^c]}{\beta} = 0 \tag{5.35}$$

This gives

$$-2\rho_{V,V^a}\sigma_V\sigma_{V^a} + 2\beta\sigma_{V^a}^2 = 0 \tag{5.36}$$

The optimal value of β that minimizes the variance of the controlled estimator is

$$\beta_{\text{opt}} = \frac{\rho_{V,V^a}\sigma_V\sigma_{V^a}}{\sigma_{V^a}^2} \tag{5.37}$$

With this value of β, the minimum variance of the controlled estimator is

$$\text{var}[\overline{V}^c]_{\min} = \text{var}[\overline{V}](1 - \rho_{V,V^a}^2) \tag{5.38}$$

If the control variate estimator and the uncontrolled estimator were perfectly correlated, we would be able to compute the value of the instrument we are interested in with one Monte Carlo cycle. This makes sense, because if both the instrument we want to price and the control variate instrument were perfectly correlated, then the control variate would simply be a rescaling of the instrument we are pricing. This implies that pricing the control variate instrument was essentially the same as pricing the instrument we want, save for a constant. This situation would not materialize in practice, but we can get fairly close to it.

Efficiency of Control Variates

The acceleration factor, Equation 5.21, becomes

$$y = \eta \frac{\text{var}\,[\overline{V}]}{\text{var}\,[\overline{V}^c]} = \frac{\eta}{1 - \rho^2} \tag{5.39}$$

In order to benefit from the control variate, the correlation coefficient between the instrument and the control instrument must be arranged such that

$$\frac{\eta}{1 - \rho^2} > 1 \tag{5.40}$$

Equivalently,

$$\rho > \sqrt{1 - \eta} \tag{5.41}$$

If it took as much time to sample the control instrument as the original instrument, $\eta = \frac{1}{2}$, and the minimum correlation coefficient for which the control variate technique will work is $\sqrt{1 - 0.5}$,

$$\rho_{min} = 0.707 \tag{5.42}$$

This is a fairly severe limitation. The reason is that the correlation coefficient between control and instrument enters as ρ^2. We need to have very tight correlations in order to gain significantly in speed. The minimum value of ρ increases rapidly as the incremental effort to compute the control variate increases.

Case Study: Application of Control Variates to Discretely Sampled Step-Up Barrier Options

This simple example shows some of the practical issues to be considered in applying control variates. The traditional approach to control variates has been to select a highly correlated financial instrument as a control variate, for which the price is known, preferably analytically. This approach is typically limited to academic examples (the best-known one is the arithmetic Asian option computed with the geometric Asian as control variate).

A much more practical approach is to select a control variate that can be solved numerically very accurately with a simple and reliable implementation, by simulation or other methods, such as finite differences or trees. This numerically "priced" control variate can then be used repeatedly to price variations of the instrument of interest. We put priced in quotes because, as we said earlier, the control variate does not need to be a meaningful financial instrument, although in most cases it will be. We now use a discretely sampled barrier option to illustrate this case.

Consider the pricing of a weekly monitored European knockout call with maturity one year, such that in the first half of the year the barrier, H, is set to \$125, and in the second half of the year it is set to \$127. Assume the underlying process is log-normal with risk-free rate $r = 0.07$, dividend yield $d = 0.02$, and volatility $\sigma = 0.2$. This problem is very simple to solve by simulation. If the spot price $S(0) = 100$, the price of the option is about \$3, and the variance of the uncontrolled estimator is approximately 35. This means that the number of cycles needed to estimate the price within \$0.01 is $\frac{35}{0.01^2} \approx 350,000$.

There are several ways to select an effective control variate. Intuitively, we can think that a discretely sampled barrier option with a constant barrier could be a reasonable control variate. This is very attractive, because the case of a discretely sampled constant barrier can be solved almost analytically by applying a correction to the continuously sampled case (Broadie, Glasserman, and Kou, 1996). However, the approximate nature of this solution will contaminate the expectation of the controlled estimator. A more practical and robust approach is to use a discretely sampled constant barrier option that has been priced using finite differences. If the finite difference technique works well for the constant barrier option, why not use it also for the case we are interested in? We can certainly do this. However, there are three reasons why we may still want to use simulation for our case and finite differences for the control variate. One reason is that applying finite differences to a constant barrier option is extremely simple; another is that the price obtained with finite differences is reliable and very accurate; and yet another reason is that this control variate can be reused for different configurations of the instrument we are interested in. The main requirement of a good control variate is that the price must be known very accurately. A fast computation of the control's price is welcome, but it is not a critical requirement if the control can be used more than once.

The fact that our problem contains a barrier that steps up in the second half of the year means that the second half of the barrier will be less likely to be hit when compared with the second half of the barrier of the control, if everything else stays the same. If we can somehow change something about the control to *decrease* the likelihood that the barrier will be hit in the second half of the year, it is possible that we will get a better control variate. One way we can accomplish this is to use a different underlying process for the control. For example, if we use a process with a lower volatility for the control instrument, the likelihood of the barrier being hit in the second half of the year will decrease, and we would expect that a slightly less volatile underlying will lead to a more efficient control. Another way to accomplish a similar effect is to increase the dividend yield of the control underlying. If we do this, the underlying price of the control variate will grow less on the average in the risk neutral world, and will therefore be less likely to hit the barrier compared with the case of lower dividend yield.

For the parameters we are discussing here, this is a very effective way of producing a control variate. Figure 5.1 shows the correlation coefficient of the uncontrolled estimator and the control variate estimator for varying dividend yield of the price process used in the control variate. We see that if the control variate is constructed with the same process as that of the problem we are trying to solve, the correlation coefficient between the uncontrolled estimator and the control variate is approximately 0.87. Assuming that the control variate doubles the computational effort (very much the case here), this translates into an acceleration factor approximately equal to 2. If we solve the

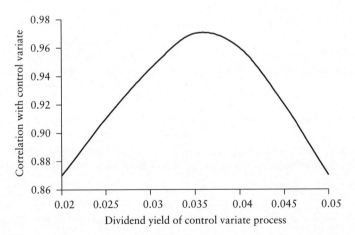

FIGURE 5.1 Effect of yield of control variate process on correlation between uncontrolled estimator of discretely sampled barrier and control variate. European knockout call with $H = 125$ for $t < 0.5$ and $H = 127$ for $t > 0.5$, $S(0) = 100$, $K = 100$, $r = 0.07$, $d = 0.02$, $\sigma = 0.2$, T = 1. Control variate parameters are identical except for the barrier: $H = 125$ for $0 \leq t \leq T$ and the dividend yield varies as shown.

control variate with an underlying price process with a dividend yield of 0.035, the correlation coefficient goes up to approximately 0.97. This means that the acceleration factor is now approximately 8.4. This is a very significant gain. We can now get the desired accuracy almost ten times faster.

In this case, the variance of the control variate is approximately 23, and the covariance of the instrument with the control variate is approximately 28. This gives $\beta \approx \frac{28}{23} = 1.22$. The controlled estimator is then,

$$\overline{V}^c_{Step\text{-}up\ barrier} = \overline{V}_{Step\text{-}up\ barrier} + 1.22(V_{Constant\ barrier} - \overline{V}_{Constant\ barrier})$$

(5.43)

The value of the step-up barrier option is 2.962. The expectation of the control variate with $d = 0.035$ is 2.452.

IMPORTANCE SAMPLING

The basic idea of *importance sampling*, also known as the *measure transformation approach*, consists of computing expectations by sampling from a different distribution than the original distribution, chosen in such a manner that the variance of the mean estimator is reduced. By sampling from a distribution other than the original one and properly adjusting the samples, it is possible to get an estimator that has the same mean as the original one but with less variance. This adjustment consists of making a measure transformation such that the expectation of the estimator is preserved. As a result, importance sampling is a particular application of the Girsanov theorem. Although many textbooks in simulation don't refer explicitly to the connection of importance sampling with the Girsanov theorem, we will emphasize this aspect here because this connection is particularly relevant in financial pricing.

To introduce the concept of importance sampling, consider the value of a derivative as an expectation of a suitably discounted payoff function, $F(S(T))$, where $S(T)$ is the underlying process at maturity. For simplicity, we assume the normalizing asset is incorporated in the definitions of $V(0)$ and $F(S(T))$:

$$V(0) = E_0[F(S(T))]$$ (5.44)

Assume now that the probability density function of $S(T)$ consistent with Equation 5.44 is $p(.)$. If the normalizing asset were the money market account, this probability density would be the risk neutral probability density. The expectation can be written as follows:

$$V(0) = \int_{S(T)} F(\xi)p(\xi)d\xi$$ (5.45)

The integral in this equation is a Lebesque integral, but we will not worry about this here. For the purpose of this discussion, we can assume that this is a regular Riemann integral. The simple Monte Carlo implementation of this expectation is

$$V(0) = \frac{1}{n} \sum_{i=1}^{i=n} F(S_i) \tag{5.46}$$

where we have n replications and S_i are realizations of independent random variables with probability density $p(.)$.

We now select another probability density, $\hat{p}(.)$, that does not vanish where $F(\xi)p(\xi) \neq 0$, and write the expectation as

$$V(0) = \int_{S(T)} F(\xi) \frac{p(\xi)}{\hat{p}(\xi)} \hat{p}(\xi) d\xi \tag{5.47}$$

The Monte Carlo implementation of the expectation in the last equation is

$$V(0) = \frac{1}{n} \sum_{i=1}^{i=n} F(\hat{S}_i) \frac{p(\hat{S}_i)}{\hat{p}(\hat{S}_i)} \tag{5.48}$$

where $\hat{S}_i$ are realizations of independent random variables with probability density $\hat{p}(.)$.

By properly selecting $\hat{p}(.)$, in some cases we can achieve

$$\mathrm{var}\left[F(\hat{S}) \frac{p(\hat{S})}{\hat{p}(\hat{S})} \right] \ll \mathrm{var}[F(S)]$$

where $\hat{S}$ has p.d.f $\hat{p}(.)$ and S has p.d.f $p(.)$. If we achieve this, depending on the cost of computing the $\frac{p(\hat{S})}{\hat{p}(\hat{S})}$, we may obtain a significant gain in computational efficiency when computing $V(0)$.

Usually, $p(.)$ is called the *nominal probability density,* and $\hat{p}(.)$ is referred to as the *importance probability density.*

The quantity $\frac{p(\hat{S})}{\hat{p}(\hat{S})}$ is called the *likelihood ratio* and is related to the Radon-Nikodym derivative we introduced in Chapter 2. Equations 5.45 and 5.47 imply

$$\hat{\mathrm{E}}\left[F(\hat{S}) \frac{p(\hat{S})}{\hat{p}(\hat{S})} \right] = \mathrm{E}[F(S)] \tag{5.49}$$

Remembering from Chapter 2, the expectation in two measures is related as follows:

$$\hat{E}\left[\frac{F(\hat{S})}{Z}\right] = E[F(S)] \tag{5.50}$$

To make the connection with the Girsanov theorem is a good idea in financial pricing because it gives us a means to compute the process Z. We can then use this process to convert to a more suitable measure for taking the expectation.

Optimal Importance Density

A natural question arises: What is the importance probability density, $\hat{p}(.)$, that minimizes the variance of $F(\hat{S})\frac{p(\hat{S})}{\hat{p}(\hat{S})}$? If $F(.)$ is a positive function, it is very simple to see that the optimal importance density is

$$\hat{p}_{optimal}(\xi) = \frac{F(\xi)p(\xi)}{V(0)} \tag{5.51}$$

To verify that this is the case, consider the definition of variance:

$$\begin{aligned}
\text{var}\left[F(\hat{S})\frac{p(\hat{S})}{\hat{p}(\hat{S})}\right] &= E\left[F(\hat{S})\frac{p(\hat{S})}{\hat{p}(\hat{S})}\right]^2 - \left(\underbrace{E\left[F(\hat{S})\frac{p(\hat{S})}{\hat{p}(\hat{S})}\right]}_{=V(0)}\right)^2 \\
&= \int\left[F(\xi)\frac{p(\xi)}{\hat{p}(\xi)}\right]^2 \hat{p}(\xi)d\xi - V(0)^2 \\
&= \int\frac{(F(\xi)p(\xi))^2}{\hat{p}(\xi)}d\xi - V(0)^2
\end{aligned} \tag{5.52}$$

Replacing Equation 5.51 in the last equation, we get

$$\begin{aligned}
\text{var}\left[F(\hat{S})\frac{p(\hat{S})}{\hat{p}(\hat{S})}\right] &= \int\frac{(F(\xi)p(\xi))^2}{\hat{p}(\xi)}d\xi - V(0)^2 \\
&= V(0)\int\frac{(F(\xi)p(\xi))^2}{F(\xi)p(\xi)}d\xi - V(0)^2 \\
&= V(0)\underbrace{\int F(\xi)p(\xi)d\xi}_{=V(0)} - V(0)^2 \\
&= V(0)V(0) - V(0)^2 \\
&= 0
\end{aligned} \tag{5.53}$$

If we select Equation 5.51 as our importance density, we get an estimator of the mean with zero variance! This means that we could solve the pricing problem with only one Monte Carlo replication. Of course, this is not really very helpful because Equation 5.51 contains $V(0)$, and if we knew $V(0)$ we would have already solved the problem.

There are several ways of selecting a suitable importance density. In financial pricing applications, there are two main approaches.

- Rather than focusing on computing a formula for the importance density, we can alter the underlying process and use Girsanov's theorem to get the appropriate measure transformation. Since in financial pricing we usually work with Wiener processes, this approach is particularly appealing. We present an in-depth discussion of an example showing this technique.
- We can try to model the importance density directly by considering a different version of the problem with more suitable properties. The difference between this approach and the previous one is that here we don't alter the parameters of the original problem. This can be very effective in pricing default-related instruments. We will also discuss an example of this approach in detail.

Applying the Girsanov Theorem to Importance Sampling: European Call Option

To illustrate the Girsanov approach to importance sampling in financial pricing, consider the case of a European call option on a non-dividend paying stock with the risk neutral log-normal price process,

$$\frac{dS}{S} = r\,dt + \sigma d\,W(t) \tag{5.54}$$

where r is the risk-free rate, assumed to be constant. K denotes the strike, and T is the time to maturity. The value of the option is, then,

$$V(0) = \mathrm{E}\exp\left(-rT\right)[S(T) - K]^{+} \tag{5.55}$$

In order to solve this problem by simulation, we construct trajectories of the stock price process from $t = 0$ to $t = T$. Because this is a European call with no events happening between $t = 0$ and $t = T$, these trajectories have only two time points of interest, 0 and T. Let's call the end points of these trajectories $S^j(T)$, $j = 1, \ldots, J$ (we use a superscript to be consistent with the notation introduced in Chapter 4):

$$V(0) \approx \frac{1}{J} \sum_{j=1}^{j=J} \exp\left(-rT\right)[S^j(T) - K]^{+} \tag{5.56}$$

With the discounted payoff $F(S) = \exp(-rT)[S - K]^+$,

$$V(0) \approx \frac{1}{J} \sum_{j=1}^{j=J} F(S^j(T)) \tag{5.57}$$

It seems intuitively clear that we are likely to get better performance by changing the process $S(t)$ in such a way that we increase the proportion of states at time T that are in the money. That is, if we can change $S(t)$ in such a way that a larger proportion of the right-hand side of Equation 5.56 are nonzero, we would expect better efficiency. As we will see shortly, this intuition is only partially right and in some cases may be quite wrong.

One way to get a larger proportion of trajectories to be in the money at time T is to increase the drift of the stock price process. If we do this, the stock price will then move upward more quickly and trajectories will be more likely to end up in the money. We can change the price process as follows:

$$\frac{dS}{S} = (r + c)dt + \sigma\left(dW(t) - \frac{c}{\sigma}dt\right) \tag{5.58}$$

where c is a positive constant. Defining

$$d\hat{W} = dW - \frac{c}{\sigma}dt \tag{5.59}$$

the stock process can be written as

$$\frac{dS}{S} = (r + c)dt + \sigma\hat{W}(t) \tag{5.60}$$

We know from Chapter 2 that $\hat{W}(t)$ is a Brownian motion in a measure defined by the relationship,

$$Z(0)\hat{E}[F(S(T))] = E[F(S(T))Z(T)] \tag{5.61}$$

where

$$Z(t) = \exp\left(-\frac{1}{2}\int_0^t \theta^2(\xi)d\xi - \int_0^t \theta(\xi)dW(t)\right) \tag{5.62}$$

with $\theta = -\frac{c}{\sigma}$. Replacing this in the last equation, we get

$$Z(t) = \exp\left(-\frac{1}{2}\frac{c^2}{\sigma^2}t + \frac{c}{\sigma}W(t)\right) \tag{5.63}$$

In order to use Equation 5.61, we express it as

$$E[F(S(T))] = Z(0)\hat{E}\left[\frac{F(S(T))}{Z(T)}\right] \tag{5.64}$$

The reason for this is that the expectation on the left is the value of the derivative and is in the same measure as the expectation in Equation 5.55. The value of the derivative is

$$V(0) = Z(0)\hat{E}\left[\frac{F(S(T))}{Z(T)}\right] \tag{5.65}$$

We are now ready to compute the expectation on the right-hand side of Equation 5.65 with Monte Carlo. To do this, we must make sure that all processes in the argument of $\hat{E}$ are expressed in terms of $\hat{W}$, not in terms of W. This is necessary so that we can treat the W's as Wiener processes.

The underlying stock price can be solved from Equation 5.60:

$$S(t) = S(0)\exp\left(\left(r + c - \frac{1}{2}\sigma^2\right)t + \sigma\hat{W}(t)\right) \tag{5.66}$$

To get the argument in Equation 5.65, we must express $Z(t)$ in terms of $\hat{W}(t)$:

$$\begin{aligned}
Z(t) &= \exp\left(-\frac{1}{2}\frac{c^2}{\sigma^2}t + \frac{c}{\sigma}W(t)\right) \\
&= \exp\left(-\frac{1}{2}\frac{c^2}{\sigma^2}t + \frac{c}{\sigma}\left(\hat{W}(t) + \frac{c}{\sigma}t\right)\right) \\
&= \exp\left(\frac{1}{2}\frac{c^2}{\sigma^2}t + \frac{c}{\sigma}\hat{W}(t)\right)
\end{aligned} \tag{5.67}$$

Replacing Equations 5.66 and 5.67 in Equation 5.65 and noticing that $Z(0) = 1$, we get the expectation that we will compute by Monte Carlo simulation:

$$V(0) = \hat{E}\left[\exp(-rT)\frac{\left[S(0)\exp\left(\left(r + c - \frac{1}{2}\sigma^2\right)T + \sigma\hat{W}(T)\right) - K\right]^+}{\exp\left(\frac{1}{2}\frac{c^2}{\sigma^2}T + \frac{c}{\sigma}\hat{W}(T)\right)}\right] \tag{5.68}$$

To have a better understanding of what to expect, let's look at what the value of the derivative in the original measure would be had we not done any adjustments to the price process drift:

$$V(0) = \mathrm{E}\left[\exp\left(-rT\right)\left[S(0)\exp\left(\left(r - \frac{1}{2}\sigma^2\right)T + \sigma W(T)\right) - K\right]^+\right] \qquad (5.69)$$

Notice that while the modification of the drift we did should cause more paths to end up in the money, the appearance of the exponential in the denominator in Equation 5.68 complicates the situation. There are two sources of difficulty. The $\frac{c^2}{\sigma^2}T$ term in the denominator will decrease the effect of the drift distortion we introduce. The negative effect of this term depends on the time to maturity and the volatility. The second source of difficulty is the $\sigma\hat{W}(t)$ term in the denominator. Although the drift modification we made by adding c to the original drift will tend to make more $S(t)$ paths land in the money, the Wiener process in the denominator will have the equivalent effect of bending those trajectories down, as far as the expectation is concerned. For a given volatility, this effect becomes increasingly more pronounced for higher drift distortions.

These facts are clearly visible in the following results. We will call the estimator without importance sampling the *nominal* estimator. Figure 5.2 shows the distributions of the random variable in the expectation of Equation 5.68 for a call option with the parameters quoted in the caption.

For small drift upward distortions, the distribution is closely centered around the strike, as expected. For moderate values of c the distribution is skewed to the right. It is at these values of c that significant gains in performance are achieved. For high values of c the distribution becomes skewed

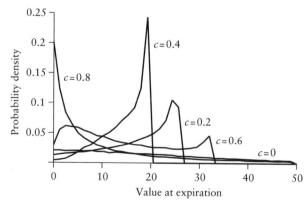

FIGURE 5.2   Effect of drift adjustment on payoff distribution. European call with $S(0) = 100, K = 100, r = 0.1, \sigma = 0.3, T = 0.75$ years.

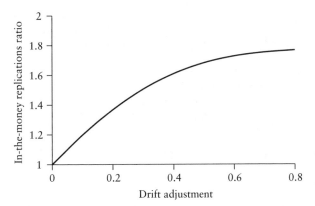

FIGURE 5.3 Effect of drift adjustment on in-the-money cycles at payoff time. Ratio of in-the-money replications at payoff for simulation with and without importance sampling for European call with $S(0) = 100$, $K = 100$, $r = 0.1$, $\sigma = 0.3$, $T = 0.75$ years.

to the left. This is the situation where terms in the $Z(T)$ begin to dominate the upward drift induced by c.

Figure 5.3 shows the ratio of in-the-money replications of the importance sampling case over the nominal case. For large values of c the fraction of in-the-money replications is much larger than in the nominal case, but this does not translate into increased numerical efficiency for the reasons discussed above.

Figure 5.4 indicates the reduction in variance that we can achieve by distorting the drift upward. The plot shows the ratio of the variance of the

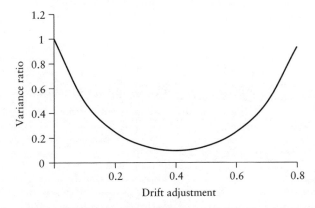

FIGURE 5.4 Effect of drift adjustment on the variance. Ratio of variance with importance sampling to variance without importance sampling for European call with $S(0) = 100$, $K = 100$, $r = 0.1$, $\sigma = 0.3$, $T = 0.75$ years.

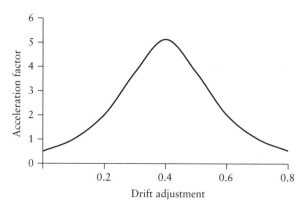

FIGURE 5.5 Effect of drift adjustment on importance sampling acceleration factor. Acceleration factor assuming $\eta = 0.5$ for European call with $S(0) = 100, K = 100$, $r = 0.1, \sigma = 0.3, T = 0.75$ years.

estimator with importance sampling to that of the nominal estimator. The plot shows a clearly defined minimum. The shape of the curve suggests that the counteracting effect of $Z(T)$ is fairly symmetrical with the beneficial effect of $S(t)$ in the importance sampling measure.

Finally, Figure 5.5 shows the acceleration factor that can be achieved with importance sampling in this case. As we discussed earlier, the acceleration factor is given by

$$y = \eta \frac{\sigma_1^2}{\sigma_2^2} \tag{5.70}$$

In our case,

$$\sigma_1^2 = \text{Variance of nominal estimator}$$

$$\sigma_2^2 = \text{Variance of importance sampling estimator}$$

$$\eta = \frac{\text{CPU of nominal replication}}{\text{CPU of importance sampling replication}}$$

$$\approx \frac{1}{2} \tag{5.71}$$

In this case we can assume that the additional work of computing $Z(T)$ is approximately the same as the work of computing $F(S(T))$. The figure shows that c must be greater than approximately 0.1 and less than approximately 0.7 for this technique to work as implemented (with a constant drift distortion). At its best, this technique as applied to this case will give us a five-fold increase in performance.

Importance Sampling by Direct Modeling of the Importance Density: Credit Put

As another application of importance sampling, we consider the case of cash flows that occur as a result of a default event. Since this is a particularly powerful application of this technique, we explore in detail the pricing of a credit put. A credit put is an instrument that pays an amount, which may or may not be known in advance, when a default event happens. The probability of a default event happening within the maturity of the instrument is extremely low. For this reason, using naive Monte Carlo to price a credit put (or other instruments that pay on default events) can be very costly. The vast majority of the effort computing the estimator will be wasted, since the relevant event occurs with very low probability.

Assume a credit put that pays a known amount $P(t)$ if a default event happens at time $t = \tau$. Assuming that any processes involved are in the risk neutral measure, the value at time $t = 0$ of this instrument is

$$V(0) = E_0\left[\frac{P(\tau)}{\beta(\tau)}\right] \tag{5.72}$$

where $\beta(\tau)$ is the money market account evaluated at default time $t = \tau$. The expectation in Equation 5.72 is taken over all default times τ. The standard model for the default process (this topic will be covered in greater detail in Chapter 7) is the Poisson process. In the Poisson model, the probability that a default event occurs after time t is given by

$$\text{Prob}(\tau > t) = E_0 \exp\left(-\int_0^t h(\xi)d\xi\right) \tag{5.73}$$

where $h(t)$ is called the *default intensity* and can be a stochastic process.

Denote by ϕ the probability density of τ. By definition of probability density,

$$\phi(t) = \frac{d\text{Prob}(\tau < t)}{dt} = -\frac{d\text{Prob}(\tau > t)}{dt} \tag{5.74}$$

Replacing for $\text{Prob}(\tau > t)$ we get

$$\phi(t) = -\frac{d}{dt}E_0 \exp\left(-\int_0^t h(\xi)d\xi\right) = +E_0 h(t)\exp\left(-\int_0^t h(\xi)d\xi\right) \tag{5.75}$$

where we use the fact that the expectation is a linear operation. ϕ is the *nominal probability density of default*. To get the likelihood ratio, we want to construct this probability. In a fairly general way, we can assume that the default intensity follows a stochastic process of the form

$$dh(t) = a_h(h, t) + b_h(h, t)dW_h \tag{5.76}$$

where a_h is a drift, b_h is a volatility, and W_h is a Wiener process. With this degree of generality, we will not typically know the nominal probability of default analytically, but we can approximate it numerically very accurately. To do this, we can compute the expectation in Equation 5.75 for an array of discrete times $t_i \in [0, T]$, $t_i < t_{i+1}$, $i = 1,...,I$, where T is a sufficiently large time to cover the times of default of interest. We now define

$$\phi(t_i) = E_0 h(t_i) \exp\left(-\int_0^{t_i} h(\xi)d\xi\right) i = 1,...,I \tag{5.77}$$

This equation can be solved very efficiently using the techniques explained in Chapter 4. Once the array $\phi(t_i)$ is known, we can compute the nominal density at default time, $\phi(\tau)$, $\tau \neq t_i$, using an appropriate interpolation technique. This is very effective and suitable for Monte Carlo simulations.

To construct the importance density, define now another default intensity function, $\hat{h}(t)$, which produces default times with probability density $\hat{\phi}(t)$. If we let $\hat{\tau}$ denote the default times drawn from $\hat{\phi}$, we can estimate the value of the credit put as follows:

$$V(0) = \frac{1}{n} \sum_{i=1}^{i=n} \frac{P(\hat{\tau}_i)}{\beta(\hat{\tau}_i)} \frac{\phi(\hat{\tau}_i)}{\hat{\phi}(\hat{\tau}_i)} \tag{5.78}$$

As we discussed before, the ratio $\frac{\phi(\hat{\tau}_i)}{\hat{\phi}(\hat{\tau}_i)}$ is the *likelihood ratio*.

There are several choices to select $\hat{h}(t)$.

■ Assume a stochastic process for $\hat{h}(t)$ with the same initial values and drift but higher volatility than that of $h(t)$.
■ Assume a stochastic process for $\hat{h}(t)$ with the same volatility but higher initial value and drift than that of $h(t)$.
■ Assume $\hat{h}(t)$ is a deterministic function.
■ Assume that $\hat{h}(t)$ is a process unrelated to that of $h(t)$.

Of these possibilities, the simplest one, namely, setting $\hat{h}(t)$ to a deterministic function of time, is usually quite effective. The first one and the last ones are unlikely to be effective.

Assume we choose $\hat{h} = $ const. This gives us a simple analytical expression for the importance default density:

$$\hat{\phi}(t) = e^{-\hat{h}t}\hat{h} \qquad (5.79)$$

To start the simulation, we select default times from $\hat{\phi}(\tau)$. To do this, we equate $\lambda\tau$ to an exponential variate. Denote by U_i a draw from the uniform distribution in [0, 1]. Then,

$$\hat{\tau}_i = -\frac{1}{\hat{h}}\log(U_i) \qquad (5.80)$$

With this, the estimation of the value is as follows:

$$V(0) = \frac{1}{n}\sum_{i=1}^{i=n}\frac{P(\hat{\tau}_i)}{\beta(\hat{\tau}_i)}\frac{\phi(\hat{\tau}_i)}{e^{-\hat{h}\hat{\tau}_i}\hat{h}} \qquad (5.81)$$

To understand the power of this approach, we consider a simple case where the credit put pays a constant amount in case of default, and where the money market account is $\beta(t) = \exp(rt)$, with r constant. Figure 5.6 shows the acceleration factors that can be obtained when the default intensity is 0.01. Figure 5.7 shows the acceleration factors when the default intensity is 0.02. Both figures were done on the same scale to visualize the different performance of importance sampling when the default intensity changes.

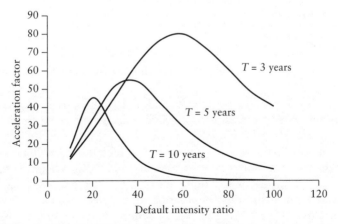

FIGURE 5.6 Credit put pricing by importance sampling. Acceleration factors assuming $\eta = 1$ for $h = 0.01$, 10 percent discount rate, constant payments on default, and maturities of 3, 5, and 10 years. Default intensity ratio is $\frac{\hat{h}}{h}$.

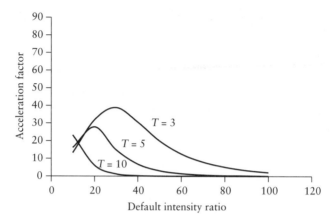

FIGURE 5.7 Credit put pricing by importance sampling. Acceleration factors assuming $\eta = 1$ for $h = 0.02$, 10 percent discount rate, constant payments on default, and maturities of 3, 5, and 10 years. Default intensity ratio is $\frac{\tilde{h}}{h}$.

From these figures, we see that importance sampling as described here is more efficient for short maturities and low default intensities. This is very fortunate because low default intensity and short maturities are the most challenging cases if no acceleration is used.

We should expect much greater benefits from this technique if there is significant work in computing the payments on default, or in getting the discount factor. This would be the case when the interest rate is stochastic, or when the model used for the discount curve involves the numerical integration of a stochastic differential equation.

MOMENT MATCHING

When constructing trajectories (in the simplest case each trajectory may consist of just two points, the starting and end values), we use basic random variables. Typically, these basic random variables are standard normal variables generated from uniform deviates. Since we build a finite number of trajectories, we use a finite number of (typically) normal random variables to build our scenarios. The *moment matching technique* consists of altering the basic random variables used in building the scenarios such that some of the moments of the finite set of these random variables are the same as the moments of their population. If our basic random variables are standard normals, there are two ways to implement the moment matching technique. We can require that the mean of our sample of standard normals must be zero and not worry about their variance, or we may require that their mean should be zero and their variance should be one.

If we use a set of n standard normals Z_i, $i = 1, \ldots, n$, using their sample mean and variance,

$$E[Z] = \frac{1}{n} \sum_{i=1}^{i=n} Z_i \qquad (5.82)$$

$$\mathrm{var}\,[Z] = \frac{1}{n} \sum_{i=1}^{i=n} (Z_i - E[Z])^2 \qquad (5.83)$$

we can define new random variables, $\hat{Z}$, with zero mean,

$$\hat{Z}_i = Z_i - E[Z] \qquad (5.84)$$

or new random variables, $\hat{Z}$, with zero mean and unit variance,

$$\tilde{Z}_i = \frac{Z_i - E[Z]}{\sqrt{\mathrm{var}\,[Z]}} \qquad (5.85)$$

The evaluation of the derivative price is done by replacing the Z_i with $\hat{Z}_i$ or $\tilde{Z}_i$.

Although this appears trivial, implementing this technique in simulation algorithms requires some care. The new random variables are not independent. One consequence of this is that we can no longer use the variance of the samples to determine the standard error. Instead, we must resort to *batching*. This means that we must compute the standard error of the estimated option price by simulating the estimated option price. Since this amounts to a Monte Carlo within a Monte Carlo, the computational time involved can be significantly larger than the case where we deal with iid random variables. Another consequence is that a naive substitution of a normal random number generator with the transformed variates $\hat{Z}$ or $\tilde{Z}$ may lead to bad output. To illustrate this point, consider what happens when we price a discretely sampled Asian option. Such an option pays on the difference between the arithmetic average of the underlying price as sampled discretely between inception and maturity. An efficient implementation using standard normals would consist of generating price trajectories and building the average value as the trajectory is built. Once the payoff is evaluated, the trajectory information is no longer needed and the memory space used for that trajectory is used for the next trajectory. To advance the trajectory from one sampling time to the next, we need to invoke a normal random number generator repeatedly. In the case of a log-normal price process,

$$S(t_{i+1}) = S(t_i)\exp\left(\left(r - \frac{1}{2}\sigma^2\right)(t_{i+1} - t_i) + \sqrt{t_{i+1} - t_i}\,\sigma Z_i\right) \quad i = 1, \ldots, I \quad (5.86)$$

TABLE 5.1   Effect of moment matching on standard deviation of European call option price.

σ_C without MM	σ_C with mean matching	σ_C with full MM
0.33	0.186 (accel. 1.77)	0.048 (accel. 6.87)

Note: $\sigma = 0.4$, spot = 100, strike = 100, risk-free rate = 0.1, maturity 1 year.

where I is the number of monitoring points. To properly capture path dependency, the Z_i must be independent and normally distributed. If we are using standard normals to draw the Z_i, we can build the trajectories according to Equation 5.86 one after another, and the function that generates the Z_i does not need to know about the trajectories themselves. To match moments, however, Equation 5.86 would have to be written as

$$S^j(t_{i+1}) = S^j(t_i)\exp\left(\left(r - \frac{1}{2}\sigma^2\right)(t_{i+1} - t_i) + \sqrt{t_{i+1} - t_i}\,\sigma\hat{Z}_{i,j}\right)$$

$$i = 1,\ldots, I, j = 1,\ldots, J$$

(5.87)

where J is the number of Monte Carlo replications (or number of trajectories). Here, the $\tilde{Z}_{i,j}$ have had their moments matched in the j direction, not in the i direction. This guarantees that the cross-sectional basic random variables are independent. Clearly, this says that now the algorithm that generates the modified basic random variables needs to know about trajectories. This has some effect on algorithm design and implementation.

Moment matching is not guaranteed to be helpful, but in some cases it is remarkably helpful. Table 5.1 shows the standard error of a simple European call option, simulated with 10000 Monte Carlo replications. The standard deviation of the option price, σ_C, was computed by batching the simulation 200 times.

Table 5.2 shows similar results for a European discretely sampled arithmetic Asia call. Clearly, the moment matching technique is far more effective with the standard European call than with the arithmetic Asian call. This is a common situation, where the effectiveness of the technique must be evaluated on a case-by-case basis.

TABLE 5.2   Effect of moment matching on standard deviation of European discretely sampled Asian call option price.

σ_C without MM	σ_C with mean matching	σ_C with full MM
0.178	0.104 (accel. 1.71)	0.093 (accel. 1.91)

Note: $\sigma = 0.4$, spot = 100, strike = 100, risk-free rate = 0.1, maturity 1 year, monitoring interval = 0.1 year

In summary, we can say the following about moment matching.

- Works by making the properties of the input random variables consistent with the population.
- Easy to implement, but may have algorithm design consequences.
- Transformed variables are no longer independent. Must use batching to get standard error.
- In implementation, care must be taken to preserve independence of cross-sectional random variables.
- There is no guarantee of performance. Must be tested on a case-by-case basis.

STRATIFICATION

Stratification is a technique that shares some of the conceptual ideas of importance sampling and low discrepancy sequences. In importance sampling, we accelerate the simulation by sampling from a distribution (the importance distribution) different from the original distribution, but which emphasizes the regions of greater importance. Stratification does not modify the distribution, but allocates the sampling points such that important regions are better captured. As in low discrepancy sequences, stratification avoids the clustering typical of naive Monte Carlo.

The basic idea in stratification is to divide the region where the random variable is defined into disjoint subregions. The expectation is then computed as the sum of the expectations in each subregion. The subregions are called *strata* or *stratification regions*. This is illustrated in Figure 5.8. Here, the subregions are one-dimensional intervals. In

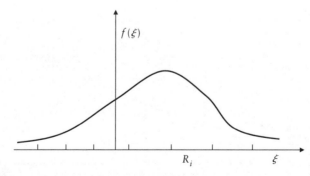

FIGURE 5.8 **Stratification in one dimension.** The region where the random variable is defined is divided into subregions R_i, where the payoff function is sampled. $f(\xi)$ is the probability density function of ξ.

multiple dimensions, the idea is similar, but the subregions are multidimensional cells.

Assuming that the stratification subregions R_i are given, our task is to determine how to distribute the sampling points across the subregions, or, in other words, how to allocate sampling points to different strata, such that the variance of the expectation estimator is minimized. Denote the underlying stochastic variable by ξ and the function whose expectation we want by $F(\xi)$. In pricing a derivative, $F(\xi)$ is a discounted payoff function. Depending how we pose the problem, ξ can be the underlying price, the Wiener process used to construct the underlying price, the standard normal variable used to construct the Wiener process, or the [0, 1] uniform random variates used to generate the standard normals. The expectation of the discounted payoff in a subregion is

$$V_i = E[F(\xi)|_{\xi \in R_i}] \tag{5.88}$$

and the derivative value is

$$V = \sum_{i=1}^{i=m} V_i \tag{5.89}$$

where we assume that there are m subregions.

To analyze stratification we define subpayoff functions, $F_i(\xi)$, such that $F_i(\xi) = F(\xi)$ if $\xi \in R_i$ and $F_i(\xi) = 0$ if $\xi \notin R_i$. This is shown graphically for the one-dimensional case in Figure 5.9.

With this, Equation 5.88 can be written as

$$V_i = p_i \hat{E}[F_i(\xi)] \tag{5.90}$$

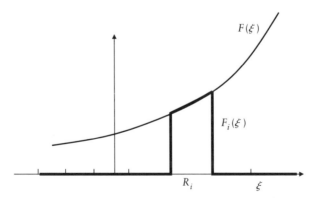

FIGURE 5.9 Stratification in one dimension. The subpayoff function $F_i(\xi)$ agrees with $F(\xi)$ in subregion R_i and is zero elsewhere.

where p_i is the probability mass in R_i, and the expectation is taken with respect to a probability density equal to $\frac{f(\xi)}{p_i}$ if $\xi \in R_i$ and equal to 0 otherwise (with this definition, this probability density integrates to 1 over the range of ξ). Replacing in Equation 5.89 we get

$$V = \sum_{i=1}^{i=m} p_i \hat{E}[F_i(\xi)] \tag{5.91}$$

We can now estimate the expectation in Equation 5.91 by averaging the samples of $F_i(.)$ over the entire range of ξ. However, the only nonzero values of F_i are for $\xi \in R_i$, where $F_i = F$. This gives us:

$$\overline{V} = \sum_{i=1}^{i=m} p_i \frac{1}{n_i} \sum_{j=1}^{j=n_i} F(\xi_j) \tag{5.92}$$

To compute the variance of $\overline{V}$ we use the fact that the random variables on the right-hand side of Equation 5.92 are independent:

$$\text{var}[\overline{V}] = \sum_{i=1}^{i=m} \frac{p_i^2 \sigma_i^2}{n_i} \tag{5.93}$$

In Equation 5.93, σ_i^2 is the variance of $F(\xi)$ over R_i. The analytical expression for this variance is

$$\sigma_i^2 = \hat{E}[(F(\xi))^2] - \hat{E}^2[F(\xi)]$$

$$= \int_{R_i} F(\xi)^2 \frac{f(\xi)}{p_i} d\xi - \frac{V_i^2}{p_i^2}$$

$$= \frac{1}{p_i} \left(\int_{R_i} (F(\xi))^2 f(\xi) d\xi - \frac{V_i^2}{p_i} \right) \tag{5.94}$$

To determine the best allocation of n_i to the strata R_i, we must solve the following constrained minimization problem:

$$\min_{n_i} \left(\sum_{i=1}^{i=m} \frac{p_i^2 \sigma_i^2}{n_i} \right) \tag{5.95}$$

subject to the constraint

$$\sum_{i=1}^{i=m} n_i - n = 0 \tag{5.96}$$

This problem is easy to solve using Lagrange multipliers (Courant and John, 1974). Introducing the Lagrange multiplier λ, we must solve the system of equations,

$$\frac{\partial}{\partial n_j}\left(\sum_{i=1}^{i=m} \frac{p_i^2 \sigma_i^2}{n_i} + \lambda\left(\sum_{i=1}^{i=m} n_i - n \right) \right) = 0, \quad j = 1,\ldots, m$$

(5.97)

$$\sum_{i=1}^{i=m} n_i - n = 0$$

This is a system of $m + 1$ equations and $m + 1$ unknowns (n_i and λ). From the first equation in Equation 5.97 we get

$$n_i = \frac{p_i \sigma_i}{\sqrt{\lambda}}$$

(5.98)

Replacing n_i in the second equation in Equation 5.97 we get

$$\sqrt{\lambda} = \frac{\sum_{i=1}^{i=m} p_i \sigma_i}{n}$$

(5.99)

Replacing $\sqrt{\lambda}$ in Equation 5.98 we get the following formula for the optimal allocation of sampling points in subregions:

$$n_i = \frac{n p_i \sigma_i}{\sum_{j=1}^{j=m} p_j \sigma_j}, \quad i = 1,\ldots, m$$

(5.100)

where p_j is the probability mass of the jth region and σ_j is the standard deviation of the random variable over the jth region. If sampling points are allocated according to Equation 5.100, it is easy to verify that the variance of the mean estimator is

$$\sigma_{\bar{V}}^2 = \frac{1}{n}\left(\sum_{i=1}^{i=m} p_i \sigma_i \right)^2$$

(5.101)

How useful is this in practice? Of course, the σ_i are not known in advance. The analytical expression given by Equation 5.94 assumes that we already know V_i. If we knew this, we would not bother any further with the problem. One potential approach is to conduct a preliminary simulation to roughly assess what the σ_i should be. This is along the lines of the preliminary estimation of the covariance in the control variate approach we discussed earlier.

We will not elaborate on this. Instead, we will now discuss two practical approaches for implementing stratification for financial pricing.

In practice, stratification is implemented in the $[0, 1]^d$ hypercube, which is the range of independent uniform variates used to generate correlated normals. The simplest thing to do is to divide the $[0, 1]^d$ hypercube into uniform cells and allocate one sampling point to each cell. In doing this, we don't worry about the approach being implemented optimally, but we do concentrate on simplicity.

This simple form of stratification is extremely efficient in one dimension, but the data requirements grow very quickly with the number of dimensions. Why would this be preferable to simply dividing the domain in uniform cells and performing a deterministic integration? One reason is that although this is a crude approach, unlike deterministic integration it is a simulation and allows us to determine a standard error. To determine the standard error we cannot simply increase the number of strata. The outcomes that result from increasing the number of strata are not independent. As a result, we must use batching, where the computation is repeated a number of times with different starting conditions.

Stratified Standard Normals in One Dimension

If U_i, $i = 1, ..., n$ are independent uniforms on $[0, 1]$, the following transformation gives us uniforms in the intervals $\left[\frac{i-1}{n}, \frac{1}{n}\right]$, $i = 1, ..., n$:

$$\tilde{U}_i = \frac{i - 1 + U_i}{n}, \quad i = 1, ..., n \tag{5.102}$$

We obtain the stratified standard normals through the transformation

$$Z_i = \Phi^{-1}(\tilde{U}_i) \tag{5.103}$$

where $\Phi(.)$ is the cumulative standard normal distribution function. The following two figures illustrate one-dimensional stratification on the standard normal distribution. Figure 5.10 shows a histogram of 1000 samples without stratification. Figure 5.11 shows a histogram of 1000 normals with the simple stratified sampling we are discussing. Not surprisingly, stratification produces a much better description of the distribution.

Although the most obvious application of one-dimensional stratification is the pricing of options that depend on a single underlying process, this does not mean that the use of one-dimensional stratification is limited to one-dimensional problems. As we discussed in Chapter 4, the construction of trajectories is actually a multidimensional problem, meaning that we need to simulate the Wiener process at intermediate times between onset and maturity.

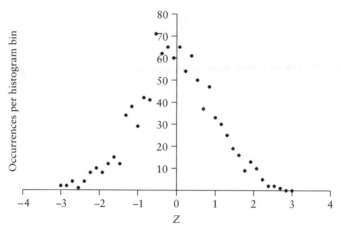

FIGURE 5.10 Simulation histogram of standard normals. Histogram consists of 40 bins from −3 to +3. 1000 replications.

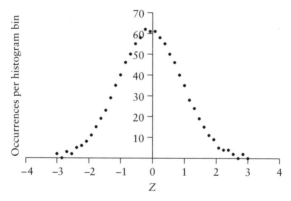

FIGURE 5.11 Simulation histogram of stratified standard normals. Histogram consists of 40 bins from −3 to +3. 1000 strata.

The use of one-dimensional stratification may be useful in constructing trajectories using the Brownian bridge approach. In this case, we first get the end values of the Wiener process using one-dimensional stratification, and then we fill in the intermediate values of the Wiener process using the Brownian bridge and sampling without stratification. Since, as we discussed in Chapter 4, most of the variability is captured by the Wiener process at maturity, this approach could be an attractive alternative for path-dependent options.

Another variation would be to use a two-dimensional stratification for the first two dimensions of the Brownian bridge construction (the terminal and middle points of the Wiener process). Next we discuss a procedure closely related to this type of stratification.

Latin Hypercube Sampling

Latin hypercube sampling (LHS) (Press et al., 1992) is a technique for implementing stratified sampling. Unlike the simple form of stratified sampling we discussed in the last section, which places one sample point on each cell in the unit hypercube, LHS places one sample point in each column and in each row of cells. No cell has more than one sample point. Figure 5.12 shows how four sample points are allocated in two dimensions. In LHS, increasing the number of sampling points means increasing the number of rows and columns.

Figure 5.13 shows 128 Latin hypercube samples in two dimensions.

Picking a point in multiple dimensions with Latin hypercube sampling is equivalent to sampling randomly from stratification in each dimension without replacement. Figure 5.14 shows how this works.

This idea can be encoded into the following algorithm for generating up to n uniform sample points in d dimensions:

$$\tilde{U}_i^j = \frac{\pi_j[i] - U_i^j}{n}, \quad i = 1,\ldots,n, j = 1,\ldots,d \tag{5.104}$$

where each π_j is an array of random permutations of $1,\ldots,n$, and $\pi_j[i]$ is the ith element of the array.

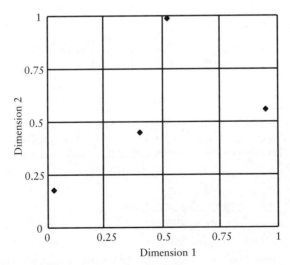

FIGURE 5.12 Latin hypercube sampling in two dimensions. 4 sample points are allocated to 4 rows and 4 columns.

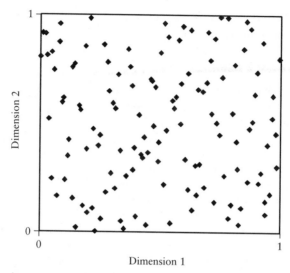

FIGURE 5.13 Latin hypercube sampling in two dimensions. 128 sample points are allocated to 128 rows and 128 columns.

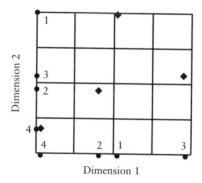

FIGURE 5.14 Latin hypercube sampling in two dimensions constructed from two one-dimensional stratifications. The round symbols are points from the one-dimensional stratifications. The numbers indicate a possible random sequence for selecting the points in each direction.

Case Study: Latin Hypercube Sampling
Applied to Exotic Basket Option

The fact that LHS places one sampling point per row and column has the intuitive outcome that LHS will work best when there is little interaction among dimensions. In financial pricing, interaction among the dimensions of the problem have two sources. One source is the correlation between underlying processes. The other source encompasses both the payoff condition and the boundary conditions. Of these, the payoff condition is likely to be the most significant source of interaction among underlying processes in most cases. Unfortunately, interesting financial derivatives have payoff conditions that tend to induce significant interaction among the underlying processes. The one derivative that does not introduce any interaction among the underlying processes is a basket forward, not a particularly exotic case.

We can explore some of the properties of the LHS method by looking at a basket call option with the following features. Given assets S_i, $i = 1, \ldots, n_s$, and two strike prices K_1 and K_2, the payoff is defined as follows:

$$F(T) = \min \left[\left(\sum_{i=1}^{i=n_s} \max \, [S_i(T) - K_1, 0] \right), K_2 \right] \qquad (5.105)$$

This option is a basket of calls with a binary cap. The basket consists of n_s calls with strike K_1, one on each asset S_i. If the sum of the individual calls at maturity exceeds K_2, the holder receives the amount K_2. Otherwise she receives the basket of calls. We assume that all spots are equal, such that $S_i(0) = S_0$, $i = 1, \ldots, n_s$.

This option is an interesting test example because by changing K_1 and K_2 we can encompass three features.

- If $K_1 \to 0$ and $K_2 \to \infty$, the option becomes a basket forward. In this case there is no interdependence among assets induced by the payoff.
- If $K_1 = \mathcal{O}(S_0)$ and $K_2 \to \infty$, the option becomes a basket of calls. In this case there is no interdependence among assets induced by payoff, but the payoff is nonlinear in each dimension.
- If $K_1 = \mathcal{O}(S_0)$ and $K_2 = \mathcal{O}(\Sigma(S(0) - K_1))$, the option payoff induces strong interdependence.

We will consider a case of eight log-normal assets, with risk-free rate 0.05, volatility 0.3, and time to maturity 1 year. We consider two correlation matrices, one with 0.2 and one with 0.8 correlation between asset returns, respectively. Table 5.3 shows the standard deviations of the value estimator for standard Monte Carlo and LHS. The runs were done with 1000 replications. The standard deviations for the LHS case were computed with 20 batches. These numbers are only a guide, but they clearly reveal that the LHS method becomes increasingly more desirable as the importance of the nonlinear features of the payoff decreases.

Table 5.4 shows the case where $K_1 \to 0$ and $K_2 \to \infty$. It is clear now that the effectiveness of the LHS is much greater than that of standard

TABLE 5.3   Standard error of standard MC and LHS for exotic basket call.

20 percent correlation			80 percent correlation		
K_2	ϵ_{MC}	ϵ_{LHS}	K_2	ϵ_{MC}	ϵ_{LHS}
100	2.4	1.9	100	3.5	3.0
200	1.8	1.2	200	2.8	1.5
400	2.3	0.5	400	3.7	1.3

Note: Volatility = 0.3, spots = 100, strike = 100, risk-free rate = 0.05, maturity 1 year. ϵ_{MC} and ϵ_{LHS} are the standard deviations of the value estimator in percentage. The Latin Hypercube becomes increasingly more effective as the digital feature becomes less important and the assets return become less correlated.

TABLE 5.4   Standard error of standard MC and LHS for forward basket limit.

20 percent correlation		80 percent correlation	
ϵ_{MC}	ϵ_{LHS}	ϵ_{MC}	ϵ_{LHS}
0.5	0.04	0.9	0.08

Note: Volatility = 0.3, spots = 100, risk-free rate = 0.05, maturity 1 year. ϵ_{MC} and ϵ_{LHS} are the standard deviations of the value estimator in percentage. The Latin Hypercube is an order of magnitude more effective.

Monte Carlo. As the asset returns correlation increases, the effectiveness of the LHS decreases, but so does the effectiveness of the standard Monte Carlo. The standard deviation ratios remain the same. The batching size is the same as in Table 5.3.

EFFECT OF DISCRETIZATION ON ACCURACY AND THE EMERGENCE OF COMPUTATIONAL BARRIERS

As we saw in Chapter 4, the construction of trajectories by numerical integration of the stochastic differential equations governing underlying processes introduces a discretization error. The discretization error is different, depending on whether we are referring to the accuracy with which the paths themselves or the accuracy with which functionals of the process are computed. If we focus on the accuracy of the paths, the discretization error arises from the weak convergence properties of the numerical scheme. The Euler scheme, for example, has an order of weak convergence of 0.5, meaning that the discretization error in computing paths is of order $\sqrt{\Delta t}$, where Δt is the time integration step. The discretization error on moments arises from the strong convergence properties of the numerical scheme. Using the Euler scheme we can compute moments with a discretization error of order Δt.

The only way to generate trajectories of general underlying processes that are not subject to error is to solve the stochastic differential equation analytically. In many cases of practical importance this is not possible. This is particularly the case when we work with implied local volatility functions (the $\sigma(S, t)$ in $\frac{dS}{S} = \mu dt + \sigma(S, t)dW$). In such cases we must construct trajectories by numerical solution of the stochastic differential equation.

If we use a numerical scheme (such as the Euler scheme) to build approximate trajectories of the underlying process and then use Monte Carlo simulation to price an option that depends on that underlying process, we confront a complication in defining the convergence of our Monte Carlo simulation. Our simulation will converge at the rate $\frac{1}{\sqrt{n}}$, where n is the number of Monte Carlo replications, to a value that is consistent with the *approximate* trajectories calculated with the numerical scheme. Clearly, this value, to which the Monte Carlo converges, is not the true value we seek. That true value will be consistent with exact solutions of the SDE governing the underlying process, not with the approximate solutions given by the numerical integration scheme.

Two questions arise.

- How far should the Monte Carlo be pushed, given that the trajectories it uses are approximate?
- How does the computational effort of the Monte Carlo scale with the true accuracy of the solution?

As far as the first question goes, it does not make sense to try to extract more accuracy out of the simulation than is embedded in the approximate nature of the trajectories. An elaboration of this idea gives us the answer to the second question. We will see that when there is numerical discretization error of order Δt, the scaling law between accuracy and computational effort jumps from $\frac{1}{\text{accuracy}^2}$ to $\frac{1}{\text{accuracy}^3}$. This is extremely important and means that when using a numerical scheme such as Euler, eventually we have to use *eight* times more effort to double the accuracy of our calculation. Of course, this transition from the second to the third power of the accuracy may occur *after* we have attained the accuracy we want. However, if the accuracy we want, given the discretization parameters we are currently using, places our computation in the $\frac{1}{\text{accuracy}^3}$ scaling, we confront what we call a *computational barrier,* where further increases in accuracy come at much higher computational expense.

We now quantify these ideas. We are solving a pricing problem by simulation and we will assume we build trajectories of the underlying process, $S(t)$, by numerically solving

$$dS(t) = a(S, t)dt + b(S, t)dW \tag{5.106}$$

using the Euler scheme, with an order of weak convergence Δt. The error in computing functionals of $S(t)$ will be

$$\epsilon_{\Delta t} = \beta \Delta t \tag{5.107}$$

where β is a constant. The error due to the Monte Carlo convergence is

$$\epsilon_{MC} = \frac{\sigma_C}{\sqrt{n}} \tag{5.108}$$

where σ_C is the standard deviation of our option value estimator. Since it makes sense that these two errors should be of the same order, we set $\epsilon_{MC} = \epsilon_{\Delta t}$ and get the relationship

$$\frac{\Delta t}{T} = \frac{1}{T\beta} \frac{\sigma_C}{\sqrt{n}} \tag{5.109}$$

where T is the maturity over which we solve the underlying stochastic differential equation numerically. Since there are $\frac{T}{\Delta t}$ evaluations of the underlying process in each Monte Carlo replication, the computational effort, W_C, in the simulation scales as follows:

$$W_C \propto \frac{T}{\Delta t} n \tag{5.110}$$

Since the error in the computation, ϵ, is assumed to be of the same order as the Monte Carlo and discretization errors, with Equations 5.109 and 5.110 we get

$$W_C \propto T\beta \frac{\sigma_C^2}{\epsilon^3} \tag{5.111}$$

If there were no discretization of the underlying process involved, the computational effort would scale like $\frac{\sigma_C^2}{\epsilon^2}$ *regardless* of the level of accuracy we seek.

In the next subsbsections we will determine the number of Monte Carlo replications beyond which no further improvement in accuracy is possible without a much larger computational effort. Doing this analysis for general cases of nonlinear stochastic differential equations is difficult and is not done in practical applications. The purpose of the analysis that follows is to gain an understanding of what may happen when discretization error and the standard Monte Carlo error are equally dominant.

We will do the analysis on the standard log-normal process integrated with the Euler scheme. Of course, in practice we don't have to integrate the log-normal process approximately with a numerical scheme because the solution to the stochastic differential equation is known analytically. But our objective is to illustrate the fundamentals. To this end, the simple log-normal process is ideal.

We will consider two cases in detail. First, we look at the discretization error of the mean and variance of the log-normal process when the SDE is integrated with the Euler scheme. Then, we consider the error induced by the discretization when trajectories of a price process are used to price a European call option.

Discretization Error for the Log-Normal Process

Consider the log-normal process described by

$$\frac{dS}{S} = \mu dt + \sigma dW(t) \tag{5.112}$$

where μ and σ are constant and $W(t)$ is a Wiener process.

Consider now the process defined by the following difference (not differential) stochastic equation, which results from applying the Euler scheme to Equation 5.112:

$$\hat{S}(t + \Delta t) - \hat{S}(t) = \hat{S}(t)\mu\Delta t + \hat{S}(t)\sigma\Delta W \tag{5.113}$$

where Δt is finite and constant. The solution $\hat{S}(t)$ is an approximation to the exact solution $S(t)$. We will determine how the expected value and variance of process $\hat{S}(t)$ differ from the expected value and variance of $S(t)$ using a simple first order perturbation technique.[1]

The exact process $S(t)$ and the approximate process $\hat{S}(t)$ are related as follows:

$$\hat{S}(n\Delta t) = S(n\Delta t) + \epsilon(n\Delta t), \quad n = 1, 2, \dots \tag{5.114}$$

---

[1]Actually, in the simple case of the log-normal process, the expectation and variance of the approximate process can be computed exactly. We will use the perturbation technique, however, because it is a method of general validity.

where n is the integration step number and $\epsilon(.)$ is an error term, itself a stochastic process (this ϵ is not the same as the one in the previous section). We will interpret the functions $E[\hat{S}(t)]$ and $\text{var}[\hat{S}(t)]$ as continuous functions of time that agree with the expectation and variance of the the process $\hat{S}(t)$ at $t = n\Delta t$, $n = 1, 2, \ldots$

Discretization Error of the Mean Taking expectation of both sides of Equation 5.113, the mean of the approximate log-normal process satisfies

$$E[\hat{S}(t + \Delta t)] - E[\hat{S}(t)] = E[\hat{S}(t)]\mu\Delta t \qquad (5.115)$$

where we remember to assume μ is a constant. The mean of the exact process follows the differential form of the last equation:

$$\frac{dE[S(t)]}{dt} = E[S(t)]\mu \qquad (5.116)$$

Expanding the left-hand side of Equation 5.115 to second order in Δt we have

$$\frac{dE[\hat{S}(t)]}{dt} + \frac{\Delta t}{2}\frac{d^2E[\hat{S}(t)]}{dt^2} = E[\hat{S}(t)]\mu \qquad (5.117)$$

Replacing

$$E[\hat{S}(t)] = E[S(t)] + E[\epsilon(t)] \qquad (5.118)$$

in Equation 5.117 we get

$$\frac{dE[S]}{dt} + \frac{dE[\epsilon]}{dt} + \frac{\Delta t}{2}\frac{d^2E[S]}{dt^2} + \frac{\Delta t}{2}\frac{d^2E[\epsilon]}{dt^2} = E[S]\mu + E[\epsilon]\mu \qquad (5.119)$$

where we drop the arguments in $S(.)$ and $\epsilon(.)$ for convenience. Notice that the fourth term on the left is of higher order. Since we are doing a first-order analysis, we can neglect this term. Replacing Equation 5.116 into Equation 5.119 we get

$$\frac{dE[\epsilon]}{dt} = \mu E[\epsilon] - \frac{\Delta t}{2}\frac{d^2E[S]}{dt^2} \qquad (5.120)$$

Introducing Equation 5.116 into Equation 5.120, we get the following first-order ordinary differential equation for the error of the mean:

$$\frac{dE[\epsilon]}{dt} = \mu E[\epsilon] - \mu \frac{\Delta t}{2} \frac{dE[S]}{dt} \qquad (5.121)$$

The mean of the exact log-normal process is

$$E[S(t)] = S(0)\exp(\mu t) \qquad (5.122)$$

where $S(0)$ is the initial process value. Since the initial conditions of the approximate process, $\hat{S}(t)$, and the exact process, $S(t)$, are the same, Equation 5.121 can be written as follows:

$$\frac{dE[\epsilon]}{dt} = \mu E[\epsilon] - \mu \frac{\Delta t}{2} S(0)\exp(\mu t) \qquad (5.123)$$

Since, by definition, the initial error is zero, the solution of Equation 5.123 is

$$E[\epsilon(t)] = -\mu \frac{\Delta t}{2} S(0)t \exp(\mu t) \qquad (5.124)$$

Remember that ϵ is what we need to add to the *exact* solution to get the approximate solution. Since ϵ is negative, this equation tells us that the first-order effect of the Euler discretization on the log-normal process is to *depress* the mean. To the first order, this effect is only due to the drift (the volatility does not enter in Equation 5.124). Effectively, the discretization induces a downward drift. If the drift of the log-normal process is negative, this distortion will grow at the beginning but will eventually die out as the exponential term begins to dominate. If the drift is positive, the first-order error will grow exponentially.

This simple analysis reveals that the behavior of the discretized process is by no means intuitive. Of course, this result does not carry over to other processes and only serves to illustrate what can be expected.

Discretization Error of the Variance   A little algebra shows that the variance of the approximate process is given by

$$\frac{\text{var}\,[\hat{S}(t+\Delta t)] - \text{var}\,[\hat{S}(t)]}{\Delta t} = (2\mu + \sigma^2)\text{var}\,[\hat{S}(t)] + E^2[\hat{S}(t)]\sigma^2 \\ + \Delta t \mu^2 \text{var}\,[\hat{S}(t)] \qquad (5.125)$$

while the ordinary differential equation for the variance of the exact log-normal process is

$$\frac{d\operatorname{var}[S(t)]}{dt} = (2\mu + \sigma^2)\operatorname{var}[S(t)] + E^2[S(t)]\sigma^2 \qquad (5.126)$$

Expanding the left-hand side of Equation 5.125 and retaining up to second-order terms in Δt, we get

$$\frac{d\operatorname{var}[\hat{S}(t)]}{dt} + \frac{\Delta t}{2}\frac{d^2\operatorname{var}[\hat{S}(t)]}{dt^2} = (2\mu + \sigma^2)\operatorname{var}[\hat{S}(t)] + E^2[\hat{S}(t)]\sigma^2$$
$$+ \Delta t\mu^2\operatorname{var}[\hat{S}(t)] \qquad (5.127)$$

We define the error of the variance as follows:

$$\operatorname{var}[\hat{S}(t)] = \operatorname{var}[S(t)] + \gamma(t) \qquad (5.128)$$

Replacing Equations 5.128 and 5.114 in Equation 5.127 we get

$$\frac{d\operatorname{var}[S]}{dt} + \frac{d\gamma}{dt} + \frac{\Delta t}{2}\frac{d^2\operatorname{var}[S]}{dt^2} + \frac{\Delta t}{2}\frac{d^2\gamma}{dt^2} = (2\mu + \sigma^2)\operatorname{var}[S] + (2\mu + \sigma^2)\gamma$$
$$+ (E[S] + E[\epsilon])^2\sigma^2 + \Delta t\mu^2(\operatorname{var}[S(t)] + \gamma) \qquad (5.129)$$

Replacing Equation 5.126 into Equation 5.129 and neglecting higher-order terms, we get the following first-order ordinary differential equation for the error of the variance:

$$\frac{d\gamma}{dt} = (2\mu + \sigma^2)\gamma - \frac{\Delta t}{2}\frac{d^2\operatorname{var}[S]}{dt^2} E^2[S]\sigma^2 + 2E[S]E[\epsilon]\sigma^2 + \Delta t\mu^2\operatorname{var}[S]$$
$$(5.130)$$

The variance for the exact process can be obtained by integrating Equation 5.126:

$$\operatorname{var}[S] = S(0)^2\exp(2\mu t)(\exp(\sigma^2 t) - 1) \qquad (5.131)$$

Replacing this expression for the variance as well as $E[S(t)]$ and $E[\epsilon]$ in Equation 5.130, we can rewrite the equation for the error of the variance as follows:

$$\frac{d\gamma}{dt} = (2\mu + \sigma^2)\gamma - a\exp((2\mu + \sigma^2)t) + \exp(2\mu t)(b - ct) \qquad (5.132)$$

where

$$a = \Delta t S(0)^2\left(\mu^2 + 2\mu\sigma^2 + \frac{\sigma^4}{2}\right) \qquad (5.133)$$

$$b = \Delta t S(0)^2 \mu^2 \tag{5.134}$$

$$c = \Delta t S(0)^2 \sigma^2 \tag{5.135}$$

Solving Equation 5.132 subject to the initial condition $\gamma(t = 0) = 0$, we obtain the following expression for the error of the variance, valid to first order in Δt:

$$\gamma = \Delta t S(0)^2 \exp((2\mu + \sigma^2)t)\left[\mu^2 t \exp(-\sigma^2 t) - \left(\mu^2 + 2\mu\sigma^2 + \frac{\sigma^4}{2}\right)t\right] \tag{5.136}$$

The quantity in the square bracket in the right-hand side of Equation 5.136 is negative. This tells us that the first-order discretization effect on the trajectories is a lower variance in the approximate process. As we saw in the previous section, the discretization effect is also a lower mean in the approximate process. We must emphasize that these conclusions are only applicable to the log-normal process. The main purpose of the analysis is to illustrate how nonintuitive these effects can be.

Of course, instead of working with the equation for the variance directly, we could have worked with the equations for the moments; the result would have been the same.

The next two figures show how significant the effect of discretization error can be. Figures 5.15 and 5.16 show a case where the log-normal stochastic differential equation was integrated with the Euler scheme using quarterly time steps. Especially for the variance, the numerical distortion can be very significant when the drift is large and positive.

So far we have discussed the effect of discretization on the properties of the trajectories themselves. How does this translate into pricing errors? How much accuracy can we get with the Monte Carlo method before we hit a computational barrier? We discuss this in the next section for a European call.

Discretization Error and Computational Barriers for a European Call[2]

We use the log-normal process to gain insight into the effect of discretization on the derivative price. We analyze the case of a simple European call. A European call on a process with deterministic volatility would not be

---

[2] This analysis was done jointly with Dr. Ervin Zhao.

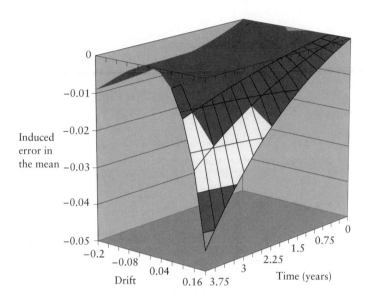

FIGURE 5.15 **Discretization error effect on the mean.** Log-normal process integrated with Euler scheme with time step 0.25, $\sigma = 0.4$. Normalized with $S(0) = 1$.

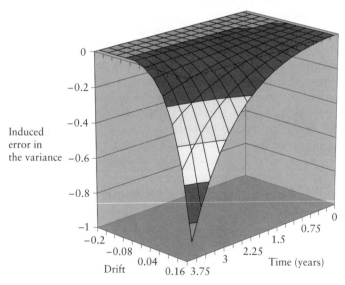

FIGURE 5.16 **Discretization error effect on the variance.** Log-normal process integrated with Euler scheme with time step 0.25, $\sigma = 0.4$. Normalized with $S(0) = 1$.

priced by simulation, but this insight can be useful in cases where we need to use a numerical scheme to construct scenarios.

This is the strategy for analysis.

- We compute the errors induced by discretization in the moments of the log-normal process.
- We construct an approximate probability density function for the simulated log-normal process using the Edgeworth expansion. This allows us to introduce the discretization error in the representation of the approximate pdf.
- The discretization error of the call price is approximately the difference between the price obtained with the approximate probability density represented by the Edgeworth expansion and the log-normal probability density.

As in the previous section, we start out with the approximate process,

$$\hat{S}(t + \Delta t) - \hat{S}(t) = \hat{S}(t)\mu\Delta t + \hat{S}(t)\sigma\Delta W \tag{5.137}$$

We define the error in the moments of the underlying process as follows:

$$E[\hat{S}^n] = E[S^n] + \epsilon_n + \mathcal{O}(\Delta t^2) \tag{5.138}$$

We will not repeat the algebraic steps, but it is straightforward to see that this error is governed by the following ordinary differential equation:

$$\frac{d\epsilon_n}{dt} - A_n\epsilon_n = \frac{\Delta t}{2}B_n E[S^n] \tag{5.139}$$

where

$$
\begin{aligned}
A_1 &= \mu \\
A_n &= n\mu + \frac{1}{2}n(n-1)\sigma^2, n > 1 \\
B_1 &= 0 \\
B_2 &= 2\mu^2 \\
B_3 &= 6\mu^2 + 6\mu\sigma^2 \\
B_n &= n(n-1)\mu^2 + n(n-1)(n-2)\mu\sigma^2 \\
&\quad + \frac{1}{4}n(n-1)(n-2)(n-3)\sigma^4, n > 3
\end{aligned}
\tag{5.140}
$$

Solving Equation 5.139 subject to the initial condition $\epsilon(0) = 0$, we get the following expression for the discretization error of the moments:

$$\epsilon_n = \frac{\Delta t}{2} S(0)^n B_n t \, \exp(A_n t) \tag{5.141}$$

To obtain an expression for the discretization error of the option price, we express the *probability density function* (pdf) of the simulated price process as an *Edgeworth asymptotic expansion* (Abramovitz and Stegun, 1964) about a log-normal pdf whose first two moments are matched to the first two moments of the discretized process. Denoting the pdf of the simulated process at the option maturity by $\hat{f}(.)$ and the log-normal pdf with the first two moments matched by $f(.)$, we have

$$\hat{f}(\xi) = f(\xi) + \sum_{i=3}^{i=\infty} \frac{a_i}{i!} \frac{\partial^i f}{\partial \xi^i} \tag{5.142}$$

with $\xi \in \mathcal{R}$, where the summation on the right-hand side starts with $i = 3$ because the first two moments are matched. Equation 5.142 is an asymptotic expansion and will not converge in general. Here we will limit this expansion to the first two terms, which means that we match the first four moments. We determine the coefficients a_i by requiring that the moments of $\hat{f}$ should equal the moments of its Edgeworth expansion.

With the definitions,

$$\hat{v}_n = \int_0^\infty \xi^n \hat{f}(\xi) d\xi \tag{5.143}$$

$$v_n = \int_0^\infty \xi^n f(\xi) d\xi \tag{5.144}$$

we get the following recursive relationship for the coefficients in Equation 5.142:

$$a_n = (-1)^n (\hat{v}_n - v_n) + \sum_{i=1}^{i=n-1} (-1)^{n-i} \binom{n}{i} a_i v_{n-i} \tag{5.145}$$

In this equation, $\hat{v}_n$ and v_n are the nth moments of $\hat{S}$ and S, respectively, evaluated at $t = T$, where T is the maturity of the call option.

We are now ready to get the effect of the numerically induced error on the option price. The values of the exact and simulated calls are

$$C = \exp(-rT) \int_K^\infty (S - K) f(S) dS \tag{5.146}$$

$$\hat{C} = \exp(-rT) \int_K^\infty (S - K)\hat{f}(S)\, dS \qquad (5.147)$$

where r is the risk-free rate and K is the strike. Using Equation 5.142, we find

$$\hat{C} = C - \exp(-rT) \sum_{i=3}^{i=\infty} \frac{a_i}{i!} \frac{\partial^i f}{\partial \xi^i}(K) \qquad (5.148)$$

The error in the price is then

$$\epsilon_C = -\exp(-rT) \sum_{i=3}^{i=\infty} \frac{a_i}{i!} \frac{\partial^i f}{\partial \xi^i}(K) \qquad (5.149)$$

To determine the number of Monte Carlo replications beyond which we cannot increase the accuracy of the simulation for a given integration time step (remember we assume we are using the Euler scheme to solve the stochastic differential equation), we equate ϵ_C to the standard error of the option price estimator. The following table (5.5) shows exact call option prices for the same underlying process discussed in the previous

TABLE 5.5 Discretization error effect on a European call.

Strike	T = 1	T = 1.25	T = 1.5	T = 1.75	T = 2
30	21.434	21.789	22.143	22.496	22.847
35	15.731	17.179	17.627	18.071	18.510
40	12.253	12.834	13.401	13.951	14.486
45	8.311	9.021	9.693	10.333	10.946
50	5.193	5.957	6.673	7.352	8.000
55	2.997	3.709	4.389	5.043	5.674
60	1.608	2.190	2.772	3.350	3.921
65	0.811	1.236	1.691	2.165	2.650
70	0.387	0.671	1.002	1.368	1.759

Note: The bolded digits represent the accuracy bound consistent with a quarterly time step. Log-normal process integrated with Euler Scheme with time step 0.25, $\sigma = 0.4$. Spot = 50, risk-free rate = 0.1. Maturities in years.

section. The integration step is quarterly. The bolded figures in the table indicate the digits that cannot be improved upon, given the fact that we are solving the trajectories by quarterly integration. Given that increasing the accuracy can only be achieved by reducing the time step, we see that moving the order of accuracy by one order of magnitude would cause the computational work to increase by a magnitude that scales like 10^3. This marks the onset of a computational barrier that becomes increasingly costly to overcome.

CHAPTER 6

Simulation for Early Exercise

E fficient pricing of instruments with early exercise features is an evolving topic of ongoing research. As of this writing, it is only recently that simulation methods of practical value have become available to the practitioner. The initial sections of this chapter follow a somewhat historical account of earlier attempts in early exercise simulation, leading up to the least squares Monte Carlo method, currently the approach of choice. This method is discussed in sufficient detail to enable the reader to produce realistic implementations.

THE BASIC DIFFICULTY IN PRICING EARLY EXERCISE WITH SIMULATION

The two greatest challenges in pricing instruments are path dependency and dimensionality. Early exercise in itself is not a particularly difficult challenge from a numerical viewpoint. The type of path dependency that creates a challenge is not the one produced by the payoff features of the instrument, but the one caused by the driving processes themselves. The reason why this type of path dependency is a challenge is that there is no corresponding partial differential equation to solve for the derivative price. This means that when we have path dependency at the process level, such as in the case of the Heath-Jarrow-Morton model for the forward rate, simulation is the only way to tackle the problem.

If the number of dimensions is small (less than four), and the underlying processes are Markovian, the finite difference approach, discussed extensively in the next chapter, is a robust strategy. This method is fast, its convergence properties are well understood, it can accommodate complex payoff requirements, and it is capable of dealing with both continuous as well as discrete exercise.

When the number of dimensions is three or larger, however, finite differences and other methodologies, such as finite elements, confront a fundamental difficulty. This difficulty has to do with data storage requirements. Assuming that the underlying processes are Markovian, it is important to realize that dimensionality is not a problem because of a burden imposed on artithmetic operations. Dimensionality is fundamentally a data problem. The reason for this is that as the number of dimensions increases, storage requirements may become unfeasible with some methodologies, such as the finite difference method.

When the number of dimensions is large, there are no satisfactory deterministic methods for pricing.

It is well known that simulation applied to the computation of expectations over a known time horizon is not affected by dimensionality. The convergence law of an expectation only depends on the variance of the price population, not on the number of stochastic dimensions of the population. Simulation, on the other hand, is a slow methodology unless clever acceleration techniques are used. The possibility of finding ways to accelerate the simulation, together with the fact that convergence is not affected by the number of dimensions, explain why Monte Carlo simulation has been so popular in pricing European derivatives.

In the case of instruments with early exercise features, the price is also given by an expectation. Unlike the case of European instruments, however, this expectation is not over a known horizon but is taken over a stochastic horizon, such as maximizing the value of the instrument. *This fact changes the picture in a fundamental way.*

The use of simulation for pricing of an instrument with early exercise features, such as a Bermudan option, is far more difficult a task than pricing the European version of the instrument. This difficulty exists even in one dimension. However the fact that other pricing methods, such as finite differences, run into trouble with a large number of dimensions has created an incentive to try to adapt simulation to be able to handle early exercise. These efforts started as early as 1993, when the first attempts to price American derivatives using simulation were undertaken. These early efforts only addressed the difficulty of early exercise, not of dimensionality. These early efforts did not succeed, but even if they had been successful, they would have remained of limited practical use unless the issue of dimensionality was properly dealt with. The reason is that if there is no dimensionality issue, finite differences easily take care of the problem (for Markovian underlying processes).

In 1997 it became possible for the first time to use a simulation-based approach to compute early exercise in several dimensions. This was an important breakthrough because for the first time, results from simulation could be guaranteed to capture the true price in a statistically meaningful way. This early successful methodology was extremely slow and could not be applied to large scale pricing.

As of this writing, there is no simulation-based approach capable of directly computing *continuous* early exercise. The approaches that exist compute discrete exercise (Bermudan) cases, and only by extrapolation can we get the continuous exercise case. This is in contrast with finite differences, where both the continuous and the discrete exercise cases can be computed.

SIMULATION APPLIED TO EARLY EXERCISE

The fundamental difficulty in applying simulation when there is early exercise is that at any exercise point we must decide between holding or exercising. The holding value of the option is itself an expectation, conditional on the information at that exercise time. This means that in order to decide between holding or exercising at an exercise opportunity, we must already have determined, by simulation, the conditional expectation of holding the option at that exercise opportunity. But this requires that we must have *converged* the simulation before we finish valuing the option by simulation. This is, of course, a contradiction. To show this explicitly, consider the value of a Bermudan option with exercise times $t_i < t_{i+1}$, $i = 1, \ldots, I$. Assume the option depends on an underlying process $S(t)$. If we express the underlying process in the risk neutral measure, the value of the option at time t_i is

$$V(t_i) = \max\left(G(t_i), \mathrm{E}_t\left[e^{-r(t_{i+1} - t_i)} V(t_{i+1})\right]\right) \tag{6.1}$$

where $G(t_i)$ is the value of exercising the option at time t_i. This is a recursive relationship. If we seek to compute the expectation in the right-hand side of this equation by producing *trajectories* of the underlying process $S(t)$, we may see that a difficulty arises. This is because we don't have a way to know which trajectories should be included at t_{i+1}. Trajectories for which the option was exercised at $t_k < t_{i+1}$, $1 \leq k < i$ should not be included. But we will not know what those trajectories are until we have recursed Equation 6.1 all the way to $t = t_1$.

This apparent difficulty is alleviated by realizing that what we need to know is not which trajectories to include in the expectation but rather which trajectories are associated with holding (or zero payoffs as a result of holding the instrument). The trajectories that are associated with zero payoffs are the ones that correspond to continuation. The ones associated with a known payoff correspond to exercise. This is conceptually simple to do if we proceed recursively backwards from maturity. The fact that we use simulation for generating the scenarios does not alter the fact that we must solve a backward recursion problem, just as in the case of trees or finite differences.

As we discussed in Chapter 3, if we knew the exercise policy of an early exercise instrument, pricing the instrument would be trivial. Knowing the exercise policy means that we know the value of the underlying process as a function of time, for which exercise should occur. This fact has motivated two fundamental approaches to simulation applied to early exercise. One approach is to parameterize the early exercise policy and then find the value of the parameters that maximize the value of the instrument. Another approach is to estimate the exercise policy directly. The second approach is the one that has proved most successful.

Dealing with Estimator Bias

Before discussing any particular approach in detail, we must realize that in most cases we will have a simulation procedure that produces a biased result. The bias can be either high or low. A simulation procedure that converges to the correct result as the number of cycles tends to infinity is called an *asymptotically unbiased procedure*. Given a simulation approach for pricing early exercise options, the first thing to do is to determine whether the method is biased high or low. If the approach as originally proposed is biased low, then it is desirable to obtain an upper bound that would be consistent with the assumptions of the original approach. If the approach is biased high, we would do the opposite. This means that given a particular approach, it is highly desirable to generate two estimators for the option value, one biased high and the other biased low. If the approach as originally proposed is biased, this is a way of getting a confidence interval that brackets the result.

Being able to bracket the result is desirable but not essential in order to profit from a simulation approach. We may be able to calibrate the approach with known results from other methodologies to have a good idea as to the quality of the results, even if the results are systematically biased. When using simulation for auditing the viability or correctness of an analytical derivation or of any other quantitative pricing method, the ability to produce upper and lower bounds may become essential.

To illustrate the issues involved in estimator bias, consider the simplest estimator of the value of a Bermudan option. This simple estimator, called the *perfect foresight path estimator*, is constructed as follows.

- Generate N paths of the underlying process.
- For each path, determine the exercise time where the payoff would be a maximum if the option were exercised at that time.
- Discount those payoffs to the present and average the results.

This procedure gives us an idea of the price of the option, but it is a very poor idea. This procedure will produce a greatly exaggerated estimation of the value of the option. To illustrate, consider the case of an at-the-money Bermudan put, with strike = $100, stock volatility 0.1, risk-free rate 0.1, maturity 1 year, and 20 exercise times. The results are shown in Figure 6.1. For comparison, the figure also shows an accurate computation of the Bermudan put value and the Black and Scholes value. As we can see, the simple path estimator grossly overstates the value of the Bermudan put. Notice that this computation is very simple to make.

What is fundamentally wrong with this estimator? At any exercise opportunity, the decision to exercise or to hold is made with the information available at that time. The perfect foresight estimator makes that decision based on knowledge of the trajectory beyond the decision time. How should this estimator be changed so that it gives a more reasonable result? This change would require that at each point where an exercise decision is made, the path should split into a large number of paths, from which expected continuation and holding values could be determined. Clearly, this first attempt to fix the simple path estimator would dramatically increase the complexity of the computation.

It is important to realize that this simple estimator does not consist in approximating the stopping times or exercise policy of the Bermudan put. By definition, a stopping time is determined by information available at the time of the decision, not at a future time.

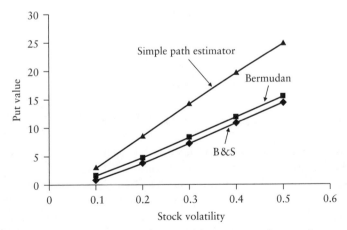

FIGURE 6.1 Perfect foresight estimator of American put value. At-the-money put with $S(0) = 100, K = 100, r = 0.1, \sigma = 0.1, T = 1$ years. This estimator greatly overstates the American premium.

What would the bias be if the estimator of the Bermudan price were based on true stopping times? It is easy to see that such an estimator would be biased low. The reason is that the value of an early exercise option is the maximum value of all possible exercise strategies. If the computation produces an approximate exercise strategy, the estimator will be biased low.

A number of simulation-based approaches for early exercise consist of averaging a number of computations, each one of which involves an average. To illustrate, consider an estimator that is based on computing the maximum of either holding the option or exercising. Assume that in order to compute the holding value of the option we must make an average over a number of future states. This procedure is repeated a number of times and the results are averaged. According to this, we would compute the estimator of the option value as follows:

$$\tilde{V}(t) = \max(\tilde{V}_c, V_e) \tag{6.2}$$

where the tilde indicates that the right-hand side is an estimator. $\tilde{V}_c$ is the estimator of the continuation value, and V_e is the exercise value. Jensen's inequality states that the expectation of a convex function of a random variable is greater than or equal to the function of the expectation of a random variable (Billingsley, 1994). A sufficient condition for Jensen's inequality to hold is that the function should have a nonnegative second derivative with respect to the random variable. This is the case with Equation 6.2. Taking expectations of both sides, we get

$$E_0[\tilde{V}(t_0)] = E_0[\max(\tilde{V}_c, V_e)]$$
$$\geq \max(E_0[\tilde{V}_c], V_e) \tag{6.3}$$

However, the value of the option is given by

$$V(t_0) = \max(E_0[\tilde{V}_c], V_e) \tag{6.4}$$

This shows that $\tilde{V}$ computed this way is biased upward. The issue of estimator bias is discussed extensively in Broadie and Glasserman (1997). As we will see, the simulated tree and the stochastic mesh algorithms produce estimators of this type but can be complemented with a biased low estimator. The least squares Monte Carlo approach produces a biased low estimator and can be complemented with a biased high estimator.

The next four subsections describe algorithms and approaches that currently can be viewed as the historical backdrop in attempts to price early exercise by simulation. This summary description, which follows closely Broadie and Glasserman's excellent survey (1997a), is included here for completeness. The interested reader can find additional information in Broadie and Glasserman's survey and the references therein. These four sections are not a requirement for the methodology of greatest practicality, the least squares Monte Carlo method described later in the chapter.

Path-Bundling Algorithms

These algorithms, which started with the pioneering work of Tilley (1993), require that the trajectories be calculated first and kept in memory. Assume we denote each path by $S^j(t)$, $j = 1,\dots, N$, where N is the number of paths. The value of the option corresponding to path $S^j(t)$ is denoted by $V(t, S^j(t))$. At maturity, $t = t_I$, the value of the option is the final payoff:

$$V(t_I, S^j(t_I)) = G(S^j(t_I)) \tag{6.5}$$

To compute the value of the option at t_{I-1}, we first determine an array of integers $k_{I-1} = 1,\dots, N$ such that

$$S^{k_{I-1}+1} > S^{k_{I-1}} \tag{6.6}$$

This ordering establishes a relationship between the index k_{I-1} and the index j of the paths. Each j has a corresponding k_{I-1}. We denote this correspondence by $j(k_{I-1})$. Figure 6.2 illustrates the idea.

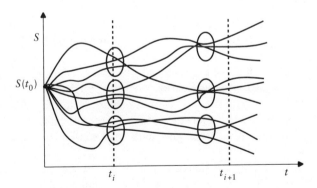

FIGURE 6.2 Path bundling. Paths are grouped in bundles. Paths within a bundle share the same continuation value. Unclear extension to higher dimensions (Broadie and Glasserman, 1997).

Once the paths are reordered according to Equation 6.6, the paths are divided into groups, or bundles, each with an equal number of paths. By grouping the paths in this way, we get paths to which we can assign a common continuation value to all the paths in each bundle. Assume that each bundle has M trajectories. The continuation value of the option at time t_{I-1} for the paths in the mth bundle is given by

$$C_m = \frac{1}{M} \sum_{k_{I-1}=1+(m-1)M}^{k_{I-1}=mM} PV\left[V\left(t_I, S^{j(k_{I-1})}(t_I)\right)\right] \qquad (6.7)$$

where PV stands for the present value at time t_{I-1}. The exercise value of the option at time t_{I-1} for a path indexed by k_{I-1} is $G(S^{j(k_{I-1})}, t_{I-1})$. The value of the option at time t_{I-1} for any paths in the mth bundle is then set to

$$V\left(t_{I-1}, S^{k_{I-1}}\right) = \max\left(C_m, G\left(S^{j(k_{I-1})}, t_{I-1}\right)\right) \qquad (6.8)$$

It is easy to see how this scheme can be recursively continued backward in time. At each exercise time, C_m is an estimation of the value of not exercising the option, conditional on a level of the underlying price representative of the paths contained in the mth bundle. At first sight, this approach appears to do what we want. The reordering of arrays and the grouping of paths into bundles takes into account the paths for which exercise has occurred. The algorithm captures the essence of early exercise.

However, we can also clearly see that this approach has a number of serious difficulties.

- The basic problem is with the estimation of the continuation value. As described, this algorithm must assign the same continuation value to all the paths included in a given bundle.
- This would not be a problem in and of itself, except that bundling the paths amounts to imposing a discretization on an already discretized problem. The continuous distribution of paths is discretized with individual trajectories, and then these trajectories are classified at another level of discretization. When this happens, it is hard to visualize how accuracy is affected.
- A significant difficulty is that it is not clear how this idea generalizes to higher dimensions. This issue is absolutely fundamental, and no algorithm that fails to address it can be seriously considered as a winner. Remember that it is not the question of early exercise per se that matters, but the handling of data volume and growth associated with many dimensions.

■ There are also some difficulties of practical nature, such as the need to store all the trajectories.

Although the path-bundling algorithm is problematic, it lays the foundation for an obvious extension.

STATE STRATIFICATION ALGORITHMS

The simplest way to visualize these methods is to consider the multidimensional space defined by the value of the underlying processes and to divide this space into cells. In a one-dimensional problem the cells would look like a grid parameterized by time (there would be a one-dimensional grid at each exercise opportunity). In a two-dimensional problem the cells would be a rectangular grid parameterized by time (one rectangular grid for each exercise opportunity). We can then generate paths and observe how these paths cross the cells as the paths go from one exercise opportunity to the next. We can now do an analysis very similar to the case of path bundling, but rather than basing the analysis on paths that are together in a bundle, we base it on the paths that emanate from a common cell at one exercise opportunity and enter the same or a different cell at the next exercise opportunity.

What is wrong with this approach? Well, if implemented this way, this approach does not conquer the problem of dimensionality. The data issue remains a problem, because the number of cells grows very quickly as the number of dimensions grows.

An alternative specification of this algorithm is to define the cells not on the underlying state, but on some aggregation or function of the underlying states. This would allow us to reduce the number of dimensions and manage the data problem. To illustrate how this would work, assume that we have a two-dimensional problem with underlying price processes $S_1(t)$ and $S_2(t)$, with I exercise opportunities. Rather than building I rectangular grids in S_1, S_2 space, we can think of building I one-dimensional grids in the one-dimensional space $S_1 + S_2$.

We can begin to suspect that if we do this, something may go wrong in a fundamental way. The value of continuation must be known for all combinations of S_1 and S_2 that may be relevant to the decision to hold or to exercise. This is accomplished by considering a two-dimensional grid, but it isn't if you look at the sum of the underlying prices.

Barraquand and Martineaux (1995) have proposed to use the payoff function as the criterion for aggregating the states. This will work if the payoff is such that there is only one decision to be made (hold or exercise) for each value of the exercise function. Unfortunately, this is not always the case.

SIMULATED RECOMBINING LATTICES

The basic idea is to repeatedly price the option using randomly generated recombining lattices and then average the results. This concept was introduced by Broadie and Glasserman (1997b), who call it the *stochastic mesh approach*. This produces an estimator of the early exercise price by simulating arrays of points in the multidimensional underlying state space for each exercise time. The array of points is illustrated in Figure 6.3. The value obtained from each mesh is a realization of the value estimator.

Stochastic meshes are essentially multidimensional recombining lattices. This is easy to see by looking at a one-dimensional version of a recombining mesh, shown in Figure 6.4.

How are the meshes generated? We can construct the mesh by sampling from the distribution of $\vec{S}$, or we can sample from some other distribution. Sampling from a different distribution amounts to performing a change in measure, and in this case we must use a likelihood ratio of the probability density of $\vec{S}$ and the probability density from which we are sampling to build the mesh. This likelihood ratio is

$$w\left(t_i; k, l\right) = \frac{p(t; k, l)}{\hat{p}(t; k, l)} \tag{6.9}$$

where $p(t; k, l)$ is the transition probabilities in the measure of $\vec{S}$ between the kth mesh points at time t_i and the lth mesh points at time t_{i+1}. $\hat{p}(t_i; k, l)$ is the

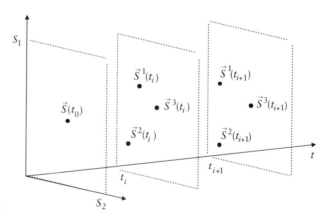

FIGURE 6.3   **Three-dimensional stochastic mesh.** Three-dimensional points are forced to recombine. Each Monte Carlo replication results from a simulated mesh (Broadie and Glasserman, 1997b).

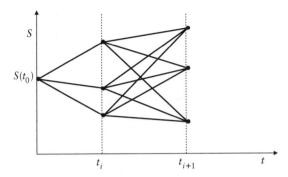

FIGURE 6.4 Two-dimensional stochastic mesh.

transition probability used to generate the mesh. If there are M nodes or mesh points at each exercise time, the estimator of the option price at time t_i conditional on state $\vec{S}(t_i)$ is

$$
V(t_i, \vec{S}^k(t_i)) = \max\left(G(t_i), \frac{1}{M}\sum_{l=1}^{l=M} e^{-r(t_{i+1}-t_i)} V\left(t_{i+1}, \vec{S}^l(t_{i+1})\right) w(t_i; k, l)\right)
$$

$$(6.10)$$

Broadie and Glasserman (1997b) have specific recommendations for choosing the transition densities.

In this approach, the estimator involves a nonlinear function of the payoff expectation. As a consequence, this estimator is biased upward, and becomes unbiased when $M \to \infty$.

In summary, we can make the following observations about the stochastic mesh approach.

- The stochastic mesh approach is equivalent to simulating recombining lattices and averaging the results. This gives an upwardly biased estimation of the derivative price.
- It is also possible to obtain a downwardly biased estimator.
- This method does not deal successfully with the issue of dimensionality.

Simulated Bushy Trees

This concept, also introduced by Broadie and Glasserman (1997), is very similar to the previous one, except that instead of using a recombining lattice to get the estimator, we use a nonrecombining multidimensional tree.

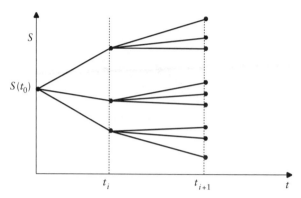

FIGURE 6.5 Simulated bushy tree. Quickly becomes unmanageable as the number of exercise opportunities grows (Broadie and Glasserman, 1997).

Figure 6.5 shows the one-dimensional case. As in the previous case, a straightforward computation of the option value by averaging an estimator of the price based on a randomly generated tree would give an upwardly biased result. Broadie and Glasserman (1997) discuss how upward and lower bounds can be generated for constructing a confidence interval of the price.

We can summarize this approach as follows.

■ The simulated bushy tree approach is robust, but becomes unmanageable as the number of exercise opportunities and the number of dimensions grow.

■ Because it is easy to produce a confidence interval for the price, this approach has been very useful in auditing the results from faster algorithms.

LEAST SQUARES MONTE CARLO

The introduction of *regression-based Monte Carlo* (also called *least squares Monte Carlo*, or *LSMC*) constituted the first definite breakthrough in pricing early exercise derivatives by Monte Carlo. The previous approaches had one fundamental fact in common. The value of continuation conditional on a particular state was calculated by working separately with each node (in the case of lattices or trees) or each bundle (in the case of the bundling method). In order for the continuation value to be meaningful, each node needs to have a sufficiently large number of branches (in the bushy tree or lattices case) or a sufficient number of paths (in the bundling method). This localized way of computing the continuation value is the basic reason why those methods don't succeed in attacking the dimensionality problem. While the straightforward computation of an expectation using Monte Carlo is not sensitive to the dimensionality of the problem, the particular way in which previous methods have tackled the computation of the continuation value reintroduces the dimensionality in the problem. On top of this problem, the simulated bushy tree is also limited by the number of exercise opportunities.

Regression-based Monte Carlo differs fundamentally from the previous methods in that the work needed for computing the continuation value at any state is done once based on the entire cross-sectional information, rather than based on each node. This work is in the form of a regression, which is then applied to each state to get the continuation value. Essentially, this approach solves the dynamic optimization problem posed by the Bellman equation (described in Chapter 3), where the value of continuation is computed on the basis of a regression on cross-sectional data.

The number of dimensions drops out from the problem, except in the computation of the regression. The regression requires the use of basis functions, which must link the various dimensions of the problem. The number of basis functions will then grow with the number of dimensions, and one could argue that the dimensionality issue creeps back in again through the number of basis functions required. However, as we will see later, in some cases this dimensionality problem is much less severe than it seems. There is also some indication that working with cross-sectional data makes the estimation of the continuation value increasingly more efficient as the number of dimensions grows. The full potential of this methodology as well as alternatives to simple regressions are yet to be explored.

The LSMC method was popularized by Longstaff and Schwartz (1998, 2000). Work along similar lines was undertaken independently by other researchers (Tsitsikilis and Van Roy, 2000). Recently, Clement, Lamberton, and Protter (2001) proved the convergence characteristics of the method.

Since this method is based on an exercise policy approach, it provides a lower bound. Andersen and Broadie (2001) proposed a way to obtain an upper bound for the LSMC.

Least Squares and Conditional Expectation

As we will discuss in the next section, the LSMC algorithm computes the conditional expectation of continuation from simulated observations of the present value of continuation through linear regression.

In this section we elucidate the connection between least squares and conditional expectation.

Assume two arrays of observations, X_j and F_j, $j = 1,..., M$. We view X_j as measurements of the variable X. We view F_j as measurements of a function $F(X_j)$ with an error. We view X_j as realizations of independent random variables. We assume that the measurements F_j are realizations of normally distributed random variables, $\tilde{F}_j$, centered around the "correct" value $F(X_j)$. Function $F(X)$ is defined in terms of some parameters $\alpha_1,..., \alpha_L$, yet to be determined. For simplicity we will only write these parameters explicitly when needed. The probability of the measurement F_j will be proportional to

$$\exp\left(-\frac{[F_j - F(X_j)]^2}{2\sigma_j^2}\right) \tag{6.11}$$

where σ_j is the standard deviation of the random variable $\tilde{F}_j$.

If there are M data points ($j = 1,..., M$), the probability of all the measured data points will be proportional to the product:

$$\prod_{j=1}^{j=M} \exp\left(-\frac{[F_j - F(X_j)]^2}{2\sigma_j^2}\right) \tag{6.12}$$

Notice that if we had a perfect model for $F(S)$, the values F_j would be the same as $F(S_j)$. This maximizes the exponential in Equation 6.12. Then we can say that a good candidate for $F(S)$ is one that maximizes the probability in Equation 6.12 with respect to any parameters that define $F(S)$. Maximizing the product in Equation 6.12 is the same as minimizing the product,

$$\prod_{j=1}^{j=M} \exp\left(\frac{[F_j - F(X_j)]^2}{2\sigma_j^2}\right) \tag{6.13}$$

which, in its turn, is the same as minimizing the logarithm of Equation 6.13.

The following minimization problem with respect to parameters α_l, $l = 1,..., L$,

$$\min_{\alpha_l,\,(l=1,...,L)} \sum_{j=1}^{j=M} \frac{\left[F_j - F(X_j; \alpha_1,..., \alpha_L)\right]^2}{2\sigma_j^2} \tag{6.14}$$

is referred to as *maximum likelihood estimation* (MLE). Although MLE is very desirable, we typically don't know the σ_j. A simple solution to this difficulty is to assume that all the σ_j are the same (Press et al., 1992). When we do this, we get the *least squares estimation* (LSE) formulation for the determination of the parameters $\alpha_l, l = 1,..., L$:

$$\min_{\alpha_l, (l=1,...,L)} \sum_{j=1}^{j=M} [F_j - F(X_j, \alpha_1,..., \alpha_L)]^2 \qquad (6.15)$$

Least squares estimation is a particular case of MLE when

- The distributions of the random variables from which the observations are assumed to be drawn are normal.
- All the standard deviations of those random variables are the same.

LSE will be less satisfactory if

- The standard deviations are not the same.
- The distributions are not normal. In financial modeling this problem is associated with "fat-tailed" distributions.

One particular form of LSE is particularly useful: *Linear least squares estimation* (LLSE). In linear least squares, the function takes the form:

$$F(X;(\alpha_1,..., \alpha_L)) = \alpha_1 f_1(X) + \alpha_2 f_2(X),..., \alpha_L f_L(X) \qquad (6.16)$$

where the $f_i(.)$ are called *basis functions*.

Notice that *linear* only refers to the parameters α_l, not to the functions $f_l(.)$. In fact, these functions are typically nonlinear. The *linear regression* is the special case where f_1 is a constant, f_2 is a linear function, and the rest of the basis functions are zero.

With Equation 6.16, our minimization problem, given by Equation 6.15, becomes

$$\min_{\alpha_1,...,\alpha_L} \sum_{j=1}^{j=M} \left(F_j - \sum_{l=1}^{l=L} \alpha_l f_l(X_j) \right)^2 \qquad (6.17)$$

This leads to the following system of equations:

$$\frac{\partial}{\partial \alpha_k} \sum_{j=1}^{j=M} \left(F_j - \sum_{l=1}^{l=L} \alpha_l f_l(X_j) \right)^2 = 0, k = 1,..., L \qquad (6.18)$$

This gives us the following linear system for $\alpha_l, l = 1,\ldots, L$:

$$\sum_{l=1}^{l=L} \alpha_{kl}\alpha_l = b_k, \ k = 1,\ldots, L \tag{6.19}$$

where

$$a_{kl} = \sum_{j=1}^{j=M} f_k(X_j)f_l(X_j), \ k,l = 1,\ldots, L \tag{6.20}$$

$$b_k = \sum_{j=1}^{j=M} F_j f_k(X_j), \ k,l = 1,\ldots, L \tag{6.21}$$

These linear equations can be solved with standard numerical routines (Press et al., 1992).

We can now make the connection between linear least squares and the conditional expected value of continuation. We have

$$E[\tilde{F}_j|X_j] = E[(F(X_j) + \text{error})|X_j] \tag{6.22}$$

Since the error is normally distributed by assumption and is centered around $F(X_j)$, we get

$$\begin{aligned} E[\tilde{F}_j|X_j] &= E[F(X_j)|X_i] \\ &= F(X_j) \end{aligned} \tag{6.23}$$

This equation establishes the connection between least squares regression and the conditional expectation. The LSMC algorithm exploits this fact.

LSMC Algorithm

The algorithm of the LSMC approach is as follows.

■ Generate N trajectories of the underlying process or processes. For illustration, we assume there is only one underlying process. The trajectories only need to be defined at exercise dates, $t_i, i = 1,\ldots, I$ and are denoted by $S^j(t), j = 1,\ldots, N$.

■ At any exercise time t_i, the value of the option is

$$V(t_i, S^j(t_i)) = \max (C_j(t_i), G(S^j(t_i), t_i)), \, j = 1, \ldots, N \qquad (6.24)$$

where $C_j(t_i)$ is the expectation of the continuation value conditional on the underlying price $S^j(t_i)$, and $G(S^j(t_i), t_i)$ is the exercise value.

■ To determine the conditional expectation of the continuation value, we first compute the present value of continuation cash flows:

$$V^j_{cont}(t_i) = \sum_{k=i}^{k=I} B^j(t_i, t_k) G(S^j(t_k), t_k) \qquad (6.25)$$

where $B^j(t_i, t_k)$ is the discount factor that applies at time t_i for the jth trajectory of a cash flow that occurs at time t_k. This discount factor will depend on the measure used to pose the problem. In general, the discount factor will be a function of the trajectory. The sum in this expression is done trajectory-wise up to a previously determined stopping time, or until maturity. As we will discuss in detail in the next section, this conditional expectation can be restricted to a suitable subset of the trajectories. In the case of a simple Bermudan put, for example, this subset is made up of the trajectories that are in the money at time t_i. In more general cases, however, this subset is chosen according to a more general criterion that we will call the *moneyness criterion*, described below.

■ Define L basis functions, $f_l(S)$, $l = 1, \ldots, L$ and regress the present value of continuation cash flows, $V^j_{cont}(t_i)$, on the underlying values $S^j(t_i)$ using least squares. This regression produces a set of coefficients α_l, $l = 1, \ldots, L$. We now interpret this regression as an estimation of the conditional expectation of the continuation cash flows. We can now evaluate the conditional expectation by evaluating the regression for each $S^j(t_i)$:

$$C_j(t_i) = \sum_{l=1}^{l=L} \alpha_l f_l(S^j(t_i)) \qquad (6.26)$$

■ Every time an exercise decision is made in evaluating Equation 6.24, we get an estimation of a stopping time. The stopping time is recorded and used in determining which elements enter in the sum in Equation 6.25.

■ In practice it is possible to carry out this cross-sectional analysis on a subset of trajectories. The selection of this subset is based on the criterion of *moneyness*, discussed in the next section. The simplest form of this criterion is to condition on trajectories that are in the money at the cross-section under consideration. Another version of the criterion is to condition on trajectories that are judged to be more representative of exercise. These are nonrigorous ways to reduce the computational burden.

Since the LSMC method is based on building an approximate exercise policy, this method gives us a lower bound of option price.

For a particular instrument, the exercise policy is encoded in a stopping rule. The stopping rule can be expressed in the form of a matrix, Θ, with entries 0 or 1. In a one-dimensional problem, this matrix has as many rows as there are trajectories, and as many columns as there are exercise times. An entry equal to 1 in the ith column and the jth row means that the jth trajectory has a corresponding stopping time at time t_i. Once this matrix is known, the value of the derivative is given by

$$V(0) = \frac{1}{M} \sum_{j=1}^{j=M} \left(\sum_{i=1}^{i=I} \Theta_{i,j} B^j(t_0, t_i) G(S^j(t_i), t_i) \right) \qquad (6.27)$$

In multidimensional problems, the stopping rule matrix is a multidimensional array. The stopping rule allows us to map the underlying trajectories onto exercise boundaries.

The fact that the LSMC is based on estimating the stopping rule does not mean that the exercise boundary must look nice in order for the computation to be accurate. As an example, consider an at-the-money Bermudan put with strike \$40 on a non-dividend paying stock with volatility 0.3, maturity 1 year, and monthly exercise opportunities. Assume that the risk-free rate is 0.06.

Figure 6.6 shows the exercise boundary for two simulations of 10,000 and 100,000 Monte Carlo cycles, respectively. The computation with 100,000 cycles gives very accurate results, although both exercise boundaries look crudely captured. This figure suggests that although the LSMC method gives a lower bound because it captures the exercise boundary approximately, we can nevertheless expect that the results can be quite good, even if the boundary is not captured accurately in a visual way. These computations were done with six monomial basis functions for the linear regression, $f_l(x) = x^{l-1}, l = 1, \ldots, 5$.

To investigate the effect of the number of basis functions on the convergence of the value, we consider the Bermudan premium of a put option with maturity 1 year, volatility 0.2, and 50 exercise times. The exact value of the Bermudan premium is not known, but we can get a very accurate assessment with a good quality finite difference computation. The results are summarized in Figure 6.7. These results are for 40,000 Monte Carlo cycles. As expected, the true value of the Bermudan premium is reached from below. Taking into account the scale of the plot, we see that the method captures the Bermudan premium reasonably well with four basis functions or more.

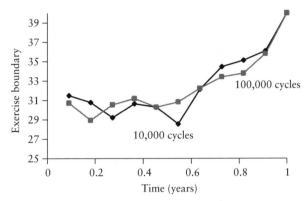

FIGURE 6.6 Bermudan put exercise boundary for 10^4 and 10^5 replications. Monthly exercise, at the money put with $S(0) = 40, r = 0.06, \sigma = 0.3, T = 1$ year.

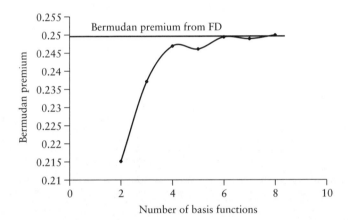

FIGURE 6.7 Effect of basis functions on Bermudan premium. At-the-money Bermudan put with 50 exercise opportunities per year, $S(0) = 40, r = 0.06,$ $\sigma = 0.2, T = 1$ year. Basis functions are monomials. The benchmark is a highly accurate finite difference computation.

We can make the following additional observations about the LSMC method.

■ The currently published versions of the LSMC are based on the use of simple linear regression for estimating the conditional expectation of the continuation value. Other techniques are also possible, such as weighted regressions, robust regressions, and so on. These alternatives have not been explored in the open literature.

- The software implementation of the LSMC is very straightforward and lends itself to recursion. In this regard, it can be programmed with a very similar architecture as the finite difference method.
- We can generate scenario trajectories by integrating the stochastic differential equations of the underlying processes numerically by sampling from the exact solution for the underlying processes, by sampling from the exact covariance matrix of the trajectory, or by Brownian bridge approximations.
- The use of quasi-random sequences (Sobol, etc.) in the Brownian bridge construction has been found to have nice convergence properties. However, no rigorous studies have been published in this area.
- All the standard variance reduction techniques of standard Monte Carlo apply to LSMC.
- The object nature of the software implementation of LSMC allows us to combine different methodologies in conducting a simulation. For example, an option that enters in the payoff of another option being priced with LSMC can be computed with finite differences, analytically, or in some other way. These combinations have not been explored so far.

The Moneyness Criterion

As we mentioned in the last section, in the simple case of a Bermudan put that it is possible to restrict the subset of trajectories used in computing the conditional expectation of continuation to those trajectories that are in the money at the time when we are computing that expectation. This idea can be generalized by defining a subset of the trajectories that are selected for computing the conditional expectation. The criterion used to select this subset will be referred to as the *moneyness criterion*. In the case of a simple Bermudan put, the moneyness criterion we have used so far selects the subset of paths for the conditional expectation if the intrinsic value corresponding to those paths is positive; in other words, the paths are selected if the corresponding intrinsic value exceeds zero. We can relax this requirement and state that the paths are selected if the intrinsic value exceeds an amount greater than zero. In such a case we say that the moneyness criterion is given by the amount the intrinsic value must exceed in order for the corresponding paths to be included in the conditional expectation set. Table 6.1 shows the impact on the price and Bermudan premium of the option from Figure 6.7 for several values of the moneyness criterion.

This table shows that the effect of changing the moneyness in this range is within the standard error of the computations.

This flexibility in selecting the subset of trajectories for the conditional expectation is not particularly significant in this simple case, but it may prove crucial in other cases. For example, if we are solving a problem

TABLE 6.1   Effect of moneyness criterion.

Moneyness criterion	$V_{Bermudan}$	Bermudan premium
0	2.3159	0.2495
1	2.3137	0.2473
2	2.2942	0.2278
3	2.3189	0.2505
4	2.3183	0.2519

Note: The conditional expectation paths are those for which the intrinsic put value is greater than the moneyness criterion. The moneyness criterion in this case is the exercise value to be exceeded by a particular trajectory in order for the trajectory to be included in the conditional expectation. At-the-money Bermudan put with 50 exercise opportunities per year, $S(0) = 40$, $r = 0.06$, $\sigma = 0.2$, $T = 1$ year. All cases done with 40,000 cycles and a standard deviation approximately equal to 0.013.

where there are many underlying processes (such as a basket option), the ability to select the subset for computing the regression may make the problem much more tractable. As we will see in another example, we will be able to limit the number of basis functions by limiting the number of assets for which the conditional expectation is computed.

Implementation Considerations

The following are some of the practical considerations in designing a pricing implementation of the LSMC method.

■ Separation between regression scenarios and pricing scenarios: Although it is not crucial to use a different set of scenarios for computing the regression and for pricing, it is a good idea to implement the approach such that this is possible. This is an indication of the robustness of the implementation.

■ Flexibility in the choice of basis functions: Some experimentation is needed to select a suitable set of basis functions. The number of basis functions and the number of simulation cycles establish an optimum balance of computational work.

■ Flexibility in selecting a moneyness criterion: Although this is not a scientifically grounded consideration, it can play an important role in keeping the computational cost (speed and memory requirements) under control.

■ Benchmarking and calibration: There are two types of benchmarks that an LSMC system should be subjected to. One is the pricing of the European version of the instrument under consideration or related instruments. This is always possible (by simulation, trees, or finite differences, depending on the number of dimensions and nature of the underlying processes). The main purpose of this benchmark is to make sure that the system is correctly pricing the European versions to arbitrary accuracy. Another benchmark is a test of the LSMC system with a low-dimensionality version of the instrument under consideration. This benchmark is more difficult than the first because it requires that a parallel method of computing early exercise should be available. The ideal way to do this is with finite differences or lattices. The main purpose of the second benchmark is to be able to select the basis functions judiciously. The case studies presented in the next sections illustrate both of these benchmarks.

In the next section we discuss in some detail two case studies of the LSMC. The information in these cases should provide the reader with a realistic feel of performance and accuracy issues.

CASE STUDY 1: BERMUDAN CALL ON BEST-OF-THREE ASSETS[1]

The call on the best performing asset of a group of assets has become a fairly standard test in multivariate option pricing (Fu et al., 2001). Here we try to determine the level of accuracy that can be achieved with the LSMC method and CPU times that can be expected in a good implementation of this method. As of this writing, the only competing method with LSMC in the case of three assets or less is the finite difference method. Beyond three dimensions, the finite difference method becomes impractical, even with powerful machines. The comparison with finite differences is meaningful for two reasons. Finite differences is the method of choice if the number of dimensions is low, and the results produced by quality implementation of finite difference methods are very reliable (we will discuss this in great detail in Chapter 7).

Specification

We consider a Bermudan call on a portfolio of three assets with price processes

$$\frac{dS_j}{S_j} = (r - y_j)dt + \sigma_j dW_j \qquad j = 1, 2, 3 \qquad (6.28)$$

---

[1]I am grateful to Dr. Curt Randall from SciComp. Inc., who provided the numerical results for this case study.

where y_j is the dividend yield. Notice that here we use subscripts to denote different assets. The assets parameters are as follows:

$$S_1(0) = S_2(0) = S_3(0) = 100$$
$$y_1 = y_2 = y_3 = 0.1 \quad (6.29)$$
$$\sigma_1 = \sigma_2 = \sigma_3 = 0.2$$

The strike, risk-free rate, and maturity are

$$K = 100$$
$$r = 0.05 \quad (6.30)$$
$$T = 3 \text{ years}$$

The payoff function of the Bermudan call at exercise time τ is

$$\text{Payoff} = \max\left(\max S_j(\tau) - K, 0\right) \quad (6.31)$$

The correlation matrix of the Wiener processes in Equation 6.28 is

$$\rho = \begin{bmatrix} 1 & -0.25 & 0.25 \\ -0.25 & 1 & 0.3 \\ 0.25 & 0.3 & 1 \end{bmatrix} \quad (6.32)$$

Basis Functions

The number of basis functions can grow quickly as the number of assets increases. Using the idea of moneyness criterion, we can restrict the number of assets to which the regression is applied. This allows us to limit the number of basis functions needed. In this case, we regress on the spots of the two highest assets.

Assume that S_1 and S_2 are the two largest assets at a given time step. The basis functions are

$$
\begin{array}{ccccc}
S_1 & S_1^2 & S_1^3 & S_1^4 & S_1^5 \\
S_2 & S_2^2 & S_2^3 & S_2^4 & S_2^5 \\
S_1 S_2 & S_1 S_2^2 & S_1 S_2^3 & S_1 S_2^4 & \\
S_1^2 S_2 & S_1^2 S_2^2 & S_1^2 S_2^3 & & \\
S_1^3 S_2 & S_1^3 S_2^2 & & & \\
S_1^4 S_2 & & & & \\
1 & & & &
\end{array}
$$

The Benchmark

The first step in a simulation study is to obtain a benchmark to be used for comparison. In this case, a highly accurate finite difference computation was used. The finite difference computation uses a grid in three space dimensions (corresponding to the three underlying assets) and time. The results are summarized in Table 6.2. The first column indicates the number of grid points in the three space dimensions. V_∞ represents the value of the Bermudan call extrapolated to an infinitely fine grid. This value can be assumed to be numerically exact. The reason

TABLE 6.2   Finite difference benchmark.

Bermudan call on best-of-three assets
Finite difference benchmark

Grid size	V	$V - V_\infty$	CPU time (sec.)
10 Exercise opportunities			
$40 \times 40 \times 40$	17.734	-0.612	5.93
$50 \times 50 \times 50$	17.774	-0.391	12.96
$60 \times 60 \times 60$	17.794	-0.277	20.12
$80 \times 80 \times 80$	17.817	-0.149	53.67
$\infty \times \infty \times \infty$	17.844	0	—
15 Exercise opportunities			
$40 \times 40 \times 40$	17.851	-0.656	7.88
$50 \times 50 \times 50$	17.896	-0.408	17.46
$60 \times 60 \times 60$	17.915	-0.299	26.97
$80 \times 80 \times 80$	17.940	-0.161	72.56
$\infty \times \infty \times \infty$	17.969	0	—
30 Exercise opportunities			
$40 \times 40 \times 40$	17.956	-0.693	13.83
$50 \times 50 \times 50$	18.002	-0.443	31.13
$60 \times 60 \times 60$	18.026	-0.308	47.35
$80 \times 80 \times 80$	18.051	-0.173	130.21
$\infty \times \infty \times \infty$	18.082	0	—

Note: PDE solutions with predictor-corrector ADI scheme. The infinite grid solution is obtained by extrapolation. Boundaries correspond to $K \exp(\pm 4 \sigma T)$. Computational grid is defined through all hyperbolic sine transformation. Boundary conditions neglect diffusion. Time step is 0.1.

for this is that in finite difference solutions (we will discuss issues like this in much greater detail in Chapter 7) the scaling of the truncation error is known precisely. In this case, since we are using a second-order spatial difference scheme,

$$V_\infty = V + c(\Delta X)^2 \qquad (6.33)$$

where c is a constant and ΔX is the grid spacing (in this case this is the same in each space dimension).

The last column shows the CPU times, in seconds, for a 1Gz computer. The computing time needed to arrive at an acceptable result using finite differences is less than is suggested by this table because the scaling of the truncation error can be easily observed. As the next tables will show, the CPU time used by the LSMC for similar accuracy is significantly lower.

Numerical Results

The next three tables summarize the LSMC simulation results. The simulation error is given as plus/minus the standard deviation estimated through batching (a batch consisted of 10 samples). When using Sobol sequences, batching is done by repeating the entire computation starting from a different starting point each time. In interpreting the results in Tables 6.3, 6.4, and 6.5, we must keep the following in mind.

- The standard error brackets the value under the assumptions of this implementation. If the number of cycles in computing the regression is maintained constant, and the number of cycles in the Monte Carlo valuation is increased, the standard error is not a bracket about the correct limit as the number of cycles goes to infinity.
- The fact that conditional expectation has been applied only to a subset of the asset trajectories also means that the limiting value will not be approached correctly.

Because of these caveats, the standard deviations we quote are only an indication of the stability of the results, not of their true accuracy.

Table 6.3 compares the results obtained with a pseudorandom and a non-Brownian bridge implementation of Sobol quasi-random sampling. In both cases, the number of cycles in the regression loop and the Monte Carlo loop are the same. As expected, the Sobol sequences offer some advantage when the number of dimensions introduced by exercise opportunities is small. As the total number of dimensions increases, the performance of the pseudorandom approach catches up with that of Sobol. The CPU time is approximately the same in both cases.

Table 6.4 shows the effect of the Brownian bridge construction. In this case there is some advantage about using Brownian bridges when the number of cycles and the number of exercise opportunities are large.

TABLE 6.3 Comparing pseudorandom numbers with Sobol.

n_r, n_v	Sobol (no BB)		Pseudorandom	
	V	CPU	V	CPU
10 Exercise opportunities				
10^4	17.792 ± 0.065	2.66	17.749 ± 0.166	2.53
310^4	17.777 ± 0.045	8.07	17.782 ± 0.098	7.56
10^5	17.803 ± 0.025	26.66	17.813 ± 0.047	24.57
15 Exercise opportunities				
10^4	17.862 ± 0.060	3.68	17.745 ± 0.165	3.51
310^4	17.914 ± 0.051	11.11	17.889 ± 0.079	10.43
10^5	17.920 ± 0.025	37.33	17.879 ± 0.051	34.78
30 Exercise opportunities				
10^4	17.955 ± 0.084	7.21	17.849 ± 0.172	6.95
310^4	17.968 ± 0.079	20.91	17.967 ± 0.106	21.05
10^5	18.017 ± 0.036	61.94	17.993 ± 0.044	57.22

Note: n_r is the number of scenarios used for correlation, n_v is the number of scenarios used for valuation. As the number of exercise opportunities increases, the advantage of the quasi-random method over standard Monte Carlo decreases.

Finally, Table 6.5 shows the effect of a different number of replications in the computation of the regression (regression module) and the Monte Carlo valuation (simulation module). Savings in CPU time result from limiting the number of cycles in the regression loop. The fact that the number of cycles are different, however, implies we must be cautious in interpreting the convergence of the results.

CASE STUDY 2: BERMUDAN SWAPTION[2]

Bermudan interest rate instruments are ideal candidates for selecting the LSMC as the solution approach. The two main reasons for this are the dimensionality that results from the number of factors in modeling the term

---

[2]This work was carried out jointly with Dr. Georg Meier of HypoVereinsbank and Mr. Dider Vermeiren of Octanti Associates.

TABLE 6.4   Effect of Brownian bridges on Sobol sequence performance.

n_r, n_v	Sobol with Brownian bridge V	Sobol without Brownian bridge V
10 Exercise opportunities		
10^4	17.779 ± 0.062	17.792 ± 0.065
310^4	17.791 ± 0.038	17.776 ± 0.045
10^5	17.804 ± 0.012	17.803 ± 0.025
15 Exercise opportunities		
10^4	17.876 ± 0.133	17.862 ± 0.060
310^4	17.893 ± 0.043	17.914 ± 0.051
10^5	17.914 ± 0.023	17.920 ± 0.025
30 Exercise opportunities		
10^4	17.951 ± 0.117	17.955 ± 0.084
310^4	18.013 ± 0.043	17.968 ± 0.079
10^5	18.0287 ± 0.017	18.017 ± 0.036

Note: n_r and n_v are the number of correlation and valuation scenarios, respectively. On the average, the Brownian bridge reduces the standard error by about half.

structure and the path dependency characteristics of the rates. The dimensionality of the term structure makes it very difficult to use alternative techniques, such as lattices or finite differences. The Bermudan swaption is a very common instrument where the need for accurate pricing is particularly important.

Specification

The Bermudan swaption used in this case study gives the holder the right to enter into a 10 year maturity annual swap at the end of years 1 through 9. We assume a flat initial forward rate term structure of 5 percent; the strike for all maturities is also 5 percent; and the volatility of the forward rates is assumed to be a constant 0.2.

Scenario Generation

We assume that the scenarios are governed by the LIBOR dynamics described in Chapter 4. We assume that there are 10 annual rates with constant correlation coefficient 0.7. The main purpose of introducing an

TABLE 6.5 Effect of regression and valuation cycles.

Matched versus unmatched number of regression and valuation paths

n_r	n_v	V	CPU	n_r	n_v	V	CPU
10 Exercise opportunities							
10^4	10^4	17.777 ± 0.082	2.70	10^4	10^4	17.779 ± 0.062	2.66
10^4	310^4	17.762 ± 0.043	4.15	310^4	310^4	17.791 ± 0.038	7.83
10^4	10^5	17.769 ± 0.014	9.41	10^5	10^5	17.805 ± 0.013	26.07
15 Exercise opportunities							
10^4	10^4	17.887 ± 0.143	3.70	10^4	10^4	17.876 ± 0.133	3.76
10^4	310^4	17.869 ± 0.053	5.85	310^4	310^4	17.893 ± 0.043	11.36
10^4	10^5	17.868 ± 0.022	13.33	10^5	10^5	17.914 ± 0.024	37.36
30 Exercise opportunities							
10^4	10^4	17.976 ± 0.130	7.06	10^4	10^4	17.951 ± 0.117	7.16
10^4	310^4	17.960 ± 0.047	11.09	310^4	310^4	18.013 ± 0.044	22.16
10^4	10^5	17.957 ± 0.024	25.24	10^5	10^5	18.028 ± 0.017	63.58

Note: Significant savings in CPU time may result from limiting the number of cycles in the regression loop.

imperfectly correlated rate structure is to study the effect of the dimensionality of the state variables. The forward rate scenarios were generated using principal component analysis on the correlation matrix, with the diagonal elements normalized to one (see Chapter 4).

Basis Functions

In the case of an interest rate product such as a swaption, there are several possibilities for choosing the correlation or conditioning state variable. In the case of a Bermudan swaption, one obvious choice is the swap rates of the underlying swaps at exercise times. Other choices are the forwards that determine the swap rates of the underlying swaps. Yet other possibilities are the European versions of the swaptions at exercise times. The selection of appropriate correlation variables is largely a matter of experience.

In general, the swap rate alone does not provide as much information about changes in the term structure as the combination of the swap rate and the forward rates. In the case of plain vanilla swaps, swap value provides the same information as the swap rate, so it won't matter which one is selected as the conditioning variable. In more complex swaps, such as amortizing swaps, selecting the swap value may be more desirable.

This study reveals that very good results can be obtained by selecting as correlation variables at a particular exercise time the swap rate (or the swap value) of the underlying swap at that time, and the forward rate nearest the exercise time.

If the stochastic dimension of the term structure is one (a term structure that moves parallel to itself), we can expect no additional improvements by combining several correlation variables.

In this case study we use the same monomials as in the previous case.

The Benchmark

As mentioned earlier, there are two benchmarks that an LSMC pricer must pass. One is the correct pricing of European versions of the instrument; the other is a satisfactory comparison with a different and reliable method. Here we discuss the Bermudan benchmark only. In the previous case study we used finite differences as a benchmark. In this case we used a highly accurate single factor lattice approach.[3] Table 6.6 shows that the

TABLE 6.6   Single factor lattice benchmark.

Bermudan swaption: Single factor lattice benchmark.

Exercise dates	Lattice value	LSMC value	Std error
1 to 9	454,273	453,981	1,455
2 to 9	444,848	444,420	1,067
3 to 9	417,716	417,938	1,255
4 to 9	377,905	379,050	1,375
5 to 9	328,490	327,616	807
6 to 9	271,756	270,205	675
7 to 9	209,335	209,133	363
8 to 9	142,523	142,522	304
9	72,387	72,431	170

Note: Differences between accurate lattice computations and LSMC results. LSMC computed with 10,000 trajectories, standard error with 10 batches. Basis functions are monomials of degree two in the swap values and the first forward rate at exercise.

---

[3]The lattice is a variation of a bushy tree with enforced recombination, proprietary technology of HypoVereinsbank, Munich.

TABLE 6.7   Convergence of Bermudan swaption value as function of correlation variables.

Bermudan swaption—10 factors
Effect of conditioning variable selection

Exercise dates	Forward Degree 2	Forward Degree 3	Forward + Swap Degree 2	Forward + Swap + European swaption Degree 2
1 to 9	391,028	391,624	404,977	405,315
2 to 9	381,275	381,898	394,970	394,985
3 to 9	360,723	360,725	372,710	372,674
4 to 9	330,223	330,274	339,714	339,828
5 to 9	290,246	290,384	298,473	298,637
6 to 9	243,037	243,122	249,241	249,370
7 to 9	191,745	191,740	194,683	194,749
8 to 9	136,176	136,198	136,196	136,186
9	72,616	72,616	72,616	72,616

Note: LSMC computed with 10,000 trajectories.

results of the LSMC compare with the results of the lattice within the standard error.

Numerical Results

Table 6.7 shows the effect of selecting different correlation variables and the degree of the monomials that define the basis functions. Notice that as the maturity of the exercise opportunity increases, the less significant the difference between choices of correlation variable and basis function degree. This is expected, since as exercise opportunities progress the importance of shape changes in the term structure on the value of the instrument decreases. At the last exercise opportunity the Bermudan swaption is no longer Bermudan, and there is no difference between choices of basis functions or correlation variables.

CHAPTER 7

Pricing with Finite Differences

T his chapter presents a summary of the finite difference method applied to pricing derivatives. The material presented here is sufficient to understand the methodology in enough detail to implement practical solutions. For a more extensive discussion, which includes a large number of numerical examples and a detailed analysis of special issues, the reader is referred to the comprehensive work by Tavella and Randall (2000).

FUNDAMENTALS

Because finite differences deal directly with the pricing equation, this technique is also referred to as a *PDE method*. The *finite difference method* has been used for derivatives pricing for a long time, but it is only in recent years that this methodology has gained significant popularity.

The work by Brennan and Schwartz (1977), for example, is an early example of the application of finite differences to pricing derivatives.

An advantage of finite differences that was understood early on is that the finite difference approach is an extremely effective way of capturing early exercise. Since, until recently, simulation methods faced serious challenges in dealing with early exercise, the finite difference method was the numerical approach of choice in many cases involving early exercise. The fact that finite differences are also able to deal effectively with jumps and paths dependencies was not fully appreciated until recently, however (Tavella and Randall, 2000). Although, as we will see in the course of this chapter, finite differences have a number of highly desirable properties, there is one fundamental obstacle that remains unsurmounted. This is the fact that the data requirements become unmanageable as the number of dimensions grows. The number of dimensions for pricing instruments on standard desktop machines under practical conditions appears to be three or less.

At the time of this writing, the simulation techniques we discussed in Chapter 6 are in tight competition with finite differences for pricing low-dimensionality instruments with early exercise features. For dimensions three or larger, the simulation approach quickly takes the lead regarding speed. However, as we saw in Chapter 6, even for a small number of dimensions, the least squares Monte Carlo method may compete favorably with finite differences. Given these facts, why would we want to use finite differences? Here are some of the reasons why.

- In finite differences there is a clearly understood scaling between computational effort and accuracy. This is not always the case with Monte Carlo, where this scaling may jump from $\frac{1}{\sqrt{n}}$ to $\frac{1}{n^{1.5}}$, for example (see Chapter 5). For this reason, finite differences provide reliable results that can be used as benchmarks, as we did in Chapter 6. The impact of truncation error on Monte Carlo simulation is very difficult to interpret. In many cases, the truncation error in finite differences is relatively easy to interpret.
- Finite differences can handle early exercise, discrete sampling, and complex boundaries and barriers.
- Finite differences capture truly continuous early exercise features. This stands in contrast to the simulation methods we discussed in Chapter 6, which capture discrete exercise. At the time of this writing, with those methods, the continuous exercise is obtained by extrapolating to infinitely frequent exercise.

These are the two primary difficulties with finite differences.

- The driving processes must be Markovian. The contingencies, however, don't have to be Markovian. In fact, finite differences are very effective at dealing with many forms of path dependencies.
- The number of dimensions must be small. This is the primary disadvantage of finite differences. This is not a numerical issue as much as a data issue. The fact that finite differences rely on grids means that storage requirements present a fundamental barrier as the number of dimensions grows.

We can argue that a particular form of finite differences is the most popular tool for derivatives pricing. As we will see later, trees can be viewed as a specific implementation of a very restricted form of finite differences. The form of finite differences that trees represent have highly limiting features, which are at the root of the rigidities that characterize trees. For this reason, even if you don't use finite differences in practice, the material in this chapter is essential for understanding the limitations of trees.

As we saw in Chapter 3, the pricing equation is a recasting of the expectation that gives us the derivative's price. What is the fundamental difference between solving this expectation using simulation or a tree and solving it using finite differences? When we solve the problem by simulation, we construct trajectories of the underlying that assume the underlying has a given initial value. The same idea applies to trees. This means that the results of simulation or of tree calculations are valid for a given value of the initial spot price. If we want to know the value of the derivative for a different initial spot price, we have to repeat the calculation. This is not the case with finite differences. Since in finite differences the spot price is viewed as a space coordinate, the computation gives us the derivative's price for all the values of the initial spot price within the computational domain. This is also true of the hedging parameters, which obey their own pricing equations.

The typical pricing equation, as we discussed in Chapter 3, is as follows:

$$
\frac{\partial V}{\partial t} + \overbrace{a\frac{\partial V}{\partial S} + b\frac{\partial V}{\partial r} + c\frac{\partial V}{\partial I}}^{Convection} + \overbrace{d\frac{\partial^2 V}{\partial S^2} + e\rho\frac{\partial^2 V}{\partial S\partial r} + f\frac{\partial^2 V}{\partial r^2}}^{Diffusion}
$$

$$
= rV - \underbrace{h\left(\underbrace{\int \eta(\xi)V(\xi)d\xi}_{Convolution} - V \right)}_{Jump} \overbrace{}^{Source} \tag{7.1}
$$

The most common form of Equation 7.1 is one where the term $\frac{\partial V}{\partial I}$, which is associated with path dependency, and the convolution jump in the source term, which is associated with jumps, are missing. In this case, the pricing equation becomes the classical Black and Scholes equation. The Black and Scholes equation is a parabolic partial differential equation in reverse time. By *reverse time* we mean that we must solve this equation starting from maturity and advancing backward toward earlier time. The reverse time aspect reflects the fact that in finance, information about payoffs becomes more concentrated as time goes by. While the underlying processes diffuse forward, the information about contingent payments increases. *Parabolic* is one of the three classifications of partial differential equations.[1] The fact that the pricing equation is parabolic allows us to use finite difference techniques that were developed for diffusion-dominated problems in physics and engineering, which are also parabolic. The basic implication of a parabolic partial differential equation

---

[1]The other two are *hyperbolic* and *elliptic*.

is that if we know the solution at a number of discrete points at time t, we can advance the solution to time $t - \Delta t$, where Δt is known as the *time step* (the advancement is to a smaller time because our equation is in reverse time). This advancement is a relatively simple algebraic problem. In the case of trees, this advancement is known as *backward induction*. In the case of finite differences applied to a parabolic PDE, this advancement is called *marching*.

Finite Difference Strategy

To do the analysis, it is convenient to work in increasing time. We accomplish this by rewriting the pricing equation in terms of time to maturity. To illustrate, consider the standard Black and Scholes equation of a derivative with a log-normal underlying:

$$\frac{\partial V}{\partial t} = -S\mu\frac{\partial V}{\partial S} - S^2\frac{1}{2}\sigma^2\frac{\partial^2 V}{\partial S^2} + rV \tag{7.2}$$

where r is the risk-free rate and where the underlying process follows the stochastic differential equation

$$dS(t) = S\mu dt + S\sigma dW(t) \tag{7.3}$$

Equation 7.2 must be solved for $V(S, t)$ subject to *end conditions* determined by the derivative payoff at maturity, $V(S(T), T) = F(S(T), T)$, and suitable boundary conditions. If T is the maturity time, we define the time to maturity $\hat{t}$ as follows:

$$\hat{t} = T - t \tag{7.4}$$

We replace $\hat{t}$ for t in Equation 7.2 to get

$$\underbrace{\frac{\partial V}{\partial \hat{t}}}_{\text{Time derivative}} = \underbrace{S\mu\frac{\partial V}{\partial S} + S^2\frac{1}{2}\sigma^2\frac{1}{2}\frac{\partial^2 V}{\partial S^2}}_{\text{Space derivatives}} - \underbrace{rV}_{\text{Source}} \tag{7.5}$$

Equation 7.5 must be solved subject to *initial conditions* given by the derivative payoff, $V(S, \hat{t} = 0) = F(S, \hat{t} = 0)$. Through the rest of this chapter, however, we don't carry the hat around and instead use t with the understanding that we mean $\hat{t}$. The form of the equations we will solve is then

$$\frac{\partial V}{\partial t} = S\mu\frac{\partial V}{\partial S} + S^2\frac{1}{2}\sigma^2\frac{\partial^2 V}{\partial S^2} - rV \tag{7.6}$$

subject to initial conditions $V(S, 0) = F(S, 0)$ and suitable boundary conditions.

To implement the finite difference strategy, we represent the partial derivatives in terms of solution values at discrete points in the S, t domain. These points are arranged in the form of a regular grid, as shown in Figure 7.1. Although this grid does not have to be regular, it is established practice to use regular grids. The reason for this will become clear as we develop the underlying theory. If there is a need for concentrating grid points in certain areas of the solution domain, the grid is defined in a domain given by a coordinate transformation of the underlying states and time. In that domain, the grid is regular. This greatly facilitates the analysis and implementation of numerical schemes.

There are two discretizations involved in setting up a finite difference solution. One discretization involves the space derivatives, the other involves the time derivative. The combination of these two discretizations gives us the *finite difference algorithm*. The finite difference algorithm establishes an algebraic relationship between the solution values at time t_n and the solution values at time t_{n+1}.

The names commonly given to finite difference schemes, such as Euler scheme, Crank-Nicholson scheme, and so on, refer to the time discretization part of the finite difference algorithm. There is a great variety of time discretization schemes from which to choose, but the ones that have established themselves are relatively few. The usual space discretizations are much less varied. Typically, we use central differences in the

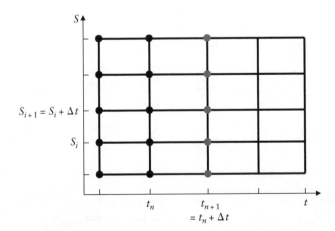

FIGURE 7.1 **Finite difference grid for a derivative with a single underlying.** Given known solution values at grid points up to time t_n, the finite difference scheme advances the solution to time t_{n+1}. Time is the remaining time to maturity. S is the underlying state or a suitable transformation. The upper and lower rows of grid points are boundary values. Boundary values can be given or computed as part of the solution.

interior of the domain and one-sided differences at boundaries. This will be fully explained shortly.

Depending on the nature of the time discretization scheme, the resulting relationship between values at t_n and t_{n+1} may be such that we can solve for the unknown solution values at t_{n+1} individually, in a straightforward algebraic fashion. Time discretization schemes that allow us to do this are called *explicit* schemes (the explicit Euler scheme is the simplest example). Time discretization schemes that require that we solve for all the values at t_{n+1} simultaneously are called *implicit* schemes (the implicit Euler scheme is the simplest example).

Constructing Finite Difference Space Discretizations

Our objective is to express the partial derivatives $\frac{\partial u}{\partial x}$, $\frac{\partial^2 u}{\partial x^2}$, and so on, as a linear combination of u evaluated at discrete points with a known truncation error. The order of the truncation error is referred to as *accuracy of the discrete approximation*. These approximations are very easy to accomplish using Taylor series expansions. To illustrate, assume we want a finite difference representation of $\frac{\partial u}{\partial x}$ evaluated at x, using discrete values to the left of x. Assume also that we want this approximation to be second order accurate. This is an example of a second-order one-sided finite difference discretization. Given a grid spacing Δx, we postulate the following expansion,

$$\Delta x \frac{\partial u}{\partial x}(x) = c_{-2}u(x - 2\Delta x) + c_{-1}u(x - \Delta x) + c_0 u(x) + \Delta x TE \qquad (7.7)$$

where TE is the truncation error. We expand the terms in the right-hand side of Equation 7.7 about x up to second order in Δx:

$$\begin{aligned}
\Delta x \frac{\partial u}{\partial x}(x) = {} & c_{-2}\left(u(x) - 2\Delta x \frac{\partial u}{\partial x}(x) + \frac{1}{2}(2\Delta x)^2 \frac{\partial^2 u}{\partial x^2}(x) + \mathcal{O}(\Delta x^3) \right) \\
& + c_{-1}\left(u(x) - \Delta x \frac{\partial u}{\partial x}(x) + \frac{1}{2}(\Delta x)^2 \frac{\partial^2 u}{\partial x^2}(x) + \mathcal{O}(\Delta x^3) \right) \\
& + c_0 u(x) + \Delta x TE
\end{aligned} \qquad (7.8)$$

We now require that the terms on the right-hand side of Equation 7.8 add up to $\Delta \frac{\partial u}{\partial x}$. We accomplish this if the coefficients c_{-2}, c_{-1}, and c_0 solve the system of equations,

$$\begin{bmatrix} 1 & 1 & 1 \\ -2 & -1 & 0 \\ 4 & 1 & 0 \end{bmatrix} \begin{bmatrix} c_{-2} \\ c_{-1} \\ c_0 \end{bmatrix} = \begin{bmatrix} 0 \\ 1 \\ 0 \end{bmatrix} \qquad (7.9)$$

Solving this system, we get

$$\frac{\partial u}{\partial x} = \frac{u(x - 2\Delta x) - 4u(x - \Delta x) + 3u(x)}{\Delta x} + \underbrace{\mathcal{O}(\Delta x^2)}_{TE} \tag{7.10}$$

We can use this approach to get higher-order discretizations (Tavella and Randall, 2000).

Four Essential Space Discretizations Most of our work with finite difference in finance can be done with just four space discretizations.

Second-order central discretizations:

$$\frac{\partial u}{\partial x} = \frac{u(x + \Delta x) - u(x - \Delta x)}{2\Delta x} + \mathcal{O}(\Delta x^2) \tag{7.11}$$

$$\frac{\partial^2 u}{\partial x^2} = \frac{u(x + \Delta x) - 2u(x) + u(x - \Delta x)}{\Delta x^2} + \mathcal{O}(\Delta x^2) \tag{7.12}$$

$$\frac{\partial^2 u}{\partial x \partial y}$$
$$= \frac{u(x + \Delta x, y + \Delta y) - u(x + \Delta x, y - \Delta y) - u(x - \Delta x, y + \Delta y) + u(x - \Delta x, y - \Delta y)}{4\Delta x \Delta y}$$
$$+ \mathcal{O}(\Delta x^2) + \mathcal{O}(\Delta y^2) + \mathcal{O}(\Delta x \Delta y) \tag{7.13}$$

One-sided first-order discretization:

$$\frac{\partial u}{\partial x} = \frac{u(x + \Delta x) - u(x)}{\Delta x} + \mathcal{O}(\Delta x) \tag{7.14}$$

Implementation of Space Discretization

For illustration, consider the following pricing equation:

$$\frac{\partial V}{\partial t} = r\frac{\partial V}{\partial x} + \frac{1}{2}\sigma^2\frac{\partial V^2}{\partial x^2} - rV \tag{7.15}$$

where r and σ are constants. We construct a grid of equally spaced points $\{x_i\} = \{x_0, x_1, \ldots, x_I\}$, such that $x_{i+1} = x_i + \Delta x$, and replace the space derivatives in Equation 7.15 with the finite difference representations in Equations 7.11 and 7.12.

$$\frac{\partial V}{\partial t}(x_i) = r\frac{V(x_{i+1}) - V(x_{i-1})}{2\Delta t} + \frac{1}{2}\sigma^2\frac{V(x_{i+1}) - 2V(x_i) + V(x_{i-1})}{\Delta x^2}$$
$$- rV(x_i) - TE \tag{7.16}$$

where TE is the truncation error that results from the discrete space approximations. We now denote by u_i the solution at grid point x_i that incorporates the trunction error. u_i is a function of time, not a function of x. We rewrite Equation 7.16 as follows:

$$\frac{du_i}{dt} = \frac{r}{2\Delta x}(u_{i+1} - u_{i-1}) + \frac{1}{2}\frac{\sigma^2}{2\Delta x^2}(u_{i+1} - 2u_i + u_{i-1}) - ru_i \tag{7.17}$$

Notice that now we have a total derivative with respect to time on the left-hand side. As the truncation error approaches zero, the discrete solution u_i approaches the exact solution $V(x_i)$. If we now focus on interior points only, $\{x_1,..., x_{I-1}\}$, we can write a system of $I - 1$ ordinary differential equations, one for each interior grid point. Rearranging Equation 7.17, we get

$$\frac{du_i}{dt} = \left(-\frac{r}{2\Delta x} + \frac{1}{2}\frac{\sigma^2}{\Delta x^2}\right)u_{i-1} + \left(-\frac{\sigma^2}{\Delta x^2} - r\right)u_i + \left(\frac{r}{2\Delta x} + \frac{1}{2}\frac{\sigma^2}{\Delta x^2}\right)u_{i+1}, \tag{7.18}$$
$$i = 1, ..., I - 1$$

This is a tridiagonal *rectangular* system; there are $I + 1$ unknowns, and there are $I - 1$ equations. u_0 and u_I are at the lower and upper boundaries, respectively. There are several things we can do to deal with u_0 and u_I.

- ■ We may be able to know an exact value or expression or a suitable approximation for the boundary values. For example, if we are pricing a call option, the lower boundary may be zero and the upper boundary may be given by the present value of the intrinsic value at maturity. If we replace u_0 and u_I with known values, the first and last columns of the rectangular system go away and the system becomes square. We can now hopefully solve for the interior values.
- ■ We may be able to express the boundary values in terms of interior values by making suitable statements about the shape of the solution near boundaries. In this case, the first and last columns of the rectangular system also go away and the system becomes square.
- ■ We may be able to add additional equations for u_0 and u_I. In this case we enlarge the system by adding two rows and making it square.
- ■ We can do a combination of the above. We will discuss this in greater detail later on.

After we introduce proper assumptions about boundaries, Equation 7.18 is written as

$$\frac{du}{dt} = Au \qquad (7.19)$$

where $u = \{u_0,\ldots, u_I\}$ and A is a matrix called the *discretization matrix*. We would like to solve this system subject to initial conditions (these are determined by the payoff). Unfortunately, this system cannot be solved analytically (except in very rare cases). To solve this system we must use a numerical *time discretization* scheme. We can now define the finite difference problem as follows. *The finite difference problem is the formulation and implementation of a scheme for the time discretization of Equation 7.19.*

As we will see, the properties of the discrete solution result from the interaction of the discretization matrix, A, and the time discretization scheme. Before proceeding, let's briefly remark on the difference between European pricing and early exercise pricing.

- In pricing a European option, we have a finite difference problem as described.
- In pricing options with early exercise (American or Bermudan), we have a discrete linear complementarity problem. From an implementation viewpoint, the early exercise and the European cases are almost identical. We will discuss this in detail later in the chapter.

One aspect crucial to the numerical efficiency of finite differences is the fact that the matrix A is *sparse*. This means that most of the entries in the matrix are zero. In addition, the discretization matrix typically has a structure that contributes to the numerical efficiency of the resulting algorithm. Although we have illustrated the space discretization with a simple one-dimensional pricing equation, the same idea applies if there are more dimensions. How about the convolution integral? It turns out that because the convolution integral contributes to the source term in the pricing equation, it does not affect the feasibility of the numerical solution. However, the discretization of the convolution integral may cause the discretization matrix to become full, as opposed to sparse. This would have a detrimental effect on efficiency. However, there are straightforward iterative techniques that we can use to get around this problem (Tavella and Randall, 2000).

The Mechanics of Finite Differences

The system in Equation 7.19 is discretized in time. To do this, we define a time step, Δt, and define time points $t_n = n\Delta t$. We use the following notation:

$$u^n = u(t_n) \qquad (7.20)$$

We now define a time scheme that approximates the total derivative $\frac{du}{dt}$. This time scheme gives the name to the resulting finite difference algorithm. The simplest time scheme is the so-called "explicit Euler scheme." When applied to Equation 7.19, this scheme is

$$\frac{du}{dt}(t) = \frac{u(t + \Delta t) - u(t)}{\Delta t} = Au(t) + TE_{\Delta t} \tag{7.21}$$

where the last term is a truncation error (the subscript in the truncation error indicates that this is the truncation error due to time discretization, as opposed to space discretization). Using our notation given by Equation 7.20,

$$\frac{u^{n+1} - u^n}{\Delta t} = Au^n + TE_{\Delta t} \tag{7.22}$$

Let's now consider the following vector equation, where $\tilde{u}$ incorporates the truncation error:

$$\frac{\tilde{u}^{n+1} - \tilde{u}^n}{\Delta t} = A\tilde{u}^n \tag{7.23}$$

Notice that at this point we have introduced two sources of numerical error. The first source is the discretization of the space derivatives. The second is the discretization of the time derivative.

Remembering that $\tilde{u}^n$, $\tilde{u}^{n+1}$ are vectors, we can rewrite this equation as

$$I\tilde{u}^{n+1} = (I + \Delta t A)\tilde{u}^n \tag{7.24}$$

where I is the identity matrix. Equation 7.24 is a particular case of a system of linear equations of the form

$$A_L\tilde{u}^{n+1} = A_R\tilde{u}^n \tag{7.25}$$

where A_L and A_R are matrices (the subscripts stand for left and right matrices.) These matrices are usually very large (equal to the number of grid points) and very sparse. The solution of Equation 7.25 has the following iterative structure:

$$b = A_R\tilde{u}^0$$
$$A_L\tilde{u}^1 = b$$
$$b = A_R\tilde{u}^1 \tag{7.26}$$
$$A_L\tilde{u}^2 = b$$
$$\vdots = \vdots$$

The vector b results from a simple and very efficient vector matrix multiplication. The solution of the system $A_L \tilde{u}^n = b$ can be extremely efficient if the sparse structure of A_L can be exploited. *This is an important reason for the preference to use second-order central differences for the approximation of the space derivatives.* In the case of a simple one-dimensional pricing equation, second-order central differences preserve the tridiagonal structure of the discretization matrix. Ideally, we would like to solve this system exploiting the sparse structure and using a direct method. For a direct method to work effectively, it must be highly specialized. Using a direct standard linear solver from a numerical library is not typically a good choice. If this approach is not possible, we can use efficient iterative techniques, as we will discuss shortly.

In the simple case illustrated by Equation 7.24, the solution of $A_L \tilde{u}^n = b$ is trivial, because $A_L = I$. In this case,

$$\begin{aligned}
\tilde{u}^{n+1} &= A_L^{-1}(I + \Delta t A)\tilde{u}^n \\
&= I^{-1}(I + \Delta t A)\tilde{u}^n \\
&= (I + \Delta t A)\tilde{u}^n
\end{aligned} \tag{7.27}$$

In this case we can get the components of $\tilde{u}$ one after the other without actually solving a linear system. *This is what characterizes an explicit method.*

To illustrate an implicit method, consider what happens if we evaluate the right-hand side of Equation 7.23 at t_{n+1}:

$$\frac{\tilde{u}^{n+1} - \tilde{u}^n}{\Delta t} = A\tilde{u}^{n+1} \tag{7.28}$$

This can be rewritten as follows:

$$(I + \Delta t A)\tilde{u}^{n+1} = I\tilde{u}^n \tag{7.29}$$

Now we must solve a linear system to advance from t_n to t_{n+1}. *This is what characterizes an implicit method.*

STABILITY AND ACCURACY ANALYSIS

To understand the reason why stability is central to the analysis of finite difference schemes, we must consider three fundamental issues.

■ Consistency: Refers to the convergence of the finite difference solution to the PDE solution as the time step and the grid size vanish.

■ Convergence: There is convergence if the finite difference solution error at a fixed point tends to zero as the time step and the grid size vanish.

■ Stability: The finite difference solution is stable if it remains bounded as the number of time steps grows.

These three issues are connected through the Lax equivalence theorem:

Given a consistent finite difference scheme applied to a properly posed initial value problem, stability is the only requirement for convergence.

Richtmeyer and Morton (1967) give a proof of this theorem.

We will only be using consistent schemes. The Lax equivalence theorem essentially means that if we are solving the right problem with a stable scheme, we can get the accuracy level we want. This also means that error and stability analyses are essential for the design of new schemes for understanding the behavior of existing ones.

There are two basic approaches to stability analysis.

■ Fourier approach: This is fairly simple and is the approach we find in most textbooks on numerical analysis. In the Fourier approach we replaced the discretized finite difference solution with Fourier modes and derive the conditions for growth of the Fourier coefficients (Tavella and Randall, 2000). The conditions under which those coefficients remain bounded determine the stability constraints. This approach is simple, but it does not take boundary conditions into account.

■ Matrix approach: This approach is based on the analysis of the eigenvalues of the discretization matrix. It is far more comprehensive than the Fourier approach and allows us to gain a deep understanding of the properties of the scheme and of the way stability is affected by boundary conditions.

We will limit our discussion to the matrix approach. The mathematics required is straightforward and the insights that can be reached are profound. The reader interested in the Fourier approach may consult Tavella and Randall (2000) for details.

Remember that the discretization of the space derivatives turns our PDE into a system of ODEs:

$$\frac{du}{dt} = Au \tag{7.30}$$

where A is the discretization matrix. We assume that A is nonsingular and has a set of linearly independent eigenvectors. If X is the matrix of eigenvectors of

A, and λ is a diagonal matrix with the eigenvalues of A, the following relationship holds (Strang, 1988):

$$X^{-1}AX = \lambda \tag{7.31}$$

We can now decouple the system in Equation 7.30 as follows. We multiply Equation 7.30 on the left by X^{-1} and take into account that $XX^{-1} = I$ to get

$$X^{-1}\frac{du}{dt} = X^{-1}AXX^{-1}u \tag{7.32}$$

We now introduce a local time linearization and assume that the elements of X are time independent:

$$\frac{dX^{-1}u}{dt} = X^{-1}AXX^{-1}u \tag{7.33}$$

Using Equation 7.31, we have

$$\frac{dX^{-1}u}{dt} = \lambda X^{-1}u \tag{7.34}$$

Introducing the definition,

$$v = X^{-1}u \tag{7.35}$$

the system of ODE in Equation 7.34 becomes

$$\frac{dv}{dt} = \lambda v \tag{7.36}$$

This is now an uncoupled system of ordinary differential equations whose solution vector, v, has elements

$$v_j = c_j \exp(\lambda_j t) \tag{7.37}$$

where c_j are constants determined by initial conditions. We will use Equation 7.36 to determine the stability characteristics of schemes.

Notice that if we solve Equation 7.36, we can recover the values we are interested in from the transformation $u = Xv$. We don't do this in an actual implementation of finite differences. The purpose of working with Equation 7.36 is only for stability analysis. The actual implementation of finite difference schemes is as described in the last section. The stability and accuracy of the implementation, however, can be inferred by analyzing the time discretization of Equation 7.36.

To determine the stability and accuracy of a scheme, we consider only one of the components of v. We determine the stability and accuracy of schemes by looking at the time evolution of the *time-discretized* solution of

$$\frac{dv_j}{dt} = \lambda_j v_j \tag{7.38}$$

We denote the discrete time solution of Equation 7.38 by $\tilde{v}_j$. The scheme will be stable if every $\tilde{v}_j$ remains bounded. To determine the time accuracy of the scheme, we consider the difference between the exact and the approximate solution of Equation 7.38, $v_j - \tilde{v}_j$. When we talk about the accuracy of a scheme, we normally refer to *time accuracy*. Time accuracy is the order of the time step to which the discrete and the exact solutions of the uncoupled system agree. This means that the order of accuracy, p, is given by

$$v_j - \tilde{v}_j = \mathcal{O}(\Delta t^{p+1}) \tag{7.39}$$

Locally, the exact solution of Equation 7.38 is

$$
\begin{aligned}
v_j &= \exp(\lambda_j t) \\
&= \exp(\lambda_j n \Delta t) \\
&= \left(1 + \lambda_j \Delta t + \frac{1}{2}(\lambda_j \Delta t)^2 + \cdots\right)^n
\end{aligned} \tag{7.40}
$$

The time discretization error is given by

$$
\begin{aligned}
v_j - \tilde{v}_j &= \exp(\lambda_j t) - \tilde{v}_j \\
&= \left(1 + \lambda_j \Delta t + \frac{1}{2}(\lambda_j \Delta t)^2 + \cdots\right)^n - \tilde{v}_j
\end{aligned} \tag{7.41}
$$

If we get an expansion for $\tilde{v}_j$ in terms of $\lambda_j \Delta_t$, we can substitute this expansion in Equation 7.41 and get an expression for the time discretization error.

We will discuss how we get an analytical expression for $\tilde{v}_j$. We will use this expression for determining stability and accuracy.

To analyze the effect of time discretization, we introduce the concept of shift operator, E^i. Given the definition,

$$v^{(n)} = v(n\Delta t) \tag{7.42}$$

the shift operator is defined through the relationship

$$E^i v^{(n)} = v^{(n+i)} \tag{7.43}$$

where the i in E^i is interpreted as a power, while the n in $v^{(n)}$ is interpreted as an index. We use parentheses to differentiate between an index and a power. (Don't confuse the shift operator with the expectation operator.) We are interested in polynomials of the shift operator because the time discretization of Equation 7.38 will introduce such polynomials.

Define a polynomial of the shift operator as

$$P(E) = \sum_{i=0}^{i=n} a_i E^i \tag{7.44}$$

where a_i are constant coefficients. An equation of the form

$$P(E)v^{(n)} = 0 \tag{7.45}$$

is known as a *homogeneous difference equation* and has the solution (Mickens, 1990):

$$v^{(n)} = \sum_{k=1}^{k=K} b_k (\Lambda_k)^n \tag{7.46}$$

where the b_k are constants and Λ_k are the roots of the polynomial equation,

$$P(\Lambda) = 0 \tag{7.47}$$

We now have the tools to get an analytical expression for $\tilde{v}_j$. If we discretize the time derivative in

$$\frac{dv_j}{dt} = \lambda_j v_j \tag{7.48}$$

we get a polynomial of the displacement operator with $\lambda_j \Delta t$ as a parameter:

$$P(E; \lambda_j \Delta t) = 0 \tag{7.49}$$

To illustrate how this happens, assume we discretize Equation 7.48 using the explicit Euler method. In this case, $\tilde{v}_j^{(n)}$ is the solution of

$$\tilde{v}_j^{(n+1)} - \tilde{v}_j^{(n)} = \Delta t \lambda_j \tilde{v}_j^{(n)} \tag{7.50}$$

which can be rewritten as

$$E^1(\tilde{v}_j^{(n)}) - \tilde{v}_j^{(n)}(1 + \Delta t \lambda_j) = 0 \tag{7.51}$$

Remember that $\tilde{\nu}$ incorporates the truncation error in the discretization. In this case the polynomial in the shift operator is

$$P(E; \lambda_j \Delta t) = E(\tilde{\nu}_j^{(n)}) - \tilde{\nu}_j^{(n)}(1 + \Delta t \lambda_j) \tag{7.52}$$

and the roots are obtained by solving

$$\Lambda_j - (1 + \Delta t \lambda_j) = 0 \tag{7.53}$$

In this simple case, the exact solution of the difference Equation 7.50 is

$$\begin{aligned} \tilde{\nu}_j^{(n)} &= c_j (\Lambda_j)^n \\ &= c_j (1 + \Delta t \lambda_j)^n \end{aligned} \tag{7.54}$$

where c_j is a constant determined from initial conditions.

We can now proceed with the general case. In general there will be K Λ-roots for each eigenvalue. The exact solution to the difference equation that results from the time discretization of Equation 7.48 is

$$\tilde{\nu}_j^{(n)} = \sum_{k=1}^{k=K} c_{jk} (\Lambda_{jk})^n \tag{7.55}$$

where c_{jk} are constants and the Λ_{jk} are solutions of

$$P(\Lambda_{jk}; \lambda_j \Delta t) = 0 \tag{7.56}$$

We now establish the connection between ν_j and $\tilde{\nu}_j$. The exact solution, from Equation 7.40, is

$$\nu_j^{(n)} = c_j \left(1 + \lambda_j \Delta t + \frac{1}{2}(\lambda_j \Delta t)^2 + \cdots \right)^n \tag{7.57}$$

The Λ_{jk} depend on λ_j and Δt only through the product $\lambda_j \Delta t$. If $\tilde{\nu}_j^{(n)}$ from Equation 7.55 is to converge to $\nu_j^{(n)}$ from Equation 7.57 as $\Delta t \to 0$, at least one of the Λ_{jk} must converge to the expansion on the right of Equation 7.57. This means that at least one of the Λ_{jk} for some k must be expressible as

$$\Lambda_{jk} = 1 + \lambda_j \Delta t + \frac{1}{2}(\lambda_j \Delta t)^2 + \cdots \mathcal{O}(\Delta t^{p+1}) \tag{7.58}$$

where the pth term is the first one that deviates from the Taylor expansion on the right-hand side of Equation 7.57. As discussed earlier, p is called the *order of accuracy* of the scheme. For each j, the Λ_{jk} that do not converge to the exponential expansion as $\Delta t \to 0$ are called *spurious roots* or *spurious amplification factors*. The spurious roots contribute to the error of the scheme and may limit the stability bounds.

For a scheme to be stable, the absolute value of all the Λ_{jk} corresponding to each eigenvalue λ_j must be less than one. This fact is determined by the combined effects of the λ_j and the choice of time discretization scheme. The λ_j are determined by the discretization matrix. The discretization matrix is determined by the choice of space discretization and by the treatment of boundary conditions.

The discretization matrix introduces a spectrum or distribution of eigenvalues λ_j. Some of these eigenvalues are relevant to the solution, some are not. The ones that are not relevant are called *parasitic eigenvalues*. The eigenvalues describe scales in the solution. For example, near expiration a call option has rapidly varying scales near the strike. To describe this solution properly we need a rich spectrum of eigenvalues. Far away from expiration, however, the solution is smoother and has fewer scales, therefore fewer eigenvalues are needed to describe the solution. The parasitic eigenvalues are scales created by the numerical algorithm. They represent high frequency modes not relevant to most of the solution. But these eigenvalues are there because they are a consequence of the space discretization, which we cannot avoid. The main difference between implicit and explicit schemes is the way they respond to these eigenvalues.

■ Implicit schemes tolerate a broad spectrum of eigenvalues. This includes both the relevant and the parasitic eigenvalues. For this reason, implicit schemes are flexible and stable.
■ Explicit schemes don't tolerate a broad spectrum of eigenvalues (either relevant or not). For this reason, implicit schemes are rigid and easily become unstable.

We can now make a preliminary remark about the connection between finite differences and trees.

■ Standard trees (binomial or trinomial) are a form of explicit scheme.
■ Trees have difficulty overcoming the rigidities created by themselves. These rigidities are their intolerance to parasitic eigenvalues and have nothing to do with the problem being solved.
■ For this reason, working with trees may require much more effort than is justified by accuracy requirements.

We will elaborate on this later.

The following section is summarized from Tavella and Randall (2000), which contains detailed analysis of other algorithms.

Analysis of Specific Algorithms

The purpose of this section is to illustrate how the framework developed in this chapter can be used to analyze individual algorithms. Following these steps, the reader can easily scrutinize alternative algorithms (including their own).

The construction of a finite difference scheme consists of two parts. One part is the space discretization, the other is the time discretization. In the matrix approach, the analysis of a particular algorithm starts out by mapping the relationship between the Λ_{jk} and the λ_j. In other words, the analysis starts with the time discretization part. This leads to the definition of regions in the λ_j complex plane where the resulting scheme will be either stable or unstable. Space and time discretizations must be such that the resulting scheme is both stable and has suitable convergence properties.

Example 1: The Explicit Euler Scheme   Consider one of the ordinary differential equations in eigenvector space resulting from space discretization:

$$\frac{dv}{dt} = \lambda v \tag{7.59}$$

Introducing the explicit approximation,

$$\left.\frac{dv}{dt}\right|^n = \frac{v^{n+1} - v^n}{\Delta t} \tag{7.60}$$

we get the following representation of the finite difference problem:

$$v^{n+1} = v^n + \lambda \Delta t v^n \tag{7.61}$$

Equivalently,

$$P(E)v^n = 0 \tag{7.62}$$

where the shift polynomial is defined as follows:

$$P(E) = E - 1 - \lambda \Delta t \tag{7.63}$$

This method has only one amplification factor:

$$\Lambda = 1 + \lambda \Delta t \tag{7.64}$$

To compute the accuracy of this method, we compare Equation 7.64 with the expansion of $e^{\lambda \Delta t}$.

$$e^{\lambda \Delta t} = 1 + \lambda \Delta t + \frac{1}{2}(\lambda \Delta t)^2 + \cdots \tag{7.65}$$

The discrepancy between the right-hand sides in Equation 7.65 and Equation 7.64 is

$$e^{\lambda \Delta t} - \Lambda = \frac{1}{2}(\lambda \Delta t)^2 + \mathcal{O}(\lambda \Delta t)^3 \tag{7.66}$$

Because the leading order term is $\mathcal{O}(\Delta t^2)$, this is a first-order accurate method. The stability region is determined by the condition $|\Lambda| \le 1$.

For the diffusion equation

$$\frac{\partial u}{\partial t} = \nu \frac{\partial^2 u}{\partial S^2} \tag{7.67}$$

discretized with central space differences, it can be shown that the most extreme eigenvalue is $\frac{-4\nu}{\Delta s^2}$ (Smith, 1985) (under the assumption that $u(S, t)$ is zero at the boundaries). It follows that for stability we require

$$\left| 1 - \frac{4\nu \Delta t}{\Delta S^2} \right| \le 1 \tag{7.68}$$

This means that the time step must be restricted as

$$\Delta t \le \frac{\Delta S^2}{2\nu} \tag{7.69}$$

Notice that if we double the number of spatial grid points, we obtain four times more spatial accuracy at the expense of four times more time steps. This, however, requires eight times more computational work. In many cases, this requirement from stability causes the time step to become much smaller than would be needed to control time discretization accuracy. We can postulate an alternative interpretation of this restriction. The inverse of each of the $|\lambda_j|$ can be viewed as a characteristic diffusion time. The smallest of such times is proportional to the square of the spatial grid spacing. Denoting this diffusion time by τ_d, the stability constraint becomes simply

$$\Delta t \le 2\tau_d \tag{7.70}$$

This means that the time step is determined by a characteristic time that is typically irrelevant to the problem under consideration. This is an illustration of the serious limitations of explicit schemes. This limitation carries over to trees.

Example 2: The Implicit Euler Scheme   Now consider the following implicit approximation to the derivative in Equation 7.59:

$$\left.\frac{dv}{dt}\right|^{n+1} = \frac{v^{n+1} - v^n}{\Delta t} \tag{7.71}$$

$$v^{n+1}(1 - \lambda\Delta t) = v^n \tag{7.72}$$

Equivalently,

$$P(E)v^n = 0 \tag{7.73}$$

where the shift polynomial is

$$P(E) = E(1 - \lambda\Delta t) - 1 \tag{7.74}$$

This method also has only one Λ root,

$$\Lambda = \frac{1}{1 - \lambda\Delta t} \tag{7.75}$$

where λ is negative. We can expand this expression in terms of $\lambda\Delta t$

$$\Lambda = 1 + \lambda\Delta t + (\lambda\Delta t)^2 + \mathcal{O}(\lambda\Delta t)^3 \tag{7.76}$$

We compute the accuracy of this method by comparing this expansion with the expansion of $e^{\lambda\Delta t}$. The discrepancy between the two expansions is

$$e^{\lambda\Delta t} - \Lambda = -\frac{1}{2}(\lambda\Delta t)^2 + \mathcal{O}(\lambda\Delta t)^3 \tag{7.77}$$

This indicates that this is also only a first-order method. Since the requirement for stability, $|\Lambda| \leq 1$, is satisfied for all values of $\lambda\Delta t$ from Equation 7.75, this is an unconditionally stable method.

This method is free from the constraint imposed by Equation 7.69. That constraint was imposed entirely by the discretization of the space dimension and was not connected with the phenomenon described by the partial differential equation. Notice that the relationship between accuracy and computational effort is less clear than in the previous case. Now advancing the solution requires solving a linear system at each time step. If we assume that the solution of the linear system requires effort linearly proportional to the number of spatial grid points, then we can quadruple the spatial accuracy by doubling the computational effort. This happens in the particularly simple case when we have a tridiagonal matrix to invert at each time step. The relationship between accuracy and computational effort is more complex (and typically less favorable) if the linear system must be solved by more general direct or iterative solvers, as is the case in multiple dimensions.

The fact that the method is unconditionally stable does not necessarily mean that the solution will make sense for large time steps. It simply means that the numerical solution will not blow up.

Example 3: The Crank-Nicholson Scheme   This method incorporates both explicit and implicit features. It is unconditionally stable but may exhibit undesirable qualities if the time step is very large. Despite this, the Crank-Nicholson scheme has been extremely popular for numerical solutions in finance. The main appeal of the method is its second-order accuracy and stability, which are achieved with a minor increase in computational cost compared to the implicit method.

Consider an approximation to the derivative in Equation 7.59 that combines explicit and implicit components:

$$\frac{1}{2}\left(\left.\frac{dv}{dt}\right|^{n} + \left.\frac{dv}{dt}\right|^{n+1}\right) = \frac{v^{n+1} - v^{n}}{\Delta t} \tag{7.78}$$

This gives the representation,

$$v^{n+1} = v^{n} + \frac{1}{2}\lambda\Delta t(v^{n+1} + v^{n}) \tag{7.79}$$

Equivalently,

$$P(E)v^{n} = 0 \tag{7.80}$$

where the shift polynomial is

$$P(E) = E\left(1 - \frac{1}{2}\lambda\Delta t\right) - \left(1 + \frac{1}{2}\lambda\Delta t\right) \tag{7.81}$$

This method also has only one Λ root:

$$\Lambda = \frac{1 + \frac{\lambda\Delta t}{2}}{1 - \frac{\lambda\Delta t}{2}} \tag{7.82}$$

We can expand this expression in terms of $\lambda\Delta t$:

$$\Lambda = 1 + \lambda\Delta t + \frac{1}{2}(\lambda\Delta t)^{2} + \frac{1}{4}(\lambda\Delta t)^{3} + \mathcal{O}(\lambda\Delta t)^{4} \tag{7.83}$$

The discrepancy between this expansion and the expansion of $e^{\lambda\Delta t}$ is

$$e^{\lambda\Delta t} - \Lambda = -\frac{1}{12}(\lambda\Delta t)^3 + \mathcal{O}(\lambda\Delta t)^4 \qquad (7.84)$$

This indicates that this is a second-order method. As was the case with the implicit Euler method, the requirement for stability, $|\Lambda| \leq 1$, is satisfied for all values of $\lambda\Delta t$ from Equation 7.82. This is also an unconditionally stable method.

The Crank-Nicholson scheme has been shown to have undesirable properties under some circumstances. To understand this, consider what happens for $\Delta t \gg \tau_d$. In this case, the amplification factor has the limit:

$$\Lambda \to -1 + 2\frac{\tau_d}{\Delta t} \qquad (7.85)$$

This means that the solution components for which $\Delta t \gg \tau_d$ may not decay appreciably, but simply oscillate in time. These components originate in discontinuities in initial conditions or in shocks such as those induced by discretely sampled barriers. Although these components do decay, we are not interested in an accurate description of their time evolution. For a satisfactory solution, these components should disappear after a relatively small number of time steps. After q time steps, Equation 7.85 implies that the amplitude of these components will have decayed by the factor:

$$\Lambda^q \approx (-1)^q \exp\left(-\frac{q\tau_d}{\Delta t}\right) \qquad (7.86)$$

This means that we can get a reduction of these components by a factor of about 2.7 after q time steps if we select Δt as follows:

$$\Delta t = q\tau_d \qquad (7.87)$$

We can select the time step to ensure that such components are damped significantly within a given number of time steps. Usually, but not always, it is not difficult to find a time step that causes the quick disappearance of these unimportant oscillations.

TIME ADVANCEMENT AND LINEAR SOLVERS

The implementation of time advancement in a finite difference solution consists of solving the iterative problem:

$$A_L \tilde{u}^{n+1} = A_R \tilde{u}^n \qquad (7.88)$$

where, as explained in the previous section, the A_L and A_R matrices result from the choice of time discretization scheme and discretization matrix.

Before discussing the methods of solution in detail, let's summarize some important features of this system.

■ Matrix A_L can be extremely large. For example, in a two-dimensional problem with a grid of 100 points along each dimension, the total number of entries in A_L would be $(100 \times 100)^2 = 10^8$.

■ Matrix A_L is also typically very sparse. If we use second-order central differences for the space derivatives and appropriate boundary conditions, this matrix is tridiagonal.

■ The sparseness of the system may be ruined by the convolution integral in the source term. If this is the case, we can use iterative techniques that rely on lagging the source terms to get around the lack of sparse structure in A_L.

■ In the case of multidimensional problems, the system will typically be sparse but will not have a tridiagonal structure. This is caused both by the multidimensionality itself and the presence of cross derivatives. In this case we can use iterative solvers or techniques that transform the original system into a sequence of systems, each one of which is a tridiagonal system, such as alternating direction implicity methods (ADI).

■ The presence of cross derivatives represents a special challenge. The matrix is changed in such a way that efficient direct solvers are not readily viable. One way to solve the problem is to use iterative solvers. Another way is to use predictor-corrector techniques for the cross derivative terms.

■ The early exercise problem modifies the problem by incorporating optimal exercise at each time step. To solve this problem with accuracy consistent with the accuracy of the finite difference scheme, the system must be solved iteratively. We discuss this in detail later on.

Next we discuss in some detail the two primary ways to solve the linear system that advances the solution in time: the use of direct solvers and iterative solvers.

Direct Solvers

To qualify as a direct solver an algorithm must reach the solution in a finite number of computational steps. An algorithm could be capable of reaching the solution within a finite number of steps theoretically, but to be a true direct solver it must be able to do so numerically. The most common direct solver is the tridiagonal solver using the Thomas algorithm. We describe this solver in detail, since this is the algorithm of choice in solving European problems that depend on one underlying. The tridiagonal solver is also relevant to multidimensional problems when they are treated as a succession of one-dimensional problems, such as in the case of alternating directions implicit (ADI) algorithms.

Tridiagonal Solver The purpose is to solve the tridiagonal system:

$$
\begin{bmatrix}
b_1 & c_1 & 0 & 0 & \cdots & 0 \\
a_2 & b_2 & c_2 & 0 & \cdots & 0 \\
\vdots & \vdots & \vdots & \vdots & \ddots & 0 \\
0 & 0 & 0 & a_{n-1} & b_{n-1} & c_{n-1} \\
0 & 0 & 0 & 0 & a_n & b_n
\end{bmatrix}
\begin{bmatrix}
u_1 \\
u_2 \\
\vdots \\
u_{n-1} \\
u_n
\end{bmatrix}
=
\begin{bmatrix}
f_1 \\
f_2 \\
\vdots \\
f_{n-1} \\
f_n
\end{bmatrix}
\tag{7.89}
$$

This is accomplished in two steps. The first step is a downward (upward) sweep of normalization and elimination, the second step is an upward (downward) sweep that yields the solution. The version of the algorithm with the downward sweep first is shown below.

Normalization:

$$
\begin{bmatrix}
1 & \frac{c_1}{b_1} & 0 & 0 & \cdots & 0 \\
a_2 & b_2 & c_2 & 0 & \cdots & 0 \\
\vdots & \vdots & \vdots & \vdots & \ddots & 0 \\
0 & 0 & 0 & a_{n-1} & b_{n-1} & c_{n-1} \\
0 & 0 & 0 & 0 & a_n & b_n
\end{bmatrix}
\begin{bmatrix}
u_1 \\
u_2 \\
\vdots \\
u_{n-1} \\
u_n
\end{bmatrix}
=
\begin{bmatrix}
\frac{f_1}{b_1} \\
f_2 \\
\vdots \\
f_{n-1} \\
f_n
\end{bmatrix}
\tag{7.90}
$$

Elimination:

$$
\begin{bmatrix}
1 & \frac{c_1}{b_1} & 0 & 0 & \cdots & 0 \\
0 & b_2 - \frac{a_2 c_1}{b_1} & c_2 & 0 & \cdots & 0 \\
\vdots & \vdots & \vdots & \vdots & \ddots & 0 \\
0 & 0 & 0 & a_{n-1} & b_{n-1} & c_{n-1} \\
0 & 0 & 0 & 0 & a_n & b_n
\end{bmatrix}
\begin{bmatrix}
u_1 \\
u_2 \\
\vdots \\
u_{n-1} \\
u_n
\end{bmatrix}
=
\begin{bmatrix}
\frac{f_1}{b_1} \\
f_2 - \frac{a_2 f_1}{b_1} \\
\vdots \\
f_{n-1} \\
f_n
\end{bmatrix}
\tag{7.91}
$$

Normalization:

$$
\begin{bmatrix}
1 & \frac{c_1}{b_1} & 0 & 0 & \cdots & 0 \\
0 & 1 & \frac{c_2}{b_2 - \frac{a_2 c_1}{b_1}} & 0 & \cdots & 0 \\
\vdots & \vdots & \vdots & \vdots & \ddots & 0 \\
0 & 0 & 0 & a_{n-1} & b_{n-1} & c_{n-1} \\
0 & 0 & 0 & 0 & a_n & b_n
\end{bmatrix}
\begin{bmatrix}
u_1 \\
u_2 \\
\vdots \\
u_{n-1} \\
u_n
\end{bmatrix}
=
\begin{bmatrix}
\frac{f_1}{b_1} \\
\frac{f_2 - \frac{a_2 f_1}{b_1}}{b_2 - \frac{a_2 c_1}{b_1}} \\
\vdots \\
f_{n-1} \\
f_n
\end{bmatrix}
\tag{7.92}
$$

This is continued until the system looks as follows:

$$
\begin{bmatrix}
1 & x_1 & 0 & 0 & \dots & 0 \\
0 & 1 & x_2 & 0 & \dots & 0 \\
\vdots & \vdots & \vdots & \vdots & \ddots & 0 \\
0 & 0 & 0 & 0 & 1 & x_{n-1} \\
0 & 0 & 0 & 0 & 0 & 1
\end{bmatrix}
\begin{bmatrix}
u_1 \\
u_2 \\
\vdots \\
u_{n-1} \\
u_n
\end{bmatrix}
=
\begin{bmatrix}
y_1 \\
y_2 \\
\vdots \\
y_{n-1} \\
y_n
\end{bmatrix}
\tag{7.93}
$$

The solution follows immediately in the upward sweep:

$$
\begin{aligned}
u_n &= y_n \\
u_{n-i} &= y_{n-i} - x_{n-i} u_{n-i+1}, \qquad i = 1, \dots, n-1
\end{aligned}
\tag{7.94}
$$

More Sophisticated Direct Solvers It is possible to use more sophisticated direct solvers that exploit the sparseness structure of the linear system. However, these solvers are not essential in practice. We can get robust implementations of finite differences using tridiagonal and iterative solvers. The interested reader may consult Tavella and Randall (2000) and the references therein.

Iterative Solvers

An iterative solver achieves the solution through an iterative improvement of an initial guess. There are two main types of iterative solvers. Stationary methods use iteration schemes with parameters that remain fixed during the iterations. Examples of these methods are the Jacobi, Gauss-Seidel, and successive overrelaxation (SOR) methods. Nonstationary methods use parameters that are updated as the iteration proceeds. Examples are the *conjugate gradient family* and *minimal residual methods*. The interested reader may consult Barrett et al. (1994) for an extensive reference on iterative methods.

Iterative solvers perform best if the matrix in $A_L u = b$ is diagonally dominant. The ideal diagonally dominant matrix is the identity matrix. Therefore, the closer A_L is to the identity matrix, the better the performance of the iterative solver. This suggests the following strategy. We select a matrix C and solve the equivalent system,

$$
[A_L C^{-1}] C u = b
\tag{7.95}
$$

where C is selected such that $A_L C^{-1}$ is as close to the indentity matrix as possible. Of course, the best choice for this would be $C = A_L$. But this is not practical, because if we knew A_L^{-1} we would have solved the problem already. Therefore, we resort to some approximation to get the matrix C or its inverse. Replacing the original system with Equation 7.95 is called *preconditioning*. The method used to obtain C is called a *preconditioner*. The simplest preconditioner is to set C^{-1} equal to the inverse of the diagonal of A_L. We will not elaborate on preconditioners here. The interested reader may refer to Tavella and Randall (2000) for a detailed discussion.

Next we describe three iterative techniques: the Jacobi, Gauss-Seidel, and Successive Overrelaxation (SOR) methods. The main objective is to describe the SOR method in detail. The reason for this is that the SOR method is sufficient to tackle most practical European multidimensional problems. Furthermore, a slight modification of SOR, called the *projected SOR*, is the technique of choice of early exercise (multidimensional or not). The reason for the order in the exposition is that the Gauss-Seidel method is a generalization of the Jacobi method, and the SOR method is a generalization of the Gauss-Seidel method.

The Jacobi Method   Consider the system of linear equations,

$$\sum_{j=1}^{j=N} a_{ij} u_j = f_i, \qquad i = 1, \ldots, N \tag{7.96}$$

If we solved for a particular unknown assuming that we know the values of all the others, we would have the following expression:

$$u_i = \frac{1}{a_{ii}} \left(f_i - \sum_{j \neq i} a_{ij} u_j \right) \tag{7.97}$$

This equation suggests an iterative algorithm of the form,

$$u_i^{n+1} = \frac{1}{a_{ii}} \left(f_i - \sum_{j \neq i} a_{ij} u_j^n \right) \tag{7.98}$$

where n stands for the iteration number, not to be confused with the time step (this iteration is happening within a given time step).

The Gauss-Seidel Method   The Gauss-Seidel method is a simple generalization of the Jacobi method. The only change is that the changes that occur to the unknowns are incorporated into the scheme as they occur. The algorithm is as follows:

$$u_i^{n+1} = \frac{1}{a_{ii}} \left(f_i - \sum_{j < i} a_{ij} u_j^{n+1} - \sum_{j > i} a_{ij} u_j^n \right) \tag{7.99}$$

Here also we can use the framework we presented to analyze the stability and convergence of the scheme.

The Successive Overrelaxation Method The *successive overrelaxation method (SOR)* is constructed by averaging a Gauss-Seidel iterate with a previous iterate:

$$\tilde{u}_i^{n+1} = \frac{1}{a_{ii}}\left(f_i - \sum_{j<i} a_{ij} u_j^{n+1} - \sum_{j>i} a_{ij} u_j^n\right) \tag{7.100}$$

$$u_i^{n+1} = \omega \tilde{u}_i^{n+1} + (1-\omega) u_i^n \tag{7.101}$$

The parameter ω is called the *overrelaxation parameter.* Its value strongly affects the rate of convergence of the method. The optimal value of ω is in general difficult to compute. In financial applications it is often the case that $\omega = 1$ is the safest choice.

FINITE DIFFERENCE APPROACH FOR EARLY EXERCISE

The application of finite difference schemes to price American-style derivatives is the subject of much ongoing research. Here we present a basic discussion on the finite difference discretization of the partial differential complementarity formulation introduced in Chapter 3. By discretizing the partial differential complementarity problem, we reduce the American option pricing problem to the solution of a sequence of linear complementarity problems (LCP). For greater detail, the reader is referred to the extensive work by Cottle, Pang, and Stone (1992), where convergence issues are thoroughly discussed.

The Linear Complementarity Problem

Given a matrix A and vectors b and c, the linear complementarity problem consists of finding vector x that satisfies the following conditions:

$$Ax \geq b \tag{7.102}$$

$$x \geq c \tag{7.103}$$

$$(x-c)(Ax-c) = 0 \tag{7.104}$$

To illustrate how the partial differential complementarity formulation of the option pricing problem leads to a sequence of LCPs, assume the following PDCP:

$$u(S,t) \geq F(S,t)$$

$$\frac{\partial u}{\partial t} \mathcal{L}(u) \geq 0$$

$$\left(\frac{\partial u}{\partial t} - \mathcal{L}(u)\right)(u-F) = 0 \tag{7.105}$$

$$0 \leq t \leq T, \ 0 \leq S \leq \infty$$

$$u(S,0) = F(S,0), \ 0 \leq S \leq \infty$$

where

$$\mathcal{L} = \mu_S \frac{\partial}{\partial S} + \frac{1}{2}\sigma_S^2 \frac{\partial^2}{\partial S^2} - ru \tag{7.106}$$

Consider the application of the Crank-Nicholson scheme to the PDCP above. As we saw earlier, the Crank-Nicholson scheme consists of approximating the $\mathcal{L}u$ operator as follows. (For added clarity, in the remainder of this section we will use bolded letters to indicate arrays.)

$$\mathcal{L}\mathbf{u} \approx \frac{1}{2}(A\mathbf{u}^{n+1} + A\mathbf{u}^n) + \frac{1}{2}(\mathbf{f}^{n+1} + \mathbf{f}^n) \tag{7.107}$$

where A is a matrix and $\mathbf{f}$ are boundary terms.
    Introducing the definitions:

$$M = I - \frac{\Delta t}{2}A$$

$$\mathbf{b} = \left(I + \frac{\Delta t}{2}A\right)\mathbf{u}^n + \frac{\Delta t}{2}(\mathbf{f}^{n+1} + \mathbf{f}^n)$$

and replacing in the definition of the PDCP, we get the following LCP:

$$\mathbf{u}^{n+1} \geq \mathbf{F}$$
$$M\mathbf{u}^{n+1} \geq \mathbf{b} \tag{7.108}$$

$$(\mathbf{u}^{n+1} - \mathbf{F})^T (M\mathbf{u}^{n+1} - \mathbf{b}) = 0$$
$$\mathbf{u}^0 = \mathbf{F} \tag{7.109}$$

where $\mathbf{F}$ is a discrete approximation to the intrinsic value, F. This shows that we must solve an LCP at each time step.
    An equivalent and more compact version is obtained by making the following substitutions:

$$\mathbf{z} = \mathbf{u} - \mathbf{F} \tag{7.110}$$

$$\mathbf{q} = M\mathbf{F} - \mathbf{b} \tag{7.111}$$

With this we get the representation of the LCP discussed by Cottle, Pang, and Stone (1992):

$$\mathbf{z} \geq 0$$
$$\mathbf{q} + M\mathbf{z} \geq 0 \tag{7.112}$$

$$z^T(q + Mz) = 0 \tag{7.113}$$

Two fundamental questions in the solution of an LCP refer to the uniqueness of the solution and to the formulation of a suitable method of solution. The answer to both of these questions depends primarily on the nature of the matrix M. As discussed by Huang and Pang (1998), the vector q is not particularly significant in establishing the properties of the LCP.

The LCP has a unique solution for all vectors q if and only if the matrix M is what is referred to as a *P-matrix*. A *P*-matrix is one whose real eigenvalues are all positive; this is equivalent to having all principal minors positive. A positive definite matrix is a particular case of a *P*-matrix. On the other hand, a *P*-matrix is not necessarily positive definite, since it need not be symmetric.

The second question we must consider is the selection of a method of solution. Just as it was the case with systems of linear equations, the methods of solution for the LCP fall into two categories: methods that yield the solution in a finite number of steps, called *pivoting methods*, and iterative methods. Also as is the case with linear systems, the selection of a suitable method is influenced by the size of the problem. A finite difference discretization of the PDCP will typically give rise to a very large matrix M, with the same characteristics as the matrices that arise in pricing European options. This is the primary reason why we will limit our discussion here to iterative methods.

We now motivate the derivation of iterative methods for solving the LCP by observing that a vector z is a solution to an LCP if and only if it satisfies the following relationship:

$$\min(z, q + Mz) = 0 \tag{7.114}$$

If we now represent matrix M as the sum of two matrices, B and C, and assume that a vector z^k from the kth iteration is available, the following recursive algorithm for determining z suggests itself:

$$\min(Bz^{k+1}, q + Cz^k + Bz^{k+1}) = 0 \tag{7.115}$$

Notice that here k does not refer to a point in time, but it refers to the kth iteration for the LCP we must solve at a given point in time. We can express this algorithm as a fixed point iteration:

$$Bz^{k+1} = B\tilde{z}^{k+1} \tag{7.116}$$

$$B\tilde{z}^{k+1} = Bz^{k+1} - \min(Bz^{k+1}, q + Cz^k + Bz^{k+1}) \tag{7.117}$$

Straightforward algebraic manipulations lead to the following iterative algorithm:

$$\mathbf{z}^{k+1} = \max(0, \mathbf{z}^n - B^{-1}(\mathbf{q} + M)\mathbf{z}^k) \tag{7.118}$$

Notice that there is a parallel between this iterative algorithm and the standard iterative algorithms for solving linear systems. Depending on the choice of matrix B, we obtain LCP versions of the linear system methods. For example, if B is chosen as the diagonal of M, we obtain the so-called "projected Jacobi method." It is called "projected" because the max( ) operator causes the next iterate to be positive.

The most popular algorithm for the solution of the LCP in option pricing is the *projected successive overrelaxation algorithm*. We obtain this algorithm by the following selection of the B matrix:

$$B = L + \omega^{-1}D \tag{7.119}$$

where L is the strictly lower triangular part of M, $D = \text{diag}(m_{11},\ldots, m_{nn})$, and ω is a relaxation parameter. Notice that in this case, care must be taken when applying the max( ) operator. The implementation of the PSOR algorithm to the LCP in Equation 7.108 leads to

$$\tilde{u}_i^{k+1} = \frac{1}{m_{ii}}\left(F_i - \sum_{j<i} m_{ij}u_j^{k+1} - \sum_{j>i} m_{ij}u_j^k\right) \tag{7.120}$$

$$u_i^{n+1} = \max[F_i, \omega\tilde{u}_i^{k+1} + (1 - \omega)u_i^k] \tag{7.121}$$

where $\tilde{u}$ is an intermediate value (this requires these two equations to be solved in succession for each i).

The next question to address is under what conditions does the PSOR algorithm converge. For values of ω in a range $1 < \omega \le 2$, the PSOR algorithm converges if M is an H_+-matrix (Huang and Pang, 1998). M is an H_+-matrix if the following two conditions are satisfied: The diagonal elements of M are positive, and the matrix $\tilde{M}$ is defined next as a P-matrix.

$$\tilde{m}_{ii} = |m_{ii}| \tag{7.122}$$

$$\tilde{m}_{ij} = -|m_{ij}|, \ i \ne j \tag{7.123}$$

A symmetric, positive definite matrix is a particular case of an H_+-matrix. In practical applications, we get a positive definite M if the pricing equation has been transformed into a simple diffusion equation with constant coefficients. If this is not done, the second-order discretization of the convection terms will cause the off-diagonal elements of M to be nonsymmetrical. If the matrix is not symmetric, we can no longer talk of a positive definite matrix in the traditional sense. A nonsymmetric matrix whose symmetrical part is positive definite is not necessarily an H_+-matrix.

Good performance of the PSOR method is typically associated with diagonal dominance. By observing the definition of the matrix M, it is easy to see that diagonal dominance improves as the time step is reduced. When central differences are used for both the convective and diffusion terms, it may be required that the time step be made sufficiently small for convergence to occur.

BOUNDARY CONDITIONS

The characterization and imposition of boundary conditions (BCs) must be done carefully. In many cases, bad or improperly imposed BCs will spoil the numerical solution or mask important features of the solution. In some cases, the solution may look perfectly acceptable but be fundamentally wrong. In some other cases, the solution may be so featureless that the use of bad boundary conditions may not matter. This is the case of a *vanilla call*. Bad BCs will not matter if the solution cannot propagate its effects. In the case of a vanilla call, for example, both the upper and lower boundaries may be so far removed from the region of significant diffusion (near the strike), that the solution may not be able to carry the wrong information into the area of interest. This should serve as a warning against using simple problems such as vanilla calls to check the correctness of BC implementations. We may get the right answer, even if our BCs are wrong. In other cases, one of several variations of good BCs can make the difference needed to achieve trading quality values. This is sometimes the case with bonds.

There are several criteria that we may use to determine the BCs for a specific problem. We will discuss some of these issues in greater detail in the text.

■ Solution geometry: It may happen that we know the shape of the solution in the vicinity of the computational boundaries. For example, if the solution becomes a flat surface at large distances, we may exploit this fact to produce a suitable boundary condition. This type of BC destroys the pricing equation at the boundary.

■ Asymptotic behavior: Sometimes we know limiting analytical forms of the solution near the boundaries. For example, in a call option we can derive an analytical expression for the value of the call when the spot is very large. This also gives us a way of producing a valid BC.

■ Known solution values: In some cases we may know the value of the solution at the computational boundary. For example, in the case of an up-and-out call with a known rebate, the solution value at the barrier equals the known value of the rebate. If we choose the barrier to be part of the boundary, we immediately have a suitable boundary condition by setting the solution value equal to the rebate.

■ Use of the pricing equation: The pricing equation itself may be used as a BC. In this case, the discretization of the pricing equation at boundaries must be such that only internal points are involved. Using the pricing equation as BC may or may not influence efficiency.

■ Use of modified pricing equation: Simplified forms of the pricing equation can sometimes be used at the boundaries. For example, at the boundaries we may assume that diffusion is negligible compared with convection.

Implementation of Boundary Conditions

There are three basic approaches for implementing boundary conditions. We can embed the boundary conditions in the discretization such that the known boundaries drop out of the equations; we can expand the system of equations by adding boundary equations; or we can enforce the boundary conditions through iteration.

Embedding Boundary Conditions in Discretization   By embedding the boundary conditions in the discretization matrix, we reduce the number of equations by twice the number of dimensions (there are two boundaries for each dimension). This is a common approach in textbooks. To illustrate, consider the case where the system we must solve at each time step is tridiagonal. We refer to the following system as the *discretization system*:

$$
\underbrace{\begin{bmatrix} a_{-1,0} & a_{0,0} & a_{1,0} & 0 & \cdots \\ 0 & a_{-1,1} & a_{0,1} & a_{1,1} & \cdots \\ \vdots & \vdots & \vdots & \vdots & \vdots \end{bmatrix}}_{A_L} \begin{bmatrix} u_0 \\ u_1 \\ u_2 \\ \vdots \end{bmatrix}^{n+1} = \underbrace{\begin{bmatrix} b_{-1,0} & b_{0,0} & b_{1,0} & 0 & \cdots \\ 0 & b_{-1,1} & b_{0,1} & b_{1,1} & \cdots \\ \vdots & \vdots & \vdots & \vdots & \vdots \end{bmatrix}}_{A_R} \begin{bmatrix} u_0 \\ u_1 \\ u_2 \\ \vdots \end{bmatrix}^{n} \quad (7.124)
$$

The unknowns are $u_0, \ldots, u_I$. As written, matrices A_L and A_R are rectangular (there are more unknowns than equations). The boundary conditions must be brought in to take care of u_0 and u_I. The idea is to eliminate u_0 and

u_I at $n + 1$ and create a new vector on the right-hand side. If u_0 and u_I are given, we have

$$
\begin{bmatrix} a_{0,0} & a_{1,0} & 0 & \cdots \\ a_{-1,1} & a_{0,1} & a_{1,1} & \cdots \\ \vdots & \vdots & \vdots & \vdots \end{bmatrix} \begin{bmatrix} u_1 \\ u_2 \\ \vdots \end{bmatrix}^{n+1}
$$

$$
= \begin{bmatrix} b_{-1,0} & b_{0,0} & b_{1,0} & 0 & \cdots \\ 0 & b_{-1,1} & b_{0,1} & b_{1,1} & \cdots \\ \vdots & \vdots & \vdots & \vdots & \vdots \end{bmatrix} \begin{bmatrix} u_0 \\ u_1 \\ u_2 \\ \vdots \end{bmatrix}^{n} + \underbrace{\begin{bmatrix} -u_0 a_{0,-1} \\ 0 \\ \vdots \end{bmatrix}^{n+1}}_{BC}
\tag{7.125}
$$

Here we only show the modification to the first equation, but a similar modification occurs for the last equation. The matrix on the left is now square, but the matrix on the right is rectangular.

The advantage of this approach is that we preserve the structure of A_R. There are some disadvantages, however, because we need to create an additional vector, and we need to work with a combination of square and rectangular matrices.

Implementing Boundary Conditions by Expanding Discretization System

Assume that u_0 and u_I are known. The system in Equation 7.124 can be expanded by adding one equation for u_0 and another for u_I:

$$
\begin{bmatrix} 1 & 0 & 0 & 0 & \cdots \\ a_{-1,0} & a_{0,0} & a_{1,0} & 0 & \cdots \\ 0 & a_{-1,1} & a_{0,1} & a_{1,1} & \cdots \\ \vdots & \vdots & \vdots & \vdots & \vdots \end{bmatrix} \begin{bmatrix} u_0 \\ u_1 \\ u_2 \\ \vdots \end{bmatrix}^{n+1} = \begin{bmatrix} 1 & 0 & 0 & 0 & \cdots \\ b_{-1,0} & b_{0,0} & b_{1,0} & 0 & \cdots \\ 0 & b_{-1,1} & b_{0,1} & b_{1,1} & \cdots \\ \vdots & \vdots & \vdots & \vdots & \vdots \end{bmatrix} \begin{bmatrix} u_0 \\ u_1 \\ u_2 \\ \vdots \end{bmatrix}^{n}
\tag{7.126}
$$

The solution vector on the right-hand side of Equation 7.126 is constructed with $u_1, \ldots, u_{I-1}$ at n but u_0 and u_I at $n + 1$.

As another example of this technique, assume we want to invoke zero curvature at the u_0. Since

$$
\frac{\partial^2 u}{\partial x^2} \approx \frac{u_0 - 2u_1 + u_2}{\Delta x^2}
\tag{7.127}
$$

this requirement amounts to

$$
u_0 - 2u_1 + u_2 = 0
\tag{7.128}
$$

To reflect this requirement, Equation 7.124 can be modified as follows:

$$
\begin{bmatrix}
1 & -2 & 1 & 0 & \cdots \\
a_{-1,0} & a_{0,0} & a_{1,0} & 0 & \cdots \\
0 & a_{-1,1} & a_{0,1} & a_{1,1} & \cdots \\
\vdots & \vdots & \vdots & \vdots & \vdots
\end{bmatrix}
\begin{bmatrix} u_0 \\ u_1 \\ u_2 \\ \vdots \end{bmatrix}^{n+1}
=
\begin{bmatrix}
0 & 0 & 0 & 0 & \cdots \\
b_{-1,0} & b_{0,0} & b_{1,0} & 0 & \cdots \\
0 & b_{-1,1} & b_{0,1} & b_{1,1} & \cdots \\
\vdots & \vdots & \vdots & \vdots & \vdots
\end{bmatrix}
\begin{bmatrix} u_0 \\ u_1 \\ u_2 \\ \vdots \end{bmatrix}^{n}
\quad (7.129)
$$

There are some distinct advantages to this approach. All matrices are of the same size, there is no need for creating additional vectors, and it is the natural framework for specifying a PDE at the boundary. One disadvantage is that in some cases we may ruin the original structure of the A_L matrix. This is the case in Equation 7.129, where the matrix on the left is no longer tridiagonal.

Solving Alternative PDEs at Boundaries

We need an additional condition at the boundary because central differences don't apply at the boundary. One-sided differences, however, do apply at the boundary. Therefore, at boundaries we can use the pricing equation, or a simplified version of the pricing equation, discretized with one-sided differences. Assume we are solving the one-dimensional problem:

$$
\frac{\partial u}{\partial t} + \mu \frac{\partial u}{\partial x} + \frac{1}{2}\sigma^2 \frac{\partial^2 u}{\partial x^2} - ru = 0 \text{ plus end conditions} \quad (7.130)
$$

In our discussion of stability, we assumed that we were advancing in time to maturity. To do this we made a trivial time transformation. This was done for simplicity. In practice, however, it is customary to leave the pricing equation as is and instead advance with negative time steps, starting at maturity and progressing down to valuation time. In this section we assume that we do this. The basic idea is not affected by this detail of implementation.

Pricing Equation 7.130 can be used as is at the boundary, or we can use a simpler version by eliminating the diffusion part:

$$
\frac{\partial u}{\partial t} + \mu \frac{\partial u}{\partial x} - ru = 0 \text{ plus end conditions} \quad (7.131)
$$

In the case of multidimensional problems, we have more choices. We may decide that diffusion is not important in one dimension, but that it is important in another dimension. The correct decision is a matter of insight, experience, and understanding of the problem at hand.

We now develop an example in detail by assuming that we want to use the convection part on the boundaries. The starting point is the discretization matrix.

At $i = 0$ we use one-sided differences:

$$\frac{\partial u}{\partial t} \approx -\left(\mu\frac{u_1 - u_0}{\Delta x} - ru_0\right) \tag{7.132}$$

At $1 \le i \le I-1$ we use central differences:

$$\frac{\partial u}{\partial t} \approx -\left(\mu\frac{u_{i+1} - u_{i-1}}{2\Delta x} + \frac{1}{2}\sigma^2\frac{u_{i+1} - 2u_i + u_{i-1}}{\Delta x^2} - ru_i\right) \tag{7.133}$$

At $i = I$ we use one-sided differences:

$$\frac{\partial u}{\partial t} \approx -\left(\mu\frac{u_I - u_{I-1}}{\Delta x} - ru_I\right) \tag{7.134}$$

The time-discretized problem looks as follows:

$$\frac{d}{dt}\begin{bmatrix} u_0 \\ \vdots \\ u_i \\ \vdots \\ u_I \end{bmatrix} = -\underbrace{\begin{bmatrix} -\frac{\mu}{\Delta x} - r & \frac{\mu}{\Delta x} & \cdots & 0 & 0 \\ \vdots & \vdots & \vdots & \vdots & \vdots \\ \cdots & \frac{\mu}{2\Delta x} - \frac{\sigma^2}{2\Delta x^2} & \frac{\sigma^2}{\Delta x^2} + r & \frac{\mu}{2\Delta x} - \frac{\sigma^2}{2\Delta x^2} & \cdots \\ \vdots & \vdots & \vdots & \vdots & \vdots \\ 0 & 0 & \cdots & -\frac{\mu}{\Delta x} & \frac{\mu}{\Delta x} - r \end{bmatrix}}_{A}\begin{bmatrix} u_0 \\ \vdots \\ u_i \\ \vdots \\ u_I \end{bmatrix} \tag{7.135}$$

Assuming we use the Crank-Nicholson scheme, we have

$$\underbrace{\left(I + \frac{\Delta t}{2}A\right)}_{A_L} u^{n+1} = \underbrace{\left(I - \frac{\Delta t}{2}A\right)}_{A_R} u^n \tag{7.136}$$

Replacing Equation 7.135 in the last equation, we get

$$A_L = -\begin{bmatrix} 1 + \frac{\Delta t}{2}\left(-\frac{\mu}{\Delta x} - r\right) & \frac{\Delta t}{2}\frac{\mu}{\Delta x} & \cdots & 0 & 0 \\ \vdots & \vdots & \vdots & \vdots & \vdots \\ \cdots & \frac{\Delta t}{2}\left(\frac{\mu}{2\Delta x} - \frac{\sigma^2}{2\Delta x^2}\right) & 1 + \frac{\Delta t}{2}\left(\frac{\sigma^2}{\Delta x^2} + r\right) & \frac{\Delta t}{2}\left(-\frac{\mu}{2\Delta x} - \frac{\sigma^2}{2\Delta x^2}\right) & \cdots \\ \vdots & \vdots & \vdots & \vdots & \vdots \\ 0 & 0 & \cdots & \frac{\Delta t}{2}\frac{\mu}{\Delta x} & 1 + \frac{\Delta t}{2}\left(\frac{\mu}{\Delta x} - r\right) \end{bmatrix} \tag{7.137}$$

$$
A_R = \begin{bmatrix}
1 - \frac{\Delta t}{2}\left(-\frac{\mu}{\Delta x} - r\right) & -\frac{\Delta t}{2}\frac{\mu}{\Delta x} & \cdots & 0 & 0 \\
\vdots & \vdots & \vdots & \vdots & \vdots \\
\cdots & -\frac{\Delta t}{2}\left(\frac{\mu}{2\Delta x} - \frac{\sigma^2}{2\Delta x^2}\right) & 1 - \frac{\Delta t}{2}\left(\frac{\sigma^2}{\Delta x^2} + r\right) & -\frac{\Delta t}{2}\left(-\frac{\mu}{2\Delta x} - \frac{\sigma^2}{2\Delta x^2}\right) & \cdots \\
\vdots & \vdots & \vdots & \vdots & \vdots \\
0 & 0 & \cdots & -\frac{\Delta t}{2}\frac{\mu}{\Delta x} & 1 - \frac{\Delta t}{2}\left(\frac{\mu}{\Delta x} - r\right)
\end{bmatrix}
$$

$$(7.138)$$

In this simple example, the use of the convection terms at the boundaries did not alter the tridiagonal structure of the A_L matrix. Notice that the one-sided discretization we used is first-order accurate, while the rest of the discretization is second order. If we had used second-order one-sided differencing for the convection terms, we would have altered the tridiagonal nature of the discretization matrix. Likewise, if we had used the full equation at the boundaries, one-sided discretization would have altered the tridiagonal structure of the discretization matrix.

The destruction of the tridiagonal structure is not only a problem for a direct solver. It may also alter the convergence properties of the SOR or PSOR iterations, causing them to fail. This failure occurs because the iteration matrix of the SOR or PSOR algorithm contains eigenvalues greater than one. This may occur if the grid is sufficiently fine. The implication is that while the use of a more accurate boundary condition (the full pricing equation) may be beneficial in that it better represents what happens at the boundary, which increases accuracy, this benefit may come at the price of a more likely appearance of the wrong eigenvalue in the SOR iteration matrix. The particular strategy for accuracy and efficiency is highly problem dependent.

BARRIERS

The finite difference method is an excellent approach for pricing barrier options. Barrier options are also a rich test case that illustrate a number of important complexities in finite difference computations. Because barrier options are prime candidates for finite difference computations, we discuss them in sufficient detail, including what should be expected from numerical computations.

- Barrier options clearly show how discrete sampling results can be used to obtain results for continuous sampling or other sampling frequencies without having to compute a separate problem in each case.
- Barrier options demonstrate the importance and the consequences of using coordinate transformations.

- Barrier options illustrate the use of finite difference strategies for compound options.
- Barrier options are a clear example of pricing equations with time-dependent coefficients.

We will discuss the coordinate transformation implications of pricing barrier options at this time. We will, however, discuss coordinate transformations in much greater detail in a later section.

Coordinate Transformation Versus Process Transformation

When pricing an instrument with a time-dependent barrier, it may be desirable to treat the barrier as a boundary, as shown in Figure 7.2. If we do this, the grid lines would be curved and the grid spacing would not be uniform.

It is very desirable to map the barriers to constant boundaries, as shown in Figure 7.3. This allows us to use a uniform finite difference grid.

We can view the mapping from a time-dependent barrier to a constant barrier in two equivalent ways. To illustrate, assume that the pricing equation is

$$\frac{\partial u}{\partial t} + u\frac{\partial u}{\partial x} + \frac{1}{2}\sigma^2\frac{\partial^2 u}{\partial x^2} - ru = 0 \ x \le h(t), \ u(x = h(t)) = R, \text{ plus ECs} \quad (7.139)$$

where R is the rebate. The value of this instrument is driven by

$$dx = \mu dt + \sigma dW(t) \quad (7.140)$$

To transform the problem such that the rebate is applied to a constant barrier, we can define the transformation,

$$z = h_0\frac{x}{h(t)} \quad (7.141)$$

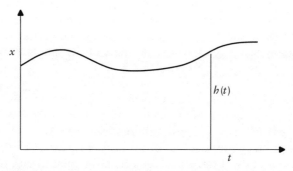

FIGURE 7.2 Barrier option with a time-dependent barrier. The underlying process is $x(t)$ and the barrier is an upper boundary.

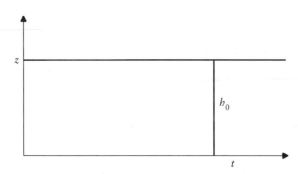

FIGURE 7.3 Barrier option with time-dependent barrier mapped to a constant. The underlying process, $z(t)$, has been selected so that it takes the value h_0 when $x(t) = h(t)$.

and use the chain rule to transform Equation 7.139 to

$$\frac{\partial u}{\partial t} + \frac{h_0}{h(t)}\left(\mu - \frac{z}{h_0}\frac{dh}{dt}\right)\frac{\partial u}{\partial z} + \frac{1}{2}\frac{h_0^2}{h(t)^2}\sigma^2\frac{\partial^2 u}{\partial z^2} - ru = 0, z \le h_0 \tag{7.142}$$

$$u(z = h_0) = R, \text{ plus ECs}$$

Another way of viewing this transformation is to define a new process,

$$dz = d\left(h_0\frac{x}{h(t)}\right)$$

$$= \frac{h_0}{h(t)}\left(\mu - \frac{z}{h_0}\frac{dh}{dt}\right)dt + \frac{h_0}{h(t)}\sigma dW(t) \tag{7.143}$$

and then use this new process to get the new pricing equation. This also results in Equation 7.142.

A general recommendation for computing barrier options is to transform the computational domains into strips bounded by the barriers. A very common case is when the payoff of the barrier option is another option. In some cases, the option that is part of the barrier payoff can be computed analytically. This would be the case in simple barrier options whose payoff is a straightforward Black and Scholes call or put option. But in cases where the payoff is a more complex option, we would like to compute the value of the payoff option using finite differences as well. In this case, there is an issue regarding the grid to be used for the barrier option and for the payoff option. Several alternatives exist here. The grid of the underlying option can be a subset of the grid of the barrier option, or they can be different grids. If the grids are different, the information of the payoff at the barrier must be transferred through interpolation from the grid of the payoff option to the barrier option.

The next few figures show finite difference results for the value, delta, and gamma of a continuously sampled up and out call on a log-normal asset with volatility $\sigma = 0.2$ and dividend yield $d = 0.02$. The maturity is one year, and the strike, K, is 100. These are highly accurate computations done with the Crank-Nicholson scheme. The reader interested in computing barrier options with finite differences should be attentive to the features shown in the following figures.

Figures 7.4, 7.5, and 7.6 show the value, delta, and gamma very near maturity. The important thing to notice is the presence of steep gradients.

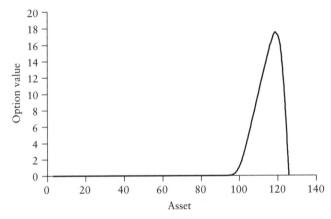

FIGURE 7.4 Continuously sampled up-and-out call. Option value at 0.02 years away from maturity. Log-normal asset process with $\sigma = 0.2$, $r = 0.07$, $d = 0.02$, $K = 100$, $T = 1$ year, barrier at 125.8.

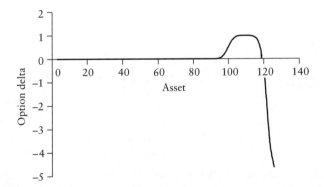

FIGURE 7.5 Continuously sampled up-and-out call. Option delta at 0.02 years away from maturity. Log-normal asset process with $\sigma = 0.2$, $r = 0.07$, $K = 100$, $T = 1$ year, barrier at 125.8.

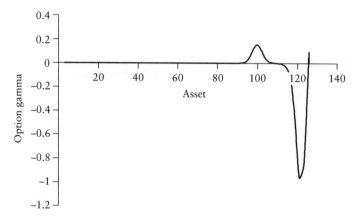

FIGURE 7.6   Continuously sampled up-and-out call. Option gamma at 0.02 years away from maturity. Log-normal asset process with $\sigma = 0.2$, $r = 0.07$, $K = 100$, $T = 1$ year, barrier at 125.8.

Figures 7.7, 7.8, and 7.9 show the value, delta, and gamma halfway to maturity. Comparing these figures with the previous ones, we see a lessening of gradients. Notice that the curves' shapes don't undergo a trivial rescaling or change as we move away from maturity. This type of detail is important in judging the quality of the numerical solution.

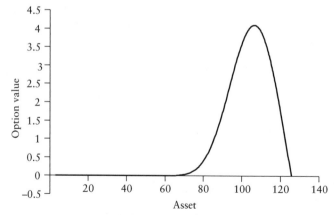

FIGURE 7.7   Continuously sampled up-and-out call. Option value at 0.5 years away from maturity. Log-normal asset process with $\sigma = 0.2$, $r = 0.07$, $d = 0.02$, $K = 100$, $T = 1$ year, barrier at 125.8.

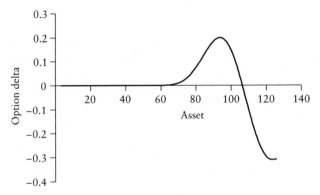

FIGURE 7.8 Continuously sampled up-and-out call. Option delta at 0.5 years away from maturity. Log-normal asset process with $\sigma = 0.2$, $r = 0.07$, $K = 100$, $T = 1$ year, barrier at 125.8.

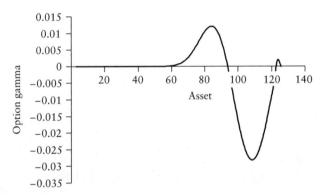

FIGURE 7.9 Continuously sampled up-and-out call. Option gamma at 0.5 years away from maturity. Log-normal asset process with $\sigma = 0.2$, $r = 0.07$, $K = 100$, $T = 1$ year, barrier at 125.8.

Discrete Sampling of Barriers

When solving a barrier option problem, we design the computational grid such that grid points are placed on the barrier. Since barrier payoff values are assigned to the discretely placed grid points on the barrier, does this mean that what we are actually solving is a discretely sampled barrier problem? *The answer is no.* We are solving a continuously sampled barrier problem. To resolve the discrete nature of the sampling properly, the solution regions between sampling points must be resolved. This requires that we place grid points between sampling points as well.

Pricing a discretely sampled barrier option can be viewed in two different ways. One way is to regard each discrete sampling of a barrier as an initial value problem. In this view, a discretely sampled barrier option is a sequence of initial value problems, each problem starting at the sampling computational time. An alternative view is to consider the discrete sampling as a Bermudan exercise, where the holder of the option receives the barrier payoff if the spot price is anywhere about the barrier at sampling time.

These two views are conceptually equivalent but have different numerical implications. The initial value view of discretely sampled barriers is the most common one. At each sampling time, new initial values for the solution of the pricing equation are created by including the barrier payoff as part of the initial values, and the solution is allowed to diffuse outside the barrier up to the next sampling point, where new initial values are created (Tavella and Randall, 2000). Near the sampling times there are strong gradients, and caution must be taken in constructing a grid that can capture these gradients. Since the sampling is captured by initial values, the solution between sampling points is a European problem, which in many cases can be solved with fast solvers (when the matrices are tridiagonals). The Bermudan view consists of regarding the sampling time as an exercise time where the holder exercises into the barrier payoff. The same issues about strong gradients arise here as well. In this case, however, the option payoff is immersed in the solution field. This requires the use of a PSOR to preserve accuracy (Tavella and Randall, 2000).

The presence of discrete sampling causes changes in the distribution of value, delta, and gamma that are not immediately obvious. We will consider an up-and-out call option as in the previous case, but it will be discretely sampled eight times between inception and maturity. We focus on the features of these distributions as we approach maturity. The following figures show results at 0.02 years away from the next sampling point.

Figures 7.10, 7.11, and 7.12 show the value, delta, and gamma with five remaining samplings to maturity (three samplings have already taken place). The important feature to notice is the apparent oscillation in the distribution of gamma in Figure 7.12. A fair question to ask is whether these "oscillations" originate in improperly damped waves in the numerical solution, or whether they are a legitimate feature of the solution. These computations were made in a way that no oscillations due to the numerics should be visible.

To understand the origin of this behavior, we look at the same parameters when only one sampling point remains. This is shown in Figures 7.13, 7.14, and 7.15.

Examination of these figures shows that they are very similar to Figures 7.4, 7.5, and 7.6, except that the plots extend beyond the barrier. The fact

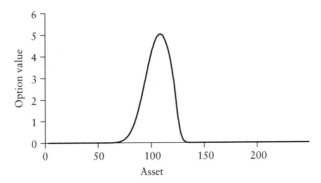

FIGURE 7.10 **Discretely sampled up-and-out call.** Option value with five samplings remaining. Log-normal asset process with $\sigma = 0.2$, $r = 0.07$, $d = 0.02$, $K = 100$, $T = 1$ year, barrier at 125.8.

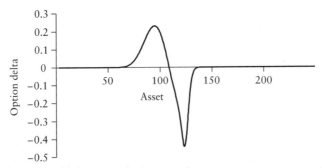

FIGURE 7.11 **Discretely sampled up-and-out call.** Option delta with five samplings remaining. Log-normal asset process with $\sigma = 0.2$, $r = 0.07$, $K = 100$, $T = 1$ year, barrier at 125.8.

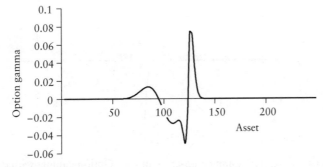

FIGURE 7.12 **Discretely sampled up-and-out call.** Option gamma with five samplings remaining. Log-normal asset process with $\sigma = 0.2$, $r = 0.07$, $K = 100$, $T = 1$ year, barrier at 125.8.

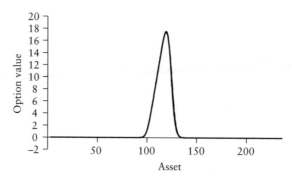

FIGURE 7.13 **Discretely sampled up-and-out call.** Option value with one sampling remaining. Log-normal asset process with $\sigma = 0.2$, $r = 0.07$, $d = 0.02$, $K = 100$, $T = 1$ year, barrier at 125.8.

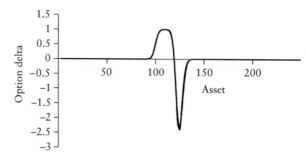

FIGURE 7.14 **Discretely sampled up-and-out call.** Option delta with one sampling remaining. Log-normal asset process with $\sigma = 0.2$, $r = 0.07$, $K = 100$, $T = 1$ year, barrier at 125.8.

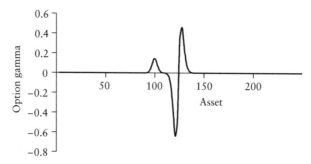

FIGURE 7.15 **Discretely sampled up-and-out call.** Option gamma with one sampling remaining. Log-normal asset process with $\sigma = 0.2$, $r = 0.07$, $K = 100$, $T = 1$ year, barrier at 125.8.

that the plots extend beyond the barrier are an indication that the solution diffuses between sampling points.

The complex shape of the gamma in Figure 7.12 is not due to numerical oscillations, but rather to the cumulative effect of sampling points that are yet to occur. As exercise information diffuses backward in time, the sampling intervals impose time scales that become visible in gamma. These scales are also present in the value and the delta of the option, but they are not readily visible in the plots. If we plotted even higher derivatives of the value, we would expect to see these scales more clearly.

We finalize this section with two issues of practical significance. In building a grid when we have discrete sampling, we must decide where to place the sampling point with respect to the grid points. As the sampling interval becomes large, the optimal location of the sampling point is between grid points. If the sampling point coincides with a grid point, the space accuracy of the scheme drops to first order. The intuition behind this fact is that discrete sampling implies describing a discontinuous function through discrete points. This is best done if the discontinuity is halfway between two points. More details on this topic can be found in Tavella and Randall (2000).

Convergence to Continuous Sampling   Computations done for a particular sampling frequency can be used to infer the value of the barrier option for other sampling frequencies, including the case of continuous sampling. The reason this is possible is that the continuous and the discrete sampling values differ in a known way as a function of the sampling interval. It is easy to see that this difference must be proportional to $\sigma\sqrt{\Delta t}$, where σ is the volatility of the underlying asset:

$$\text{discrete sampling price} - \text{continuous sampling price} = c\sigma\sqrt{\Delta t} \quad \text{as } \Delta t \to 0$$
$$(7.144)$$

where c is a constant.

There are two justifications we can invoke. A financial reason is that the incremental loss of probability of hitting the barrier as a result of discrete sampling must be proportional to the diffusion of the underlying process through the sampling interval. This diffusion is proportional to $\sigma\sqrt{\Delta t}$. Another reason comes from dimensional analysis. Discrete sampling introduces another nondimensional group in the problem proportional to $\sigma\sqrt{\Delta t}$. Any changes in the outcome of the problem due to discrete sampling must be a function of this group. When $\Delta t \to 0$, such changes must be linear functions of the nondimensional group. This discussion does not tell us what the constant in Equation 7.144 is. For an analytical treatment of this issue, see Broadie, Glasserman, and Kou (1996).

We can exploit this relationship to get the value of a discretely sampled barrier option for arbitrary sampling frequency as follows. Given numerically computed values of barrier options for sampling intervals Δ_1, Δ_2, and Δ_3, denoted by V_1, V_2, and V_3, respectively, we make a plot of $\log(V_1 - V)$, $\log(V_2 - V)$, and $\log(V_3 - V)$ versus $\log \Delta_1$, $\log \Delta_2$, and $\log \Delta_3$. The magnitude of V that turns this plot into a straight line is the extrapolated value of the barrier option for continuous sampling.

COORDINATE TRANSFORMATIONS

It is highly desirable to work with uniform grids. Except in a few simple cases, a uniform grid will not capture the most important features of the solution unless we introduce coordinate transformations. Coordinate transformations allow us to better discern important features of the solution field and at the same time maintain a uniformly spaced grid.

Coordinate transformations fulfill three basic objectives.

- Boundary control: To be able to precisely accommodate and resolve external boundaries. This is essential in barrier problems, where we transform the domain into a rectangular strip.
- Resolution of high gradient features: This refers to accurately capturing internal and end conditions features where the solution varies widely. This objective is often combined with the previous one, since in many cases the regions of high gradients are near boundaries.
- Dimensional redistribution: This is an advanced application of coordinate transformations where we can achieve higher performance by transferring resolution from dimensions where the gradients are mild to dimensions where the gradients are steep.

Coordinate transformations accomplish these objectives through two mechanisms.

- They change the eigenvalue spectrum of the discretization matrix.
- They change the solution levels to which the eigenvalues are exposed.

Coordinate transformations do not, in general, simplify the pricing equation. In fact, they typically make the pricing equation much more complex. This is not an issue, however, because transformations are typically implemented numerically, not analytically. The logarithmic transformation of the Black and Scholes pricing equation is a notable exception. This transformation leads to a simpler PDE and in many cases a better numerical problem.

To illustrate the changes in the eigenvalue spectrum introduced by coordinate transformation, consider the logarithmic transformation applied to the Black and Scholes pricing equation:

$$\frac{\partial u}{\partial t} + rx\frac{\partial u}{\partial x} + \frac{1}{2}\sigma^2 x^2\frac{\partial^2 u}{\partial x^2} = ru \qquad (7.145)$$

With the coordinate transformation $z = \log x$ the pricing equation is

$$\frac{\partial u}{\partial t} + \left(r - \frac{1}{2}\sigma^2\right)\frac{\partial u}{\partial z} + \frac{1}{2}\sigma^2\frac{\partial^2 u}{\partial z^2} = ru \qquad (7.146)$$

The transformed equation is simpler because its coefficients are constant. The fact that the coefficients are constant has a profound effect on the eigenvalues of the discretization matrix, as shown in Figure 7.16. The difference between the largest and the smallest eigenvalue in the case of Equation 7.146 is much smaller than in the case of the original Black and Scholes equation. The fact that the eigenvalues look nicer does not mean that the transformation is beneficial, however. The transformation must also concentrate grid points in regions that matter. The logarithmic transformation of the Black and Scholes equation does this in some cases but not in others. In the case of a call option, for example, the logarithmic transformation works fairly well because it concentrates points in the region where they are needed for values of the underlying of the order of the strike. In the case of a barrier option this transformation does not take the barrier into account

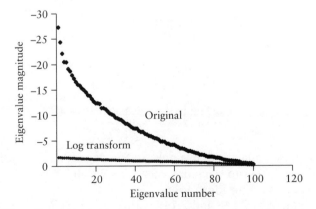

FIGURE 7.16 Effect of logarithmic transformation on eigenvalue spectrum of the discretization matrix of the Black and Scholes equation. The logarithmic transformation dramatically flattens the eigenvalue distribution.

and we would not expect it to work particularly well. In general we must select transformations purely on the basis of how they help resolve features of the solution, not on the basis of how they simplify the pricing equation.

Implementation of Coordinate Transformations

We will concentrate on one-dimensional coordinate transformations. Extension of the ideas presented here to several dimensions is trivial but it may become analytically cumbersome. For a comprehensive discussion of multidimensional coordinate transformation, the reader may consult Tavella and Randall (2000).

We will denote the original space coordinate by S and the transformed space coordinate by ξ. In simple cases it may be practical to implement the coordinate transformations analytically. In general, however, coordinate transformations are best implemented numerically. This is not only a matter of minimizing algebraic derivations but also a matter of flexibility, as we will see shortly.

Analytical Implementation of Coordinate Transformations   Defining the mapping function we get

$$\xi = f(S) \tag{7.147}$$

The analytical implementation of a coordinate transformation consists in applying the chain rule of differentiation using Equation 7.147:

$$\frac{\partial}{\partial S} = \frac{\partial \xi}{\partial S}\frac{\partial}{\partial \xi} \tag{7.148}$$

$$
\begin{aligned}
\frac{\partial^2}{\partial S^2} &= \frac{\partial}{\partial S}\left(\frac{\partial}{\partial \xi}\frac{\partial \xi}{\partial S}\right) \\
&= \frac{\partial \xi}{\partial S}\frac{\partial}{\partial S}\left(\frac{\partial}{\partial \xi}\right) + \frac{\partial^2 \xi}{\partial S^2}\frac{\partial}{\partial \xi} \\
&= \left(\frac{\partial \xi}{\partial S}\right)^2\frac{\partial^2}{\partial \xi^2} + \frac{\partial^2 \xi}{\partial S^2}\frac{\partial}{\partial \xi}
\end{aligned}
\tag{7.149}
$$

The simplest analytical example is the logarithmic transformation applied to the Black and Scholes equation. We did this before, but we repeat it here as a simple illustration.

Using Equations 7.148 and 7.149 with $\xi = \log(S)$ in

$$\frac{\partial u}{\partial t} + rS\frac{\partial u}{\partial S} + \frac{1}{2}\sigma^2 S^2\frac{\partial u}{\partial S^2} = ru \tag{7.150}$$

we get

$$\frac{\partial u}{\partial t} + \left(r - \frac{1}{2}\sigma^2\right)\frac{\partial u}{\partial \xi} + \frac{1}{2}\sigma^2\frac{\partial u}{\partial \xi^2} = ru \qquad (7.151)$$

As a result of the log transformation, the coefficients became constant and the drift changed by $\frac{-\sigma^2}{2}$. As discussed in the previous section, this transformation has two effects. It changes the eigenvalues of the discretization matrix as shown in Figure 7.16, and it concentrates points in lower values of S.

Analytical transformations are limited because we usually don't know $\xi = f(S)$. What we know is how the grid points are distributed in the ξ coordinate, where we assume the grid points are equally spaced. As a result, what we usually know is $S = f^{-1}(\xi)$. This implies that coordinate transformations are best handled numerically.

Numerical Implementation of Coordinate Transformations Figure 7.17 illustrates the situation we face. We have a uniform distribution of grid points in the transformed coordinate and a way of mapping those points to the original coordinate, such that boundaries or features we would like to resolve are properly captured. We may have obtained the distribution of points in the S coordinate by an analytically known inverse transformation, $S = f^{-1}(\xi)$, or by some other numerical procedure. The important fact is that we know the inverse transformation, not the direct transformation. We will denote the inverse transformation by $g(\xi) = f^{-1}(\xi)$.

We will illustrate the numerical implementation of coordinate transformation with the Black and Scholes equation. Given the inverse transformation

$$S = g(\xi) \qquad (7.152)$$

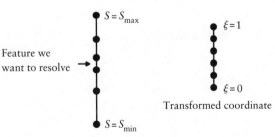

FIGURE 7.17 Coordinate transformation. We know the distribution of points in the transformed domain.

and its Jacobian,[2] defined as

$$J(\xi) = \frac{dS}{d\xi} \tag{7.153}$$

the pricing equation

$$\frac{\partial u}{\partial t} + \mu S \frac{\partial u}{\partial S} + \frac{1}{2}\sigma^2 S^2 \frac{\partial u}{\partial S^2} = ru \tag{7.154}$$

can be written as

$$\frac{\partial u}{\partial t} + \mu \frac{S(\xi)}{J(\xi)}\frac{\partial u}{\partial \xi} + \frac{1}{2}\sigma^2 \frac{S^2(\xi)}{J(\xi)}\frac{\partial}{\partial \xi}\left(\frac{1}{J(\xi)}\frac{\partial u}{\partial \xi}\right) = ru \tag{7.155}$$

It is easy to verify that if we replace $S = \exp(\xi)$ in the Jacobian, Equation 7.151 becomes Equation 7.154 with $\mu = r$.

We now discretize Equation 7.155. The diffusion term is best handled numerically as follows (for more details, see Tavella and Randall (2000)):

$$\frac{\partial}{\partial \xi}\left(\frac{1}{J(\xi)}\frac{\partial u}{\partial \xi}\right) \approx \frac{u(\xi + \Delta\xi) - u(\xi)}{J\left(\xi + \frac{1}{2}\xi\right)\Delta\xi^2} - \frac{u(\xi) - u(\xi - \Delta\xi)}{J\left(\xi - \frac{1}{2}\xi\right)\Delta\xi^2} \tag{7.156}$$

This approximation is second order in $\Delta\xi$ if we set

$$J(\xi + \Delta\xi) = \frac{S(\xi + \Delta\xi) - S(\xi)}{\Delta\xi} \tag{7.157}$$

Using the notation,

$$S_i = S(\xi_i)$$
$$S_{i\pm1} = S(\xi_i \pm \Delta\xi)$$
$$J_{i\pm\frac{1}{2}} = J\left(\xi_i \pm \frac{1}{2}\Delta\xi\right)$$

the discretized form of Equation 7.155 is

$$\frac{\partial u}{\partial t} + \frac{\mu}{\Delta\xi}\frac{S_i}{J_{i+\frac{1}{2}} + J_{i-\frac{1}{2}}}(u_{i+1} - u_{i-1}) + \frac{\sigma^2}{\Delta\xi^2}\frac{S_i^2}{J_{i+\frac{1}{2}} + J_{i-\frac{1}{2}}}\left(\frac{u_{i+1} - u_i}{J_{i+\frac{1}{2}}} - \frac{u_i - u_{i-1}}{J_{i-\frac{1}{2}}}\right) = ru_i$$

$$\tag{7.158}$$

---

[2]This idea carries over to multiple dimensions easily, where the Jacobian is a matrix and its inverse is defined as the inverse of that matrix.

The discretization matrix is tridiagonal:

$$\frac{du_i}{dt} = a_i u_{i-1} + b_i u_i + c_i u_{i+1} \tag{7.159}$$

with

$$a_i = \frac{1}{J_{i+\frac{1}{2}} + J_{i-\frac{1}{2}}} \left(\frac{\mu}{\Delta \xi} S_i - \frac{\sigma^2}{\Delta \xi^2} S_i^2 \frac{1}{J_{i-\frac{1}{2}}} \right)$$

$$b_i = r + \frac{\sigma^2}{\Delta \xi^2} \frac{S_i^2}{J_{i+\frac{1}{2}} + J_{i-\frac{1}{2}}} \left(\frac{1}{J_{i+\frac{1}{2}}} + \frac{1}{J_{i-\frac{1}{2}}} \right) \tag{7.160}$$

$$c_i = -\frac{1}{J_{i+\frac{1}{2}} + J_{i-\frac{1}{2}}} \left(\frac{\mu}{\Delta \xi} S_i + \frac{\sigma^2}{\Delta \xi^2} S_i^2 \frac{1}{J_{I+\frac{1}{2}}} \right)$$

We now discuss two simple and useful numerical transformations.

Example 1: Transformation to Place a Known Underlying Value on a Grid Point

Assume that we would like to map the range $S = 10$ to $S = 90$ in our original coordinate to the range $\xi = 0.1$ to $\xi = 0.9$ in our transformed coordinate, such that the point $S = 59$ maps to $\xi = 0.5$.

The procedure to accomplish this is as follows.

■ Construct an array representing the grid points in the transformed coordinate. In our case, this array could be $\tilde{\xi} = \{0.1, 0.2, 0.3, 0.4, 0.5, 0.6, 0.7, 0.8, 0.9\}$.
■ Construct an array of the original points that we want to map to known locations in the transformed domain. In this example, this array is $\hat{S} = \{10, 59, 90\}$.
■ Construct an array of the known mapping in the transformed domain. In our case, $\hat{\xi} = \{0.1, 0.5, 0.9\}$.
■ Do a cubic spline of $\hat{\xi}$ against $\hat{S}$ (the former is the dependent variable, the latter is the independent variable).
■ Obtain the array of S_i values by interpolating on each element of $\tilde{\xi}$. *This is our grid in the original coordinates.*
■ Using the grid points in the original coordinates, S_i, construct the Jacobians according to Equation 7.157. We can now construct the discretization matrix.

From this description it is clear that we were able to construct the grid without knowing the transformation function $\xi = f(S)$. In this case, we used a simple cubic spline. There are far more elaborate ways to construct

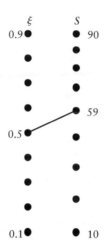

FIGURE 7.18 Mapping of known points to transformed coordinate. Points $S = 10$, $S = 59$, and $S = 90$ are mapped to $\xi = 0.1$, $\xi = 0.5$, and $\xi = 0.9$, respectively, using a cubic spline.

grids (Tavella and Randall, 2000). If we use an interpolation approach, we must be careful to respect the continuity of the derivative of the Jacobian. A cubic spline will do this.

The transformation is illustrated in Figure 7.18.

A variation of this transformation is one where you would like to place a known value of the original coordinate between two grid points. Assume that you would like the value $S = 59$ to map to $\xi = 0.5 + \frac{1}{2}\Delta\xi$, instead of $\xi = 0.5$. This is very easy to accomplish by splining the pair $\hat{\xi} = \{0.1, 0.5 + \frac{1}{2}\Delta\xi, 0.9\}$ and $\hat{S} = \{10, 59, 90\}$, instead of the pairs $\hat{\xi} = \{0.1, 0.5, 0.9\}$ and $\hat{S} = \{10, 59, 90\}$.

Example 2: Transformation to Concentrate Points Around Desired Locations

The basic idea is to work with the Jacobian, rather than with the transformation itself. A transformation that accomplishes what we want will have a Jacobian that is peaky at the location where we want to concentrate points. What we need to do is postulate a Jacobian with this property and then integrate the Jacobian (numerically or analytically) to get the grid points in the original domain. The following Jacobian, taken from Tavella and Randall (2000), leads to a concentration of points around $S = S^*$ in the range $S_{min} \leq S \leq S_{max}$:

$$J(\xi) = \sqrt{\alpha^2 + (S - S^*)^2} \qquad (7.161)$$

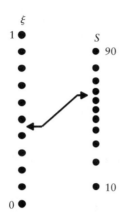

FIGURE 7.19 Concentration of points. Grid points computed with Equation 7.162 for $\alpha = 0.2(S_{max} - S_{min})$. Points are concentrated around $S^* = 59$, which maps to $\xi = 0.565$ (indicated by the arrow).

This Jacobian can be integrated analytically:

$$S = S^* + \alpha \sinh\left(\xi \sinh^{-1} \frac{S_{min} - S^*}{\alpha} + (1 - \xi) \sinh^{-1} \frac{S_{max} - S^*}{\alpha} \right) \quad (7.162)$$

The value of α controls the degree of concentration of points. If $\alpha \ll S_{max} - S_{min}$, the points will be highly concentrated; if $\alpha \gg S_{max} - S_{min}$, the points will be highly uniform. Figure 7.19 shows an example of this approach.

The complexity of transformations increases quickly as the number of dimensions increases. It is also possible to build time-dependent transformations (a simple example of this was discussed in the section on barrier options). In general, realistic financial pricing problems do not require very complex transformations. The reader interested in greater detail can consult Tavella and Randall (2000).

DISCRETE EVENTS AND PATH DEPENDENCY

The power of finite differences in solving path-dependent derivatives such as Asian options is related to the way finite differences can be used to price derivatives whose underlyings undergo jumps at known points in time.

To illustrate how this connection arises, let's consider the case of an option on a stock with a known discrete dividend payment amount. We will show that the price of this option results from a sequence of computations on nondividend paying stock. These computations involve the pricing equation for the underlying stock process *without* dividends. This idea is important because we can solve the dividend case by solving the PDE for the nondividend case. What makes this possible is the concept of *displacement shocks*. Displacement shocks (also called *continuity conditions* or *jump conditions*) connect the derivative's price before and after the underlying's jump. By increasing the frequency of dividend payments, we can approach the continuous dividend case.

Of course, the PDE for the case of a derivative on a continuously dividend-paying stock is known and not significantly different for the case of no dividends. However, this idea can be extended to cases where either deriving the pricing equation is difficult, or where the pricing equation is hard to solve. This means that we are able to solve problems that may be quite difficult through a sequence of problems that are much easier. We will discuss the case of discrete dividends as a first example.

Displacement Shocks

The value of a derivative may depend on a process subjected to jumps at known points in time. For example, the value of an option on a stock that pays discrete dividends will depend on a stochastic process that jumps down by the amount of the dividend each time a dividend payment happens. If the derivative is such that those jumps do not induce cash flows to the holder of the instrument, the derivative's price must be continuous across the points in time when the jumps occur. This continuity means that the value of the derivative immediately after the jump in the underlying, valued at the underlying level after the jump, must be the same as the value immediately before the jump, valued at the underlying level before the jump (assuming that no exercise is allowed at the dividend payment time).

Example: Call Option on Stock with Discrete Dividends

As an example, consider the case of a derivative on a stock, $S(t)$, that pays a discrete dividend d. The value of the derivative, $u(S, t)$, must obey

$$u(S, t^-) = u(S - d, t) \qquad (7.163)$$

where t^- is the instant of time right before the dividend payment happens. In computational time (or remaining time to maturity), this expression is

$$u(S, t) = u(S - d, t^+) \qquad (7.164)$$

where t^+ is the instant of time right after the dividend payment happens. We refer to a condition of this type as a *displacement shock*. Although the option value does not change as a result of the jump, the hedge characteristics change. Equation 7.164 is implemented as an initial condition and does not cause stability concerns. In between discrete dividend payments, we solve the standard Black and Scholes pricing equation.

Figures 7.20, 7.21, and 7.22 show the results for a call option with one year maturity, risk-free rate 0.05, volatility 0.3, strike = 100, and a discrete dividend payment of 4 percent of the spot value.

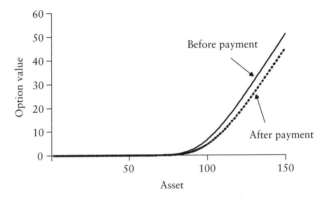

FIGURE 7.20 Discrete dividend payment effect on call value. Option value immediately before and immediately after dividend payment. (Before and after are with respect to remaining time to maturity.) $T = 1$ year, $K = 100$, $r = 0.05$, $d = 0.04$, $\sigma = 0.3$. Discrete dividend at $t = 0.25$ years.

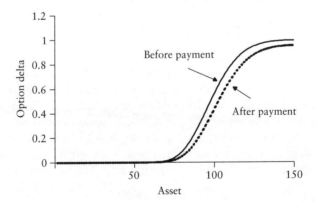

FIGURE 7.21 Discrete dividend payment effect on call delta. Option delta immediately before and immediately after dividend payment. (Before and after are with respect to remaining time to maturity.) $T = 1$ year, $K = 100$, $r = 0.05$, $d = 0.04$, $\sigma = 0.3$. Discrete dividend at $t = 0.25$ years.

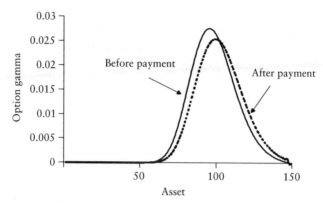

FIGURE 7.22 Discrete dividend payment effect on call gamma. Before and after refer to remaining time to maturity. $T = 1$ year, $K = 100$, $r = 0.05$, $d = 0.04$, $\sigma = 0.3$. Discrete dividend at $t = 0.25$ years.

If we imagine that we allow the number of discrete payments to go to infinity and impose the displacement shock of Equation 7.164 at each payment, we would be effectively solving the pricing equation,

$$\frac{\partial u}{\partial t} + (r - y)S\frac{\partial u}{\partial S} + \frac{1}{2}S^2\frac{\partial^2 u}{\partial S^2} = ru \qquad (7.165)$$

where y is the continuous dividend yield. This equation differs from the one that we implement between displacement shocks,

$$\frac{\partial u}{\partial t} + rS\frac{\partial u}{\partial S} + \frac{1}{2}S^2\frac{\partial^2 u}{\partial S^2} = ru \qquad (7.166)$$

in that the drift of the underlying process is different. If we wanted to solve the continuous dividend yield case, we would not actually exploit the discrete approach in the limit of infinitely many dividend payments. We would solve Equation 7.165 directly. In path-dependent derivatives involving continuous sampling, however, it may be far more advantageous to exploit the displacement shock idea rather than solving the full pricing equation. We illustrate this next for the case of an Asian option.

Path Dependency and Discrete Sampling

From a computational standpoint, we distinguish three basic types of path dependencies.

- Path dependency in the underlying stochastic processes. This is the case of the short rate in the Heath-Jarrow-Morton framework. Since in this case we don't get a PDE as a pricing equation, we are not concerned with this type of path dependency when applying finite differences techniques as discussed in this chapter.
- Path dependency imposed by boundaries. This is the case of barrier options. This is the easiest type of path dependency to treat with finite differences.
- Path dependency imposed by payment contingencies. This is the case of options with payoffs that depend on certain properties of the underlying's trajectory, such as in the case of Asian options, Parisian options, and so on. This type of path dependency is much harder to treat with finite differences than the previous one. This type will be the focus of this section.

The property of the trajectory that determines the path dependency may enter the pricing problem as an additional process. For example, in the case of an Asian option whose payoff depends on an average of an underlying process, this average is itself a process that enters as an additional dimension in the pricing equation. We can tackle this path dependency in two ways. We can derive the pricing equation specifically for this type of path dependency and apply standard finite difference techniques to that pricing equation. There are two difficulties here. One is that we need to derive the pricing equation, and this may not be an easy task. The other is that the resulting pricing equation may be much harder to solve than the standard pricing equation we have been discussing so far. To understand why this may be the case, consider an option whose payoff is a function of the continuous arithmetic average of a stock process, $S(t)$, described by $dS(t) = S\mu dt + S\sigma dW(t)$. The running arithmetic average of this stock process is

$$X(t) = \frac{1}{t}\int_0^t S(\xi)d\xi \qquad (7.167)$$

If we apply the techniques of Chapter 3 to derive a pricing equation for this option, we will find that the pricing equation is a PDE where both $S(t)$ and $X(t)$ appear as independent dimensions. However, they appear in a fundamentally different way. While $dS(t)$ has a $dW(t)$ term in it, $dX(t)$ does not. This means that in the resulting PDE the dimension X will only appear in the first-order derivatives (convective terms), not in the second-order derivatives (diffusive terms). As it turns out, the appearance of additional convective terms without a diffusive counterpart poses numerical difficulties. Not all path dependencies result in pricing equations without a diffusive component. However, our approach here will not be to derive and solve the specific PDE for a particular path-dependent option, but to use the displacement shock ideas discussed earlier. This is a far more robust and simpler approach where we capture the solution of a more complicated PDE (which we may not even know) through the limit of a sequence of solutions of a much simpler, standard PDE.

An additional appeal of the displacement shock approach is that this is the natural choice for discrete sampling of path dependency. As a result, this approach gives us two things: a way to compute path-dependent options with discrete sampling and a way to converge to the limit of continuous sampling *without having to deal with the specific PDE for the particular form of path dependency.*

How is the continuous sampling limit approached as the sampling interval vanishes? This depends on whether the increment of the path-dependent quantity has a dW term in it or not. If it does, we can argue that the continuous sampling limit should be approached with an error $\mathcal{O}(\sqrt{\Delta t})$ (this is the case of a discretely sampled Parisian option). If the increment of the path-dependent quantity does not have a diffusion part, the limit is approached like Δt (this is the case of a discretely sampled arithmetic Asian option).

Example: Discretely Sampled Arithmetic Asian Option   We define G to be the running sum of asset prices at observation times. The payoff of an arithmetic Asian call is

$$V(S, G, T) = \max\left(0, \frac{G(T)}{N} - K\right) \tag{7.168}$$

where N is the number of sampling times and K is the strike. At each sampling time, G jumps by S, and the displacement shock condition at sampling time t_i is

$$V(S, G, t_i^-) = V(S, G + S, t_i) \tag{7.169}$$

In between sampling times, the solution progresses according to the standard Black and Scholes equation. At the sampling time, new initial conditions are created following Equation 7.169. It is important to realize that although we are solving PDEs with one space dimension between sampling times, the problem is truly two dimensional. The grid point values in the G coordinate enter as parameters in the initial conditions between sampling points. This means that between sampling points we are solving as many one-dimensional problems as there are grid points in the G coordinate. The solution information that must be kept in memory must take into account the grid points in the G coordinate. In practice, this is a very efficient way of dealing with discrete sampling.

As a simple example, consider an arithmetic Asian option with the following characteristics: log-normal stock price with risk-free rate $r = 0.1$, stock volatility $\sigma = 0.4$, 10 samplings per year, strike $K = 100$, and maturity $T = 1$ year. The problem is solved with the Crank-Nicholson scheme.

The following figures indicate what the nonintuitive nature of the implementation of the displacement shocks accomplish in this case. Figure 7.23 shows the value of the option at maturity. Since the payoff is only a function of the arithmetic average measured at maturity, the payoff is independent of the spot price at maturity.

Figure 7.24 shows the value of the option at $t = 0.45$, or about half-way to maturity. Notice that the effect of the displacement shocks is to rotate the solution such that as time decreases, the importance of the spot price becomes more prevalent in comparison with the average.

Finally, Figure 7.25 shows the option value at $t = 0$. We see now that the value depends exclusively on the level of the spot (no average has taken place at $t = 0$). The solution has then rotated 90 degrees. This was accomplished by applying the displacement shock conditions ten times between $t = 1$ and $t = 0$. We were able to do this without ever inquiring what the actual pricing equation of an arithmetic Asian option is like. We could easily find the limiting value for continuous sampling by exploiting the fact that in this case the continuous sampling value must be reached linearly, proportional to the sampling interval Δt. For additional details and examples on the use of this approach to the computation of path-dependent options, the reader is referred to Tavella and Randall (2000), where many of the detailed numerical issues are discussed. In conclusion, we can remark the following.

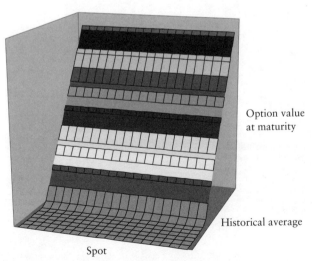

FIGURE 7.23 Payoff at maturity. Arithmetic Asian call with $r = 0.1$, $\sigma = 0.4$, 10 samplings per year, $K = 100$, $T = 1$ year.

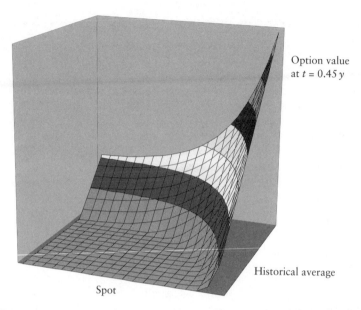

FIGURE 7.24 Option value at $t = 0.45$. Arithmetic Asian call with $r = 0.1$, $\sigma = 0.4$, 10 samplings per year, $K = 100$, $T = 1$ year.

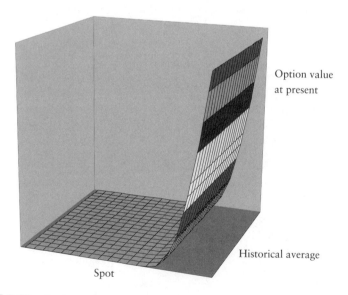

FIGURE 7.25 Option value at $t = 0$. Arithmetic Asian call with $r = 0.1$, $\sigma = 0.4$, 10 samplings per year, $K = 100$, $T = 1$ year.

- There may be more than one way to impose displacement shock conditions. For an example of this in the context of Asian options, see Tavella and Randall (2000).
- The displacement shock condition requires interpolation. Cubic splines work well, but lower quality interpolations can also be used.
- The displacement shock condition may require extrapolation. Whether this is required may depend on the formulation of the shock condition. When needed, linear extrapolation appears to work well.

TREES, LATTICES, AND FINITE DIFFERENCES

Trees are a very popular approach to implement financial pricing. We have not, however, dedicated time to trees because trees, as we will see in this short section, are particular forms of finite difference schemes. The nature of the finite difference scheme that trees represent will make it immediately clear to the reader why trees cannot perform better than some of the lowest-performing finite difference schemes. From a practical view, properly implemented finite difference code will be equally fast or faster, much more robust, and far more flexible than trees (binomial or trinomial).

Although the words *trees* and *lattices* are used almost interchangeably, here we will make a differentiation. Both a *tree* and a *lattice* are defined by an array of points in the multidimensional space whose coordinates are the underlying states and time. Beyond this geometric characterization, we will distinguish the following differences between trees and lattices.

- Trees are typically triangular arrays of points (the shape may be more complex if the tree has been cropped), where the transition probabilities result from the parameterization of the tree. Arbitrage arguments and assumptions about the recombination of the tree are used to determine the distance between nodes and the transition probabilities at the same time. The triangular shape results naturally from the way these arguments are applied.
- Lattices are not necessarily triangular arrays of points (or regular arrays, for that matter). A lattice is characterized by an array of points and transition probabilities that are not determined together with the construction of the lattice but are determined separately. When so defined, lattices are more flexible than trees in that they offer flexibility in node placement. We can build a lattice easily if we are able to compute transition probabilities directly from the underlying process. A powerful way to compute transition probabilities using

finite differences is by numerically solving the Fokker-Plank equation of probability diffusion. We have not discussed this equation or lattices in this book, but the interested reader can consult Tavella (2001) for additional ideas and information.

Our emphasis now will be in the connection between trees and finite differences. We will illustrate this connection in the context of the CRR (Cox, Ross, and Rubinstein, 1979) and Jarrow and Rudd (Jarrow and Rudd, 1983) binomial trees. The reader can explore the connection with other trees easily.

Connection Between the CRR Binomial Tree and Finite Differences

The CRR tree assumes a log-normal underlying process (we assume no dividends for simplicity),

$$\frac{dS}{S} = rdt + \sigma dW \tag{7.170}$$

where r is the instantaneous risk-free rate. The underlying price is subject to up and down moves of the form,

$$S_{up} = S \exp(\sigma\sqrt{\Delta t})$$

$$S_{down} = S \exp(-\sigma\sqrt{\Delta t}) \tag{7.171}$$

where Δt is the time spacing of the tree.

The transition probability to the up move is (the probability of a down move is one minus the probability of an up move)

$$p = \frac{\exp(r\Delta t) - \exp(-\sigma\sqrt{\Delta t})}{\exp(\sigma\sqrt{\Delta t} - \exp(-\sigma\sqrt{\Delta t}))} \tag{7.172}$$

Taylor series expansion of this expression gives

$$p = \frac{1}{2} + \frac{r}{2\sigma}\sqrt{\Delta t} - \frac{\sigma}{4}\sqrt{\Delta t} + \mathcal{O}(\Delta t^{3/2}) \tag{7.173}$$

This definition of up and down moves means two things:

- The spacing of nodes in the logarithm of the underlying process is constant and is equal to $\sigma\sqrt{\Delta t}$.
- The tree recombines at constant values of the underlying process (an up move followed by a down move leads to the original value).

With $x = \log(S)$,

$$dx = \left(r - \frac{1}{2}\sigma^2\right)dt + \sigma dW \tag{7.174}$$

The pricing equation of a European derivative is

$$\frac{\partial V}{\partial t} = \left(r - \frac{1}{2}\sigma^2\right)\frac{\partial V}{\partial x} + \frac{1}{2}\sigma^2\frac{\partial^2 V}{\partial x^2} - rV \tag{7.175}$$

where t starts at maturity, such that our initial conditions are given by the payoff function. We now define a grid spaced by Δx and apply the explicit Euler scheme to this equation. This gives us the update formula,

$$
\begin{aligned}
u_i^{(n+1)} = & \underbrace{\left(-\frac{1}{2}\frac{\Delta t}{\Delta x}\left(r - \frac{1}{2}\sigma^2\right) + \frac{1}{2}\frac{\Delta t}{\Delta x^2}\sigma^2\right)}_{A} u_{i-1}^{(n)} \\
& + \underbrace{\left(-\frac{\Delta t}{\Delta x}\sigma^2 - \Delta t r + 1\right)}_{B} u_i^{(n)} \\
& + \underbrace{\left(\frac{1}{2}\frac{\Delta t}{\Delta x}\left(r - \frac{1}{2}\sigma^2\right) + \frac{1}{2}\frac{\Delta t}{\Delta x^2}\sigma^2\right)}_{C} u_{i+1}^{(n)}
\end{aligned}
\tag{7.176}
$$

where $u_i^{(n)}$ approximates $V(t, x)$ at $t = n\Delta t$ and $x = x_i$.

If we now select the value of Δx that makes the term multiplying $u_i^{(n)}$ equal to zero, we get

$$B = 0 \Rightarrow \Delta x = \sigma\sqrt{\Delta t} + HOT \tag{7.177}$$

This is precisely the value of the node spacing in the CRR tree. If we now replace this value in the term that multiplies $u_{i+1}^{(n)}$, we get

$$C = \frac{1}{2} + \frac{r}{2\sigma}\sqrt{\Delta t} - \frac{\sigma}{4}\sqrt{\Delta t} + HOT \tag{7.178}$$

This is precisely the expression for the transition probability to the up state in the CRR tree. We can conclude that the grid of x values can be viewed as containing a binomial tree if the A, B, and C coefficients in explicit Euler finite difference approximation are interpreted as transition probabilities. Figure 7.26 illustrates this point.

Recently, Rubinstein (2000) has conducted a related analysis.

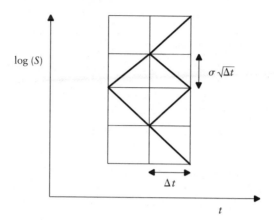

FIGURE 7.26 CRR binomial tree embedded in a finite difference grid. To first order, the explicit Euler scheme and the CRR binomial tree are equivalent if the grid spacing is selected in the appropriate relationship with the the time step.

Connection Between the Jarrow and Rudd Binomial Tree and Finite Differences

The Jarrow and Rudd binomial tree differs from the CRR tree in the parameterization. It also assumes a log-normal process, but the up and down moves are

$$
S_{up} = S \exp\left(\left(r - \frac{1}{2}\sigma^2\right)\Delta t + \sigma\sqrt{\Delta t}\right)
$$
$$
S_{down} = S \exp\left(\left(r - \frac{1}{2}\sigma^2\right)\Delta t - \sigma\sqrt{\Delta t}\right)
$$

(7.179)

and the probability of an upward move is

$$
p = \frac{\exp\left(\frac{\sigma^2}{2}\Delta t\right) - \exp\left(-\sigma\sqrt{\Delta t}\right)}{\exp\left(\sigma\sqrt{\Delta t}\right) - \exp\left(-\sigma\sqrt{\Delta t}\right)}
$$

(7.180)

A Taylor series expansion shows that this probability tends to 0.5 as $\Delta t \to 0$:

$$
p = \frac{1}{2} + \frac{1}{24}\sigma^3 \Delta t^{3/2} + \cdots
$$

(7.181)

Inspection of the up and down factors suggests that the Jarrow-Rudd tree recombines around the value $S \exp((r - \frac{1}{2}\sigma^2)t)$. This means that if we consider the transformation $S \exp(-(r - \frac{1}{2}\sigma^2)t)$, we would have a tree that recombines around S. Consequently, if we consider the transformation,

$$y = \log\left(S \exp\left(-\left(r - \frac{1}{2}\sigma^2\right)t\right)\right) \qquad (7.182)$$

we would have a tree whose nodes are equally spaced by the amount $\sigma\sqrt{\Delta t}$ and that would recombine around a constant value. This suggests that if we base our pricing equation on the transformation in Equation 7.182 and discretize this equation with the explicit Euler scheme, we would recover the Jarrow-Rudd binomial tree. Since the process for y is driftless, the pricing equation using Equation 7.182 is

$$\frac{\partial V}{\partial t} = \frac{1}{2}\sigma^2\frac{\partial^2 V}{\partial y^2} - rV \qquad (7.183)$$

The explicit Euler finite difference update of this equation is

$$
\begin{aligned}
u_i^{(n+1)} = {} & \underbrace{\left(\frac{1}{2}\frac{\Delta t}{\Delta y^2}\sigma^2\right) u_{i-1}^{(n)}}_{A} \\
& + \underbrace{\left(-\frac{\Delta t}{\Delta y}\sigma^2 - \Delta tr + 1\right) u_i^{(n)}}_{B} \\
& + \underbrace{\left(\frac{1}{2}\frac{\Delta t}{\Delta y^2}\sigma^2\right) u_{i+1}^{(n)}}_{C}
\end{aligned}
\qquad (7.184)
$$

As in the case of the CRR tree, the value of Δy that causes the middle term on the left to be zero is $\Delta y = \sigma\sqrt{\Delta t} + HOT$. Replacing this value in the expression for C, we have

$$C = \frac{1}{2} - \Delta tr + HOT \qquad (7.185)$$

This value is the same to lower order as the probability of an upward move, given by Equation 7.181. Therefore, the Jarrow-Rudd binomial tree can be viewed in the same way as the CRR tree: as being embedded in a finite difference grid when the explicit Euler scheme is used.

A similar analysis can be carried out for other tree configurations (such as trinomial trees). For additional thoughts on this subject, refer to Tavella (2000).

Implications of the Correspondence Between Trees and Finite Differences

The fact that trees are forms of explicit finite difference schemes has the implication that trees inherit all the rigidities and problems of explicit finite difference schemes (stability constraints due to an unfavorable eigenvalue spectrum). Furthermore, while in finite differences (explicit or implicit) we have great flexibility in handling boundaries, this flexibility does not exist with trees. Practitioners have invested a great deal of labor in adapting trees to handle unusual boundaries, a task that can be trivially handled by finite differences.

bibliography

Abramowitz, M., and I. Stegun. *Handbook of Mathematical Functions.* New York: Dover Publications, 1964.

Andersen, L., and M. Broadie. 2001. A Primal-Dual Simulation Algorithm for Pricing Multi-Dimensional American Options. Working paper, Columbia University.

Barraquand, J., and D. Martineau. "Numerical Valuation of High Dimensional Multivariate American Securities." *Journal of Financial and Quantitative Analysis* 30, no. 3 (1995): 383–405.

Barrett, R., M. Berry, T. F. Chan, J. Demmel, J. Donato, J. Dongarra, V. Eijkhout, R. Pozo, C. Romine, and H. van der Vorst. *Templates for the Solution of Linear Systems: Building Blocks for Iterative Methods.* Philadelphia: SIAM, 1994.

Bhar, R., and C. Chiarella. "Transformation of Heath-Jarrow-Morton Models to Markovian Systems." *European Journal of Finance* 3 (1997): 1–26.

Billingsley, P. *Probability and Measure.* New York: John Wiley & Sons, 1994.

Black, F., and M. Scholes. "The Pricing of Options and Corporate Liabilities." *Journal of Political Economy* 81 (1973): 637–659.

Bratley, P., B. L. Fox, and L. Schrage. *A Guide to Simulation.* New York: Springer Verlag, 1987.

Brennan, M. J., and E. S. Schwartz. "Convertible Bonds: Valuation and Optimal Strategies for Call and Conversion." *Journal of Finance* 32 (1977): 1699–1715.

Broadie, M., P. Glasserman, and S. Kou. 1996. A Continuity Correction for Discrete Barrier Options. Working paper, Columbia University.

Broadie, M., and P. Glasserman. "Pricing American Style Securities Using Simulation." *Journal of Economic Dynamics and Control* 21 (1997): 1323–1352.

Broadie, M., and P. Glasserman. "Monte Carlo Methods for Pricing High-Dimensional American Options: An Overview." *Net Exposure: The Electronic Journal of Financial Risk* 3 (1997a): 15–37.

Broadie, M., and P. Glasserman. 1997b. A Stochastic Mesh Method for Pricing High Dimensional American Options. Working paper, Columbia University.

Caflisch, R. E., W. Morokoff, and A. Owen. *Journal of Computational Finance* 1, no. 1 (1997): 27–46.

Clement, E., D. Lamberton, and P. Protter. 2001. An Analysis of the Longstaff-Schwartz Algorithm for American Option Pricing. Working paper, Cornell University.

Cottle, R. W., J. S. Pang, and R. E. Stone. *The Linear Complementarity Problem*. San Diego: Academic Press, 1992.

Courant, R., and F. John. *Introduction to Calculus and Analysis*. Vol. 2. New York: John Wiley & Sons, 1974.

Cox, J., J. Ingersoll, and S. Ross. "A Theory of the Term Structure of Interest Rates." *Econometrica* 53 (1985): 385–408.

Cox, J., M. Rubinstein, and S. Ross. "Option Pricing: A Simplified Approach." *Journal of Financial Economics* 7, no. 3 (1979): 229–263.

Dixit, A. K., and R. S. Pindyck. *Investment under Uncertainty*. Princeton, New Jersey: Princeton University Press, 1994.

Dotham, M. U. *Prices in Financial Markets*. Oxford, England: Oxford Financial Press, 1990.

Duffie, D. *Dynamic Asset Pricing Theory*. Princeton, New Jersey: Princeton University Press, 1996.

Duffie, D., and K. Singleton. "Modeling Term Structures of Defaultable Bonds." *Review of Financial Studies* 12 (1999): 687–720.

Embrechts, P., S. Resnik, and G. Samorodnitsky. "Extreme Value Theory as a Risk Management Tool." *North American Actuarial Journal* 3 (1999): 30–41.

Fu, M. C., S. B. Laprise, D. B. Madam, Y. Su, and R. Wu. "Pricing American Options: A Comparison of Monte Carlo Simulation Approaches." *Journal of Computational Finance* 4 (2001): 39–98.

Hammersley, J. M., and D. C. Handscomb. *Monte Carlo Methods*. New York: Chapman and Hall, 1964.

Heath, D., R. Jarrow, and A. Morton. "Bond Pricing and the Term Structure of Interest Rates: A New Methodology for Contingent Claims Valuation." *Econometrica* 60 (1992): 77–106.

Ho, T., and S. Lee. "Term Structure Movements and Pricing Interest Rate Continent Claims." *Journal of Finance* 41 (1986): 1011–1029.

Huang, J., and J. S. Pang. "Option Pricing and Linear Complementarity." *Journal of Computational Finance* 2 (1998): 31–60.

Hull, J., and A. White. "Pricing Interest Rate Derivative Securities." *Review of Financial Studies* 3 (1990): 573–592.

Ingersoll, J. E., Jr. "Approximating American Options and Other Financial Contracts Using Barrier Derivatives." *Journal of Computational Finance* 1 (1998): 85–112.

Jarrow, R., and A. Rudd. *Option Pricing*. Homewood, Illinois: Irwin, 1983.

Jorion, P. *Value at Risk*. New York: McGraw-Hill, 2000.

Karatzas, I., and S. Shreve. *Brownian Motion and Stochastic Calculus*. New York: Springer Verlag, 1988.

Kloeden, P. E., and E. Platen. *Numerical Solution of Stochastic Differential Equations*. New York: Springer Verlag, 1995.

Lamberton, D., and B. Lapeyre. *Introduction to Stochastic Calculus Applied to Finance*. New York: Chapman and Hall, 1996.

Law, A. M., and W. D. Kelton. *Simulation Modeling and Analysis*. New York: McGraw-Hill, 2000.

Longstaff, F. A., and E. S. Schwartz. 1998. Valuing American Options by Simulation: A Simple Least-Squares Approach. Working paper, University of California, Los Angeles: 25–98.

Longstaff, F. A., and E. S. Schwartz, "Valuing American Options by Simulation: A Simple Least-Squares Approach." *Review of Financial Studies* 14, no. 1 (2000): 113–147.

Lupton, R. *Statistics in Theory and Practice*. Princeton, New Jersey: Princeton University Press, 1993.

Merton, R. C. "Option Pricing when Underlying Stock Returns Are Discontinuous." *Journal of Financial Economics* 3 (1976): 125–144.

Mickens, R. E. *Difference Equations*. New York: Van Nostrand-Reinhold, 1990.

Milshtein, G. N. "A Method of Second Order Accuracy Integration of Stochastic Differential Equations." *Theory of Probability and Its Applications* XXII, no. 2 (1978): 396–401.

Niederreiter, H. *Random Number Generation and Quasi–Monte Carlo Methods*. Philadelphia, Pennsylvania: Capital City Press, 1992.

Oksendal, B. *Stochastic Differential Equations*. Berlin: Springer Verlag, 1995.

Press, W. H., S. A. Teukolsky, W. T. Vetterling, and B. P. Flannery. *Numerical Recipes in C*. 2d Ed. Cambridge: Cambridge University Press, 1992.

Protter, P. *Stochastic Integration and Differential Equations*. New York: Springer Verlag, 1995.

Richtmeyer, R., and K. Morton. *Difference Methods for Initial-Value Problems*. New York: Interscience, 1967.

Rubinstein, M. *On the Relationship Between Binomial and Trinomial Option Pricing Models*. The *Journal of Derivatives* 8, no. 2 (2000): 47–50.

Schoenbucher, P. J. 1997. Pricing Credit Derivatives. Working paper, London School of Economics, London.

Smith, G. D. *Numerical Solution of Partial Differential Equations: Finite Difference Methods*. 3d Ed. Oxford, England: Clarendon Press, 1985.

Strang, G. *Linear Algebra and Its Applications*. San Diego, California: Harcourt Brace Jovanovich, Publishers, 1988.

Tavella, D., and C. Randall. *Pricing Financial Instruments: The Finite Difference Method.* New York: John Wiley & Sons, 2000.

Tavella, D. "Empowering Lattices." *Risk* (June 2001).

Tavella, D. "The Root of Tree Trouble." *Risk* (July 2000).

Tilley, J. A. "Valuing American Options in a Path Simulation Model." *Transactions of the Society of Actuaries* 45 (1993): 84–104.

Tsitsikilis, J. N., and B. Van Roy. 2000. Regression Methods for Pricing Complex American-Style Options. Working paper, Stanford University.

Varian, H. R. "The Arbitrage Principle in Financial Economics." *Economic Perspectives* 1, no. 2 (1987): 55–72.

Vasicek, O. "An Equilibrium Characterization of the Term Structure." *Journal of Financial Economics* 5 (1977): 177–188.

Wilmott, P. *Derivatives.* Chichester, England: John Wiley & Sons, 1998.

Wilmott, P., J. DeWynne, and S. Howison. *Option Pricing: Mathematical Models and Computation.* Oxford, England: Oxford Financial Press, 1993.

Zvan, R., P. A. Forsyth, and K. Vetzal. "Robust Numerical Methods for PDE Models of Asian Options." *Journal of Computational Finance* 1 (Winter 1997–1998): 39–78.

index